Compassionate
Music Teaching

Compassionate Music Teaching

A Framework for Motivation and Engagement in the 21st Century

Karin S. Hendricks

National Association
for Music Education

ROWMAN & LITTLEFIELD
Lanham • Boulder • New York • London

Published in Partnership with the National Association for Music Education

Published by Rowman & Littlefield
A wholly owned subsidiary of The Rowman & Littlefield Publishing Group, Inc.
4501 Forbes Boulevard, Suite 200, Lanham, Maryland 20706
www.rowman.com

Unit A, Whitacre Mews, 26–34 Stannary Street, London SE11 4AB

British Library Cataloguing in Publication Information Available

Library of Congress Cataloging-in-Publication Data
Names: Hendricks, Karin S., 1971– author. | National Association for
  Music Education.
Title: Compassionate music teaching : a framework for motivation and
  engagement in the 21st century / Karin S. Hendricks.
Description: Lanham : Rowman & Littlefield, [2018] | "Published in
  Cooperation with the National Association for Music Education." |
  Includes bibliographical references and index.
Identifiers: LCCN 2017060294 (print) | LCCN 2017060402 (ebook) |
  ISBN 9781475837346 (Electronic) | ISBN 9781475837322 (cloth :
  alk. paper) | ISBN 9781475837339 (pbk. : alk. paper)
Classification: LCC MT1 (ebook) | LCC MT1 .H44 2018 (print) |
  DDC 780.71—dc23
LC record available at https://lccn.loc.gov/2017060294

♾ The paper used in this publication meets the minimum requirements of American
National Standard for Information Sciences—Permanence of Paper for Printed Library
Materials, ANSI/NISO Z39.48–1992.

Printed in the United States of America

For Alisa, Josh, Marisa, Shawn, and Yui

Contents

Preface

If you were to name the top three things you love about teaching music, what would make that list? Certain repertoire? Musical expression? Students? Parents? Performing?

It is safe to assume that, for many of us, the teaching of musical technique—on its own—would not be at the top of the list. Of course, we teach technique on a daily basis, have a bag of tricks to approach each technical issue, and preach to students at all levels that solid technique is the foundation for expressive performance. But therein lies the point: Technique is merely a means for something much bigger.

It is not the development of technique that got most of us into this business; it is the students. It is the music. It is the dynamic interplay of connecting living, changing, unpredictable beings with living, changing, often unpredictable sounds—and dancing in the space between them. It is surfing the waves of unknown events and experiencing the unexpected: lesson plans gone awry, lessons gone surprisingly well, glimpses of virtuosity from students on whom we had prematurely given up hope. It is finding the unique key to unlock the motivation and potential within each individual student. It is thrilling. It is frustrating. It is exhilarating. It is so much more than a perfect embouchure or bow hold.

Although this book is titled *Compassionate Music Teaching,* it is really about students. It is about inspiring them, motivating them, connecting with them, listening to them, *hearing* them. It is about teaching them how to connect with others. Yet this book is also about teachers: listening to our own authentic voice and being true to ourselves so that we can, in turn, provide a place for students to learn to express themselves freely—through music and in countless other ways.

Compassionate Music Teaching bridges the worlds of research and practice, discussing cutting-edge and sometimes controversial topics while also offering practical strategies that are useful *today*. Each chapter is addressed from multiple lenses, including research in music, education, psychology, sociology, and related fields; insights from various students and teachers across the United States; and an in-depth study of five "compassionate music teachers" (CMTs) whom I interviewed specifically for this project. These CMTs have worked in a variety of teaching settings throughout the United States and represent a broad range of musical styles, ages, and pedagogies. The CMTs have all simultaneously exercised compassion for their students while still maintaining the highest musical standards, no matter their preferred genres or pedagogical styles.

As a part of this research-to-practice approach, I also weave in personal narratives from my own music-teaching career as a K–12 schoolteacher, private studio teacher, university professor, researcher, performer, and especially one who has learned by making a good share of mistakes over the past thirty years. The topic and approach both come as a result of conversations with teaching colleagues who requested that I offer something to our field about the ways in which teachers can relate to and engage with students. Because I am passionate about the topic of compassionate teaching as well as the need for research to reach those who are best positioned to act, I have accepted the challenge.

This book begins by taking a close look at the meaning of "compassion" in the context of music teaching—what it is and what it isn't, and why we need it more than ever. After introducing the five CMTs in chapter 2, I devote the remainder of the book to a discussion of how six qualities of compassion—trust, empathy, patience, inclusion, community, and authentic connection—have influenced human lives and how these qualities relate to what we do as music teachers. Parker Palmer, one example of a compassionate educator, wrote:

> Teachers possess the power to create conditions that can help students learn a great deal—or keep them from learning much at all. Teaching is the intentional act of creating those conditions, and good teaching requires that we understand the inner sources of both the intent and the act.[1]

I believe "good teaching" and "compassionate teaching" are one and the same. This book is dedicated to exploring those conditions that help students not only to learn, but also to grow, thrive, and freely express themselves—and to become compassionate musicians, teachers, performers, and people as well.

NOTE

1. Parker J. Palmer, *The Courage to Teach: Exploring the Inner Landscape of a Teacher's Life* (San Francisco, CA: Jossey-Bass, 2007), 7.

Acknowledgments

I express deep gratitude to the "compassionate music teachers" (CMTs) who participated in this research project. Thank you for sharing your time, wisdom, and insights for the purposes of this book. I am committed to honoring and sharing your ideas with other teachers and scholars who may glean from the compassionate ways in which you have guided students over the years. I have learned a great deal from what you have shared. Thanks also to Dijana Ihas and Angella Ahn for providing valuable reflections and resources about Dorothy DeLay.

A thousand thanks to my brother, Steven Hendricks, an extraordinarily successful high school band director who carefully read every word of the book manuscript to ensure that it would be well received by music teachers who are, for me, the most critical audience. Thank you, Steve, for providing me with the kind of direct, honest, and specific feedback that is characteristic of compassionate music teachers like you. This final version is much improved because of your contribution.

Words cannot express my gratitude to my research assistant Chad Putka, who generously transcribed research interviews, turned my scribbled drawings into presentable figures, and took the lead on reference editing. I could not have finished the book in a timely manner without your help. Thanks also to research assistant Yank'l Garcia, whose keen attention to detail was key in creating the index, and to Anna Halverson for helping me out of a time pinch with her fast typing skills.

Thanks to Naomi Copeland, Shawn Davern, Marisa Giangregorio, Alisa Granada, Brian Hendricks, Bob Hendricks, Ryan Hourigan, Josh Kanaga, Yui Kitamura, Al Legutki, Johanne Ray-Hepp, Megan Richards, Savana Ricker, Deejay Robinson, Michael Sundblad, and Brent Talbot for reviewing select portions of the book and offering ideas. Your suggestions and encouragement were exceptionally helpful. I acknowledge the support of Gary McPherson with the material on music ability development for this book in particular, as well as in prior research under his life-changing mentorship.

I express deepest gratitude to Tawnya Smith, my colleague and soul companion, and the most compassionate music teacher I know. You have inspired this book through your remarkable work with students of all ages, stages, and musical interests. I have learned a tremendous amount about trust, empathy, patience, inclusion, community, and authentic connection merely by observing the way you so graciously interact with others. Thank you for your help with photos, artwork, proofreading, and for being a constant support and wise guide through the entire book-writing process.

Finally, I offer appreciation to my own music teachers over the years, all of whom—each in their own ways—have inspired this research and who have shown me what compassionate music teaching can look like. I acknowledge the students I have taught over the past three decades. Each of you has taught me, day by day, how to be more compassionate. This book would not exist without you.

Chapter 1

The Nature of Compassion

Compassion is not a relationship between the healer and the wounded.
It's a relationship between equals. . . . Compassion becomes real when we
recognize our shared humanity.

—Pema Chödrön[1]

THE 21st-CENTURY SHIFT IN MUSIC EDUCATION

Educational approaches in the early part of the 20th century were, in many
ways, driven by an authoritarian, "no-nonsense," product-focused philosophy, as influenced by the factory management model in industry.[2] Music
education in the United States was also influenced by a strong military band
paradigm, due in large part to the influx of war veterans and other musicians
with limited teaching experience who entered the teaching workforce and
taught the genres and in the styles they knew best.[3] These trends took hold
and held fast for decades, with countless band directors leading from the
podium like sergeants and instilling deep adoration, fear, and respect from
those they led.

While initially eclipsed by the rise in instrumental music, choir programs
found their renaissance through celebrated *a cappella* choirs in which directors also demanded the highest standards from young singers.[4] String programs experienced a more gradual rise to prominence in school music over
the course of the century, with orchestra directors similarly taking on the
distinction of maestro that had been a part of their professional traditions
for centuries.[5] This rise in music ensembles as well as in efficient, autocratic
instructional approaches created an age of veneration for the "man on the

1

stand": The 20th-century image of the ensemble director on a pedestal was, in many American programs, as fundamental as A = 440.

This paradigm worked extremely well in a time and culture where people valued authority and loyalty over self and enjoyed the comfort of having one "right" or "best" way to accomplish a goal. "Just tell me what to do and I'll do it," devoted ensemble members have said, and they have been deeply committed to doing their part exactly as directed, thereby bringing honor to the entire group. Anyone who has watched Drum Corps International (DCI) finals, enjoyed the stunning productions of a university marching band, or experienced a conservatory-level performance of a choral masterwork knows that this approach is extremely effective in getting results of precision and group virtuosity. It can be truly breathtaking—and downright magical.

Meanwhile, many 20th-century private studios have thrived on an intensely competitive atmosphere. After all, if you're going to make it as a professional performer, you've got to be tough. With hundreds of applicants for every major spot in a professional orchestra, the stakes are much too high to spend any time messing around. For the small percentage of the population who aspire to be professional performers (classical or otherwise), a stiff practice regimen is not optional.

Traditional ensemble programs and classical music studios are alive and well, and likely will be for some time. The virtuosity of performers will also likely continue to rise to levels that we presently cannot even imagine. As we step further into the 21st century, however, we are witnessing an expansion of what it means to be a music educator, and even what it means to be "musical." While also maintaining strong and stunning classical programs, music educators in the United States are ever so gradually starting to join their international colleagues to make space for more diverse musical approaches, including (but not limited to) popular musics, various international musics, technology, and community music.[6]

This broadening of what it means to be musical requires an accompanied expansion in music education approaches. Many ensemble directors are not only expanding their repertoire, but also stepping off the podium and engaging in music-making with and among their students. Other music teachers are balancing the role of *maestro* with one of "facilitator"—affording their students an equal voice in the learning process.[7] Teacher-facilitators are asking questions of learners, thereby making room for multiple perspectives and ideas—something that is both thrilling and unnerving at the same time for those of us who were trained in the classical tradition.

Yet there is no need to fear. In many ways, it's liberating. As one who started my career with feet glued to the podium and a set of "right" ways to teach technique, I am personally grateful to let go of the unrealistic and unfair expectation that I have to be perfect—something a leader has to model when demanding it of everyone else, I can instead focus on exploring a variety of means for optimal and authentic expression.

This is where compassion comes in. By making space for diverse musics, learning styles, and pedagogical approaches, we shift our attention away from exacting external standards and move toward shared music-making with others whom, despite their usually younger age and lesser experience in certain areas, we recognize to be equal to us in the collective place we call humanity.

COMPASSION: WHAT IS IT?

In general terms, compassion is defined as "a process of connecting by identifying with another person."[8] However, as I discuss later, compassion is broader than empathy, as it involves having a disposition for helping others in ways that empathy in and of itself may lack. True compassion leads to action, regardless of whether the actor gains any benefit other than the sheer pleasure of seeing good work in the life of another. In 1759, philosopher Adam Smith stated it this way:

> How selfish soever man may be supposed, there are evidently some principles in his nature, which interest him in the fortunes of others, and render their happiness necessary to him, though he derives nothing from it, except the pleasure of seeing it. Of this kind is . . . compassion.[9]

As one scholar said about medical doctors: "Compassion is the emotion that starts the process of bringing physicians close to their patients, causes them to make the healing connection, and drives their desire to help."[10] Not surprisingly, then, compassion is noted as a requisite for anyone working in a helping profession such as teaching, medicine, or psychology.[11] In a field such as music, where expression and personhood intermingle with the content itself,[12] compassion may be even more critical.

Different Views of Compassion

The meaning of compassion varies from culture to culture.[13] On one end of the spectrum we can view compassion as an act of pity, where a person who is superior to another in some way reaches "down" and generously spares time and resources to help the person in a place of inferiority. On the other end of the spectrum is an interpretation of compassion that involves an understanding between equals, where no one is superior, but in which a person knows how to help another simply because of a shared awareness between them.

Our current educational system more closely aligns with the first notion of compassion as a superiority–inferiority relationship, with teachers viewed as having superior knowledge and experience over that of students. Curricula, tests, classroom structures, and even special tax deductions for K–12 educator expenses all support the expectation of teachers to have the answers, for students to sit silently and then prove that they were listening, and for teachers to willingly sacrifice their time and resources to make up the difference as they help those "less fortunate" than themselves.

The "hero" teacher narrative is one that we have come to take for granted, often without questioning what it truly means for us or for the students we serve. Although our egos might salivate at the idea of playing Superman or Wonder Woman in the classroom, such an approach to compassion demonstrates an inherent and ironic problem with power: Not only are students seen as inferior and helpless, but teachers are, in a sense, expected to act the role of benefactor, generously teaching out of the goodness of their hearts without adequate compensation or personal respect.

The definition of compassion as one of pity does not serve us in education. As teachers are placed in a superior position to students, they are simultaneously charged with full responsibility for any and all learning, thereby potentially underestimating the wisdom and contribution of students in the learning process. Furthermore, not only does a pity-based compassion approach significantly limit learning to the creativity and resources of just one person (the teacher), but it also promotes a view in which one person remains superior to others even after the learning has taken place. In a more egalitarian view of compassion in education, teacher and student have different roles to play in the learning process, but neither role is viewed as superior or inferior to the other.

Compassion as an Equalizer

Decades ago, Paulo Freire criticized the "banking" approach to education, in which teachers were viewed as merely "depositing" knowledge into students' minds and thereby transferring the same knowledge from generation to generation.[14] Instead, he proposed a more dialogic approach, in which teachers and students talked together, with teachers asking students questions and allowing students to come to their own understandings. The rationale for Freire's approach was unequivocally rooted in discussions of power: His "pedagogy of the oppressed" was intended to liberate those who had been treated and viewed as less human than others—and who had also come to perceive themselves the same way. Freire intended that this approach would not only allow the oppressed to see themselves differently and play their own critical role in liberating themselves, but to stop the cycle of oppression in the future, no matter who ended up in authority at any particular time.

This last point is critical: As long as there is a superior–inferior relationship, there is a need to control power. And as innumerable studies in a variety of academic fields have told us, as long as there is a power struggle, true learning cannot take place—at least not the learning that is intended. Rather, what students end up learning are lessons about power, authority, embarrassment, oppression, pain, and how to "win" or "lose" in a system with particular rules that favor one person or idea over another.

A Definition for "Compassion"

In this book, I choose a more egalitarian definition of "compassion," namely, as one of shared human experience between equals. In this view, those who exercise compassion have a sense of the feelings and needs of another and are motivated by that understanding to reach out and support one another. As the quote from Pema Chödrön at the beginning of this chapter suggests, this kind of compassion is not a relationship of superior to inferior, nor is it one of pity. It is a relationship of *experience-sharing* in which one might offer support to another based on a shared understanding of feelings, hopes, and/ or desires. In this more equalizing version of compassion, we still reach out to help, and we still sacrifice, but what we risk is not the same. Perhaps some would feel that what we *do* give in this model is even more challenging to give, because it is more personal.

Shared Passion

The word *compassion* derives from the Latin *com,* meaning "with," and *passion,* meaning "suffering."[15] In a traditional sense, compassion would mean sorrowing with another in that person's moment of pain. However, in today's language, the word *passion* has taken on a more positive connotation, suggesting a strong emotion or excitement—even enthusiasm for something.[16] Based on this understanding, I propose that a compassionate music teacher (CMT) in the 21st century is one who feels, understands, and even shares *the students'* enthusiasm for music and reaches out in ways that support *the students'* passions, visions, and desires—and then further awakens passion for music in their students.

Compassionate music teachers act as guides, supports, and champions of students' self-selected dreams, using the students' own aspirations for musical expression as a catalyst for emphasizing the practice of diverse technical skills. Facilitating this kind of learning requires that we listen, that we empathize, that we truly put ourselves in students' shoes and consider what learning looks like from the student's perspective. It follows, then, that we teach in the way that is best for each student or each class in each particular moment.

Compassionate music teaching approaches allow the direction and focus of an activity to shift unexpectedly or earlier than the lesson plan intended, because we understand that forcing a certain direction upon a brain in motion is wasteful and limiting.[17] It also requires that we set our egos aside. If, for example, a teaching approach that has always worked before suddenly or unexpectedly doesn't, we (a) pause, (b) exchange a reactive stance for a reflective one, (c) consider where the students got lost in the translation, and (d) step back to meet them there.

Approaches Guided by Compassion

A set agenda and rote approach might need to go out the window, of course, and this can be frightening. However, as we begin to open up to teaching approaches that are guided by compassion—and perhaps even invite our students to design learning experiences along with us—we may find that they stay better on task because they feel an ownership of the task in the first place.[18] In a compassionate approach, we allow learning to naturally unfold, negotiating with our students the "ifs" and "whys" and "hows" that likely will—with a bit of patience and creativity—eventually lead back to where we both wanted to go anyway, but without unnecessary resistance.

Compassionate music teachers are open to learning from students. They recognize that students can teach them things about music (and life) that they never knew or perhaps had forgotten along the way. As we become more compassionate, therefore, we might need to expand our musical vocabulary and try on new musical styles. As a result of listening to students, we may come to recognize the nuances and artistry in certain musics that we once considered inferior. As we listen to and learn from students, we may be inspired to try on new pedagogical tools and approaches that bolster more effective teaching and learning. We may learn to explore. We may learn to listen better. We may learn to share in new and exciting ways. We may learn to just *be*.

COMPASSION: WHAT IT ISN'T

- *Compassionate music teaching is not weakness.* Compassion is not letting students "walk all over us." Because we care, we are firm. Because we share their passions and understand their dreams, we hold them accountable to their own goals when they slip up. But we make it clear to students that this is what we are doing—reminding them of their own self-stated goals and agendas, and questioning them as to how their current behavior or lack of focus might or might not fit with these goals. In this vein, correction isn't personal, nor is it malicious (on either part). It's just a chance for focus, revision, and redirection.

Compassion does involve taking the time to explain to students how certain choices they make may or may not fit with certain passions, values, or goals. Communication involves taking the time to outline for students the steps that are necessary for them to reach their dreams, and to check in with them from time to time about their progress and motivation as it relates to those goals. Compassion also includes recognizing when students' goals might change, and being flexible enough to make sure that educational approaches still line up with the students' present needs and adjusted dreams.

Compassion might mean withholding rewards or opportunities, because we share a passion in something bigger than what is displayed in the present moment. Course correction can be administered with gentleness—with clear explanations of why—rather than using an authoritarian or threatening approach. Compassion might mean, for example, that we delay a student's performance of a piece because we share a passion for high-quality, self-expressive music and want the student to experience moments of success and emotional safety rather than embarrassment. Compassion might mean not encouraging students to learn a particular piece as soon as they would like, because we share a passion for the student's ability to play more advanced repertoire meaningfully—and we understand in a way that the student might not yet understand how bypassing certain technical skills will lead to unnecessary challenges or anxiety in the future.[19]

When we share goals and values of musical and educational excellence with students—and execute our actions and decisions through this lens—we are being compassionate. However, when our actions are self-serving and have more to say about our friction or disconnect with students, then we may need redirection: Is it possible that our goals and values really don't match those of the student? Perhaps the student needs to find a different teacher who shares more similar musical values? Perhaps the teacher needs to consider the reasons why a student has these particular goals and values? In moments of disconnect, doing a compassion check with ourselves might help us to understand whether we share the same goals, values, and dreams—or if, perhaps, there is a better option. It's not personal—it's just about fit.

- *Compassionate music teaching is not getting overly caught up in students' lives.* While compassionate teachers relate with their students' experiences, they neither try to live their lives for them, nor do they lose their own sense of self at the expense of their students' needs. According to experts at the HeartMath Institute, exercising too much sympathy creates a scenario in which "our heads overidentify with someone in need, and we start projecting our own concerns."[20] While compassionate teachers share their students' passions, they do not allow themselves to get personally engulfed by their students' problems. These authors further explain:

Compassion, on the other hand, is regenerative, and it offers intuitive understanding and potential solutions. It lets us feel what another is feeling while holding on to our own authenticity. We can embrace [another] without falling into over-responsibility and despair.[21]

Compassionate teachers keep professional and personal boundaries and maintain appropriate relationships with their students. Compassionate teachers are compassionate with themselves first and enjoy a healthful personal life outside of teaching so that they don't place too much energy or emotion on their students either during or outside of teaching time. The practices of self-care and self-compassion enable teachers to be able to "stay on top of their game" and avoid getting too close or experiencing burnout from overserving or over-care.

- *Compassionate music teaching is not impossible in an education system run by government accountability and testing.* Many of us have endured a number of government initiatives that promised to be the renaissance of schooling, but in reality just led to increased frustration and workload. Many of us have also persisted through countless hours of music advocacy presentations in the face of administrative cuts. It's hard when you feel as though someone else is controlling your teaching and you feel as if you can't advocate for your own passions, goals, and values, let alone those of your students. But compassionate teaching may, in fact, offer hope in ways that surprise us.

As will be explored further in chapter 3, one of the characteristics of compassion is building a relationship of trust with our students—something that researchers have found to make a vast difference in student achievement.[22] Furthermore, compassionate teachers know how to be creative, how to engage their students no matter the distractions, and how to continue doing what they love while making it align with the initiative *du jour*. We can't control everything that our students will experience or be required to undertake; however, we can make a difference by modeling good character (even in the most frustrating of times) and become more involved in our communities and in politics, using that fuel of compassion to advocate for young people in every way we can.

A BRIEF EXAMPLE: COMPASSIONATE LANGUAGE

In this book, I explore a number of approaches for compassionate teaching by describing six qualities of compassion (trust, empathy, patience, inclusion, community, and authentic connection). Here is one brief example to illustrate what compassionate music teaching is—and isn't—through a discussion of language. Compassionate teaching is often recognizable by the words that teachers use, and it includes a lot of questions, such as:

- *Guiding questions* (e.g., "What did you like about that?" "What would you do differently?" "What do you want to improve?");
- *Inspiring questions* (e.g., "What does this song remind you of?" "How would you like to phrase this passage?" "Which instrument do you think would sound good with this?" "What piece would you like to pick from this list?");
- *Connection questions* (e.g., "How did your soccer game go yesterday?" "Did you get that job you applied for?" "Would you like to help [a younger student] learn this technique?"); and
- *Goal-clarification questions* (e.g., "Do you like this piece?" "I noticed that you had a hard time focusing today. Is everything okay?" "How much time can you devote to practice this semester?")

Language that is not compassionate tends to include more telling, and more external judgment about people rather than about techniques or things.[23] Of course, there are blatant examples of mean, hurtful, and inappropriate words that we don't even need to include here. But other teacher-centered phrases that are commonly used and might need to be checked for intent include, "I want you to . . . ," "Play this again for me," "*My* choir," or, depending on the circumstance, even "I like that." Even praise can be noncompassionate when it is overused, unconstructive, or focuses on the teacher's desires being met rather than emphasizing the students' specific achievements.[24]

Asking questions allows the student to be an equal partner or even a leader in the learning process, while a "telling" approach keeps the control in the teacher's hands. Questions can help us avoid unnecessary judgment. Quite often students know what we are going to say before we say it anyway, especially when they have been taught to think for themselves. By asking questions, we encourage and teach students to self-assess, thus encouraging them to be independent learners.

In brief: If approaches or words focus the students' attention on meeting the teacher's requirements or pleasing the teacher, or if they don't allow space for self-assessment or self-expression, then they do not fit under this book's definition of compassion, no matter how well intended they may be.

OUR PRESENT NEED FOR COMPASSION

At a time when technology and globalization are leading to increased connections throughout the world—yet when domestic and international conflicts continue to keep so many of us separated and even in fear of one another—discussions of compassion and shared understandings are both timely and necessary. We have some tough questions to consider in the 21st century: Are we really connecting more with others throughout the world, or are the multiple information-sharing media merely making our differences more apparent? Are we coming together as a human family, or becoming increasingly polarized in our politics and beliefs? Is there a way to truly understand others who are different from us without losing our own sense of identity? Can we respect others' conflicting paradigms while still holding on to our own clarity of purpose?

In addition to the shift in musical styles and approaches that we are witnessing, the next several decades will find us teaching students with increasingly more diverse backgrounds. As we teach and make music with students of various cultures, languages, and musical heritages, we will likely find that a "color-blind" approach does not suit compassionate music teachers, because it does not allow a space for us to truly understand the unique experiences, needs, challenges, and strengths that each individual brings to the learning space.[25]

Furthermore, as my colleague and I have written, the "Net Generation" has very different needs than those of previous cohorts:

> Advances in technology have turned the world of teacher education upside down. Whereas the old educational model featured a [teacher] imparting wisdom and hard-earned knowledge to a classroom of note-taking students, today's [students] have access to more information via the mobile phones in their back pockets than any one [teacher] could possibly provide. This shift in technology welcomes a similar shift in teaching approach—one that is democratic, organic, project-based, experimental, and experiential—one in which the [teacher] becomes the "facilitator" of differentiated yet community-based learning, and allows learners to individually explore topics in ways that are personally meaningful.[26]

In this new age, we need qualities, skills, and approaches to meet the needs of this very different—and increasingly diverse—generation of students. As compassionate teachers, we will need to listen more, ask tough questions of our students (and of ourselves), and continually assess whether our tried-and-true approach is still working—or if we need to expand our outlook and/or techniques.

Our generation of teachers needs much more than basic general education skills (e.g., pedagogical content knowledge, skills, organizational skills) to be effective.[27] According to research by University of Massachusetts professor Sonia Nieto, additional qualities are needed to make a positive impact on students, particularly those who may be marginalized in some way: "a sense of mission; solidarity with, and empathy for, their students; the courage to challenge mainstream knowledge and conventional wisdom; improvisation; and a passion for social justice."[28] These qualities represent those of compassionate teachers, as we will further explore in later chapters of this book.

COMPASSION: OUR HUMAN BIRTHRIGHT

The 21st-century shift goes beyond music and education. It is worldwide in scope—with technology and globalization affecting the way we think, perceive the world, do business, engage in politics, and interact with others. Compassion is not just something that humans do by choice: Scientists suggest that we have an innate, instinctual drive to care for others. Researchers have even found signs of compassion at the neurological level: Brain activity has shown to be similar when mothers look at pictures of their own babies, and when other individuals have been asked to imagine someone being harmed.[29] In the words of psychology professor Dacher Keltner, "Compassion isn't simply a fickle or irrational emotion, but rather an innate human response embedded into the folds of our brains."[30]

Similarly, compassion education scholar Khen Lampert has drawn on principles of various religions from Christianity to Buddhism to show as well how compassion—which is distinctly different from emotional attachment—is both individual and universal.[31] According to Lampert, compassion is "the most basic human attribute in people"; in fact, "it is the anthropological meaning of humanity."[32] If this is so, why are we not always compassionate? Unfortunately, fear and self-preservation are also inherent within our brain wiring, and social and emotional skills need to be nurtured and developed to win out.[33] That's where what Lampert calls "radical compassion" or "compassion translated into real action" can come to play,[34] and that's where compassionate music teachers can make a tremendous difference.

Recently, multiple grassroots movements have arisen to advocate for compassion in our world, sparked by a similar belief that there is bright hope for the changing future if we focus on compassion today. The Charter for Compassion International,[35] now with over 800 global partners, acts as an international home organization for other movements, such as the Fetzer Institute, the Council of Conscience, and the Compassionate Action Network.[36] According to the Charter for Compassion, compassion is "born of our deep interdependence . . . [and] essential to human relationships and to a fulfilled humanity. It is . . . indispensable to the creation of a just economy and a peaceful global community."[37]

It is good news that we already have the capacity for compassion within us, because we are at a time in history and in music education when we desperately need it. As compassionate music teachers, we can reach out with understanding to young musicians who are also future teachers, leaders, and policymakers. By teaching through compassionate approaches, we increase the possibility that our students, too, will reach out to others with compassion and understanding. By modeling compassion to those in our care, we plant seeds of compassion for the future.

Reflection Questions

1. What are your primary priorities as a music teacher? Are you able to rank these priorities? If so, why did you choose the order that you did? What circumstances or events might shift the weight of one priority to another?
2. What are some specific ways that you can simultaneously be compassionate with students' shortcomings and also encourage high musical quality?
3. What types of questions do you (or someone you admire) use to instruct and motivate students? Do you (or this person) use an effective balance of guiding, inspiring, connection, and goal-clarification questions? Is there an area of questioning that you might further explore?
4. Are there any aspects of the teaching approach described in this chapter that you hesitate to try? If so, what are they? Why do you think you might feel the way you do? What would help you to feel more comfortable in trying out this approach?

NOTES

1. Pema Chödrön, *The Places That Scare You: A Guide to Fearlessness in Difficult Times* (Boston, MA: Shambhala Publications, 2007), 47.
2. Randall Everett Allsup, "Democracy and One Hundred Years of Music Education," *Music Educators Journal* 93, no. 5 (2007): 52–56; Michael Mark and Charles L. Gary, *A History of American Music Education* (Lanham, MD: Rowman & Littlefield Education, 2007).
3. Robert A. Cutietta, "During the Renaissance I Want to Be a Suzuki Teacher" (keynote address), International Research Symposium on Talent Education, Minneapolis, MN, May 22, 2014; James A. Keene, *A History of Music Education in the United States* (Hanover: University Press of New England, 1982); Mark and Gary, *A History of American Music Education*.
4. Keene, *A History of Music Education in the United States*.
5. Keene, *A History of Music Education in the United States;* Mark and Gary, *A History of American Music Education*.
6. Janet R. Barrett, "Forecasting the Future of Professional Associations in Music Education," *New Directions in Music Education* 1, no. 1, accessed August 19, 2017, https://www.newdirectionsmsu.org/issue-1/barrett-forecasting-the-future-of-professional-associations-in-music-education; Lucy Green, *Music, Informal Learning and the School: A New Classroom Pedagogy* (Burlington, VT: Ashgate, 2008); Marie McCarthy, "Widening Horizons with a Global Lens: MENC Responds to the New

World Order, 1982–2007," *Journal of Historical Research in Music Education* 28, no. 2 (2007): 140–54; Gary E. McPherson and Graham F. Welch, eds., *The Oxford Handbook of Music Education* (New York: Oxford University Press, 2012).

7. See Randall Everett Allsup, "Mutual Learning and Democratic Action in Instrumental Music Education," *Journal of Research in Music Education* 51, no. 1 (2003): 24–37; Randall Everett Allsup, "Democracy and One Hundred Years of Music Education," *Music Educators Journal* 93, no. 5 (2007): 52–56; Lee Higgins, "The Creative Music Workshop: Event, Facilitation, Gift," *International Journal of Music Education* 26, no. 4 (2008): 326–38; Lee Higgins and Patricia Shehan Campbell, *Free to Be Musical: Group Improvisation in Music* (Lanham, MD: Rowman & Littlefield, 2010).

8. Eric J. Cassell, "Compassion," in *The Oxford Handbook of Positive Psychology,* ed. C. R. Snyder and Shane J. Lopez (New York: Oxford University Press, 2009), 395.

9. Adam Smith, *Theory of Moral Sentiments* (Indianapolis, IN: Liberty Classics, 1759/1976), 9, quoted in Cassell, "Compassion," 398.

10. Cassell, "Compassion," 402.

11. Ibid.

12. Susan A. O'Neill, "Perspectives and Narratives on Personhood and Music Learning," in *Personhood and Music Learning: Connecting Perspectives and Narratives,* ed. Susan A. O'Neill (Waterloo, ON: Canadian Music Educators Association, 2014), 1–14.

13. For a more detailed description of compassion across cultures and religions, see Khen Lampert, *Compassionate Education: A Prolegomena for Radical Schooling* (Lanham, MD: University Press of America, 2003).

14. Paulo Freire, *Pedagogy of the Oppressed, 30th Anniversary Edition* (New York: Continuum, 2007).

15. See Sherlyn Jimenez, "Compassion," in *The Encyclopedia of Positive Psychology, Volume I,* ed. Shane J. Lopez (Malden, MA: Blackwell, 2009), 209–15.

16. *Merriam-Webster Online, s.v.* "passion," August 23, 2017, http://www.merriam-webster.com/dictionary/passion.

17. Eric E. Jensen, *Teaching with the Brain in Mind* (Alexandria, VA: Association for Supervision and Curriculum Development, 1998).

18. Deborah V. Blair, "Stepping Aside: Teaching in a Student-Centered Music Classroom," *Music Educators Journal* 95, no. 3 (2009): 42–45; Susan A. O'Neill, "Youth Music Engagement in Diverse Contexts," in *Organized Activities as Context for Development: Extracurricular Activities, After-School Programs, and Community Programs,* ed. Joseph L. Mahoney, Reed W. Larson, and Jacquelynne S. Eccles (Mahwah, NJ: Lawrence Erlbaum Associates, 2005), 255–73; and James M. Renwick and Gary E. McPherson, "Interest and Choice: Student-Selected Repertoire and Its Effect on Practising Behaviour," *British Journal of Music Education* 19, no. 2 (2002): 173–88.

19. Casey McGrath, Karin S. Hendricks, and Tawnya D. Smith, *Performance Anxiety Strategies: A Musician's Guide to Managing Stage Fright* (Lanham, MD: Rowman & Littlefield, 2017).

20. Doc Childre and Howard Martin, *The HeartMath Solution* (New York: HarperCollins, 1999), 43.

21. Ibid.

22. Anthony S. Bryk and Barbara Schneider, "Trust in Schools: A Core Resource for School Reform," *Educational Leadership* 60, no. 6 (2003): 40–45; Anthony S. Bryk and Barbara Schneider, *Trust in Schools: A Core Resource for Improvement* (New York: Russell Sage Foundation, 2002); Patrick B. Forsyth, Laura L. B. Barnes, and Curt M. Adams, "Trust-Effectiveness Patterns in Schools," *Journal of Educational Administration* 44, no. 2 (2006): 122–41; Goddard, Roger D., "Relational Networks, Social Trust, and Norms: A Social Capital Perspective on Students' Chances of Academic Success," *Educational Evaluation and Policy Analysis* 25, no. 1 (2003): 59–74; Parker J. Palmer, *The Courage to Teach: Exploring the Inner Landscape of a Teacher's Life* (San Francisco, CA: Jossey-Bass, 2007); Thomas J. Sergiovanni, "The Virtues of Leadership," *The Educational Forum* 69, no. 2, (2005): 112–23.

23. Casey McGrath, Karin S. Hendricks, and Tawnya D. Smith, *Performance Anxiety Strategies: A Musician's Guide to Managing Stage Fright* (Lanham, MD: Rowman & Littlefield, 2017).

24. See Alfie Kohn, *Punished by Rewards: The Trouble with Gold Stars, Incentive Plans, A's, Praise, and Other Bribes* (Boston, MA: Houghton Mifflin, 1999); Karin S. Hendricks, Tawnya D. Smith, and Jennifer Stanuch, "Creating Safe Spaces for Music Learning," *Music Educators Journal* 101, no. 1 (2014): 35–40; McGrath, Hendricks, and Smith, *Performance Anxiety Strategies*.

25. Louis S. Bergonzi, "To See in Living Color and to Hear the Sound of Silence: Preparing String Teachers for Culturally Diverse Classrooms," in *String Teaching in America: Strategies for a Diverse Society,* ed. Jane Linn Aten (Alexandria, VA: American String Teachers Association, 2006), 77–100; Gloria Ladson-Billings, "But That's Just Good Teaching! The Case for Culturally Relevant Pedagogy," *Theory into Practice* 34, no. 3 (1995): 159–65; Gloria Ladson-Billings, "Toward a Theory of Culturally Relevant Pedagogy," *American Educational Research Journal* 32, no. 3 (1995): 465–91.

26. Karin S. Hendricks and Ann M. Hicks, "Uses of Technology in an 'Immersive Learning' Teacher Preparation Course," in *Music and Media Infused Lives: Music Education in a Digital Age*, ed. Susan A. O'Neill (Waterloo, ON: Canadian Music Educators Association, 2014), 328.

27. Sonia Nieto, "Solidarity, Courage and Heart: What Teacher Educators Can Learn from a New Generation of Teachers," *Intercultural Education* 17, no. 5 (2006): 457–73.

28. Ibid., 457.

29. Jonathan D. Cohen, "The Vulcanization of the Human Brain: A Neural Perspective on Interactions between Cognition and Emotion," *Journal of Economic Perspectives* 19, no. 4 (2005): 3–24; Joshua D. Greene, R. Brian Sommerville, Leigh E. Nystrom, John M. Darley, and Jonathan D. Cohen, "An fMRI Investigation of Emotional Engagement in Moral Judgment," *Science* 293, no. 5537 (2001): 2105–108; Jack B. Nitschke, Eric E. Nelson, Brett D. Rusch, Andrew S. Fox, Terrence R. Oakes, and Richard J. Davidson, "Orbitofrontal Cortex Tracks Positive Mood in Mothers Viewing Pictures of their Newborn Infants," *Neuroimage* 21, no. 2 (2004): 583–92, cited in Dacher Keltner, "The Compassionate Instinct," in *The Compassionate Instinct: The Science of Human Goodness,* ed. Dacher Keltner, Jason Marsh and Jeremy Adam Smith (New York: Norton, 2010), 8–15.

30. Keltner, "The Compassionate Instinct," 10.

31. Lampert, *Compassionate Education*.

32. Ibid., 172.

33. See Scott N. Edgar, *Music Education and Social Emotional Learning: The Heart of Teaching Music* (Chicago, IL: GIA Publications, 2017); Daniel Goleman, *Emotional Intelligence* (New York: Bantam, 2006); see also Collaborative for Academic, Social, and Emotional Learning, "What Is Social and Emotional Learning?" *Collaborative for Academic, Social, and Emotional Learning*, accessed August 4, 2016, http://www.casel.org/social-and-emotional-learning.

34. Lampert, *Compassionate Education,* 173.

35. Charter for Compassion International, "The Charter for Compassion," *Charter for Compassion*, accessed July 25, 2014, http://www.charterforcompassion.org.

36. Charter for Compassion International, "About the Charter for Compassion," *Charter for Compassion,* accessed July 25, 2014, http://charterforcompassion.org/about-charter.

37. Charter for Compassion International, "The Charter for Compassion," *Charter for Compassion,* accessed August 4, 2016, http://www.charterforcompassion.org/index.php/charter.

Chapter 2

Models of Compassion

I believe in being kind. I think that I have to do my job and I have to do it in a kind way and a constructive way. Even though the basic message is the same, the way it is presented is what is really important. You can tell somebody the same thing in two, three, or four different ways. One way, they can listen to you and feel terrible, and another way they can listen to you and feel wonderful.

—Itzhak Perlman[1]

This book is sprinkled with insights from several compassionate music teachers, including five whom I studied specifically for this project. Before delving into the six qualities of compassion in later chapters, I first introduce each of those teachers (hereafter referred to as "compassionate music teachers," or CMTs) to provide a background about their unique personalities and successes. Although their stories, backgrounds, and music teaching spaces are unique—something I intentionally sought out among potential participants for this research—these teachers share a common passion for music, for teaching, and for their students.

Four of the five CMTs were recommended for the project by their own students, music parents, or colleagues, who recognized the five qualities of compassion in their teaching approaches. These CMTs were also recommended because of their ability to simultaneously exemplify these compassionate qualities while also eliciting the highest levels of musicianship in their students. In these four cases I had the opportunity to work closely with the CMT and/or observe the CMT in action before conducting a personal interview. I also consulted regularly with the CMTs while preparing the manuscript, cherishing their insights as a means of providing both credence and life to the ideas presented here.[2]

Although the renowned violin pedagogue Dorothy DeLay passed away in 2002, I include information about her in this book because of the legendary ways in which she used what I call "compassionate teaching" approaches to draw out the very best in her students—students who have gone on to become some of the world's most successful violinists. In this case, I consulted a number of published sources about Miss DeLay. I reached out to violinist Angella Ahn, who graciously offered a personal reflection of her long-time former teacher. In addition, I interviewed Dijana Ihas, who has conducted extensive research with several other former students of Miss DeLay.[3] Dr. Ihas has been most generous in sharing findings of her research for inclusion in this book.[4]

The five CMTS are all remarkably accomplished in their own unique and individual ways. They are introduced in this chapter in alphabetical order. I offer a brief biography for each, followed by specific insights about how these teachers exemplify the qualities of compassionate music teaching.

Dorothy DeLay

One of the great forces in the world of violin teaching, Dorothy DeLay, . . . died at the age of 84, leaving a legacy of pupils that includes many of today's greatest violinists. . . . DeLay taught primarily at New York's prestigious Juilliard School, but her net also encompassed Sarah Lawrence College, north of New York, the New England Conservatory in Boston, the University of Cincinnati, and, during the summer, the Aspen festival.

Her teaching methods were unconventional. She was not old-school and authoritarian, thrusting the same style on to all comers. Her secret was to treat each student as an individual and to play to their strengths, encouraging each to do better and establishing great self-esteem. . . . It was an approach that caused uproar in the rarefied environment of the teaching of the musical elite. . . . For DeLay, the answer lay in teaching the student, not the subject. She felt the power and influence of a teacher's words were a terrific responsibility, and that success lay in encouraging students to believe in themselves.[5]

It is hard to determine which is more remarkable about Dorothy DeLay: the number of world-renowned virtuosos to come out of her studio, or the unique way in which she—so differently than other conservatory colleagues of her generation—empowered her students to become agents of their own learning. I would argue that these two remarkable features are not coincidental, but that her teaching approach had everything to do with her students' success. It was, perhaps, for this reason that so many Juilliard violin students, Itzhak Perlman among them, chose to move to DeLay's violin studio when she parted ways with the legendary Ivan Galamian, whom she had previously assisted.[6]

Figure 2.1. Dorothy DeLay teaching a young Angella Ahn at the Aspen Music Festival and School, Aspen, Colorado. Figure courtesy of Angella Ahn.

Galamian and DeLay are both remembered as legendary teachers who, although they taught in the same school, used teaching approaches that were miles apart. Galamian, ever the authoritarian, is remembered to have used the same approach with every student, with hardly any variation, focusing only on particular techniques and repertoire that he taught well and with which he had great success. There was only one way to learning in Galamian's studio, and other ways, concerns, or repertoire was not to be explored. His approach was systematic, codified, and his demeanor gruff and distant. According to Itzhak Perlman, Galamian's motivational approach could be coined as "Scare You to Death" in that he used intimidation to demand the highest level of playing from his students.[7]

Dorothy DeLay, on the other hand, fostered the highest levels of virtuosity through a much more flexible and nurturing approach. She routinely asked students questions, was willing to entertain their requests for specific technical help, was open to hearing new repertoire they would bring, and turned each lesson into one of mutual learning and exploration. Even the simplest instructions (e.g., "Sugarplum, what is your concept of F-sharp?" or "Why is [this note] out of tune?") were ones in which students were empowered—and charged—to think for themselves.[8]

Many of DeLay's students, such as Nadja Salerno-Sonnenberg and others who were used to a more authoritarian approach, had to adjust to DeLay's flexibility when joining her studio. Salerno-Sonnenberg described her initial frustration at not being given all the answers, as well as her eventual recognition about how valuable this approach was in helping her become an independent virtuoso:

> Sometimes I'd get so mad I'd yell, "I don't know [the answer to your question]! Why are you getting paid? What is this, I'm teaching myself?" [In hindsight] I was right. She was teaching me to teach myself—and that's why she is a great teacher.[9]

DeLay's teaching and mentorship went far beyond violin technique, as she was genuinely and deeply concerned about the personal and professional lives of her students. She continued in long-term relationships with her students after they left her studio, playing an active role in their employment and professional success.[10]

Dorothy DeLay was unique among conservatory-level teachers in that she did not have a particular method but instead worked on an individual-need basis with her students. She explored and learned along with them, even correcting a student who said that she loved teaching by stating "I love to *learn*."[11] She subscribed to the power of positive affirmation, exposing students to a number of approaches, communicating openly, motivating through pleasure rather than fear, involving students in goal-setting, and using empathy as a means of determining the best way to approach individual student needs.[12]

Angella Ahn, who studied with Dorothy DeLay for fourteen years, described the lasting impact that DeLay had on her playing, teaching, and life:

> I'm going into my 8th year of teaching at Montana State University. Not one day goes by while working with my students when I don't ask myself, "What would Ms. DeLay do? How would she explain this?" I have an ongoing conversation with my late teacher: How do I help student A improve on pitch without discouraging him about his ability to hear accurately? How can I show the best way to produce a fuller tone to student B without pressing on her bow? How do I explain the importance of not just playing what's on the page but telling a story?
>
> Fourteen years of studying with the same teacher really leaves an imprint on you. She taught me not only to play the violin to my best ability, but also to be assertive, kind, thoughtful, and caring. There isn't a more compassionate teacher than Ms. DeLay. Some of her students say she had a dual role as a psychiatrist and a violin teacher, and I would have to agree. She had a knack for finding every student's individual strengths. And she had so many students!
>
> She guided every student in a unique way. If the student needed more encouragement, she gave it. If the student needed more modesty, she worked on that.

If the student had a strong left hand but needed help with his/her bow arm, she knew how to focus on that. She encouraged her studio to be supportive, compassionate, and empathetic towards each other. She taught us so much more than just violin playing. She taught us how to be professionals.[13]

Steve Massey

Stephen C. Massey, chairman of the music department in the Foxborough (MA) Public Schools, supervises an extensive music curriculum for grades 1–12. His high school wind ensembles, concert bands, and jazz ensembles have consistently received state, regional, and national recognition. Mr. Massey's ensembles have made ten recordings and hosted dozens of world-class guest artists, conductors, and composers. The Foxborough HS Jazz Ensemble and Wind Ensemble have consistently received gold medals at district, state, national, and international music festivals over the last three decades.

In 1997 the Jazz Ensemble attended the Essentially Ellington *High School Jazz Band Competition & Festival at Jazz at Lincoln Center for the first time and won the competition. They have since qualified for the finals eleven times, which is the most of any high school group in the country. The 1999 Foxborough High School Wind Ensemble was one of sixteen ensembles nationwide invited to the Bands of America Concert Band Festival in Indianapolis. In 2009 the Foxborough Jazz Ensemble was the only amateur group at a pre-inaugural event at the Kennedy Center in Washington, DC, with other performers in attendance including Wynton Marsalis, Dianne Reeves, Paquito D'Rivera, and Dave Brubeck, who performed with the Foxborough Jazz Ensemble.*

Mr. Massey has guest-conducted numerous district and all-state concert bands and jazz bands, including the All Northwest Jazz Band in Portland,

Figure 2.2. Steve Massey. Figure credit: Brian Doherty.

Oregon, and the New York, Rhode Island, New Hampshire, and Massachu-
setts All State Jazz Bands. The Massachusetts Music Educators Association
presented Mr. Massey with the Lowell Mason Award for Leadership in Music
Education in 1997, and the Massachusetts Instrumental Conductors Association
honored him with the Conductor of the Year Award in 1994. The Massachusetts
Unit of the International Association of Jazz Educators recognized Mr. Massey
with a lifetime achievement award in 2005.[14]

Even in the moment that I inserted Steve Massey's biography into this manuscript, I noted how quintessentially "Steve Massey" it is: Very little of the extended biography from which I drew this smaller excerpt centered around Steve, but instead focused on the accomplishments of his students. Massey would not have it any other way. For forty-six years as a school band director, he has tirelessly centered his life and career around his students—who now include children of former students—dedicating his efforts to teaching them how to be independent learners and leaders.

Massey is the mastermind behind a district music program that runs like a well-oiled machine, bringing together students, school faculty, administrators, parents, and other community members and teachers who each contribute with pride to the program's success. Over the past three decades, Massey has become so respected in his community that, should you ask a Foxborough, Massachusetts local who the hometown celebrity is, Tom Brady and Bill Belichick might be their second and third choice. Massey, in the meantime, has not only influenced the music scene in Foxborough to become one that regularly hosts jazz superstars, but his educational approach has changed the way a sizeable portion of the population views life, leadership, and responsibility.

A large part of Massey's success has to do with the way in which he empowers and trusts his students to take on critical leadership roles. I am not talking about student officers who merely order T-shirts and plan parties; rather, students are engaged at every possible level in *musical* endeavors, from concert logistics to teaching and mentoring other students to be successful musicians. The music itself is the highest priority in the Foxborough culture, and Massey is the leader of a *musical* culture where everyone—including students, music faculty, and parents—has a particular role to play to make the music everything it can be.

To maintain this process of leadership, Massey holds student leadership classes every Friday morning before school, in which he teaches his students leadership skills such as teaching music to others, motivating other students to practice, fostering a caring ensemble, and developing empathy for others. Not only do the students show up each Friday morning, but they also regularly take home their newfound wisdom and share it with their parents. At one school concert I attended, a parent shared with me how her son would regularly share "Mr. Massey wisdom" with the family at dinner, encouraging the family to incorporate some of the leadership principles in their own home.

In one of Steve Massey's final performances before his retirement in the spring of 2017, jazz legend Wynton Marsalis—a longtime friend and collaborator of Massey—made a surprise visit to honor (and play with) Massey and the Foxborough Jazz Ensemble. Wynton Marsalis gave a personal tribute to Massey, speaking of the integrity, love, sacrifice, soul, and generosity of spirit that Marsalis had witnessed in Massey over their many years of knowing one another:

> Integrity is a word we hear all the time, but we see it very seldom, because integrity costs. [Steve Massey] possesses tremendous integrity. . . . When he walks into a room, all of our music is brought into the room with him because of the level of his integrity and the depth of it. . . . He loves his kids. That's why they play the way that they play. He loves the music. He's willing to sacrifice for it, and he knows about it. Love manifests itself in knowledge, and he has been dedicated for such a long time. . . . Soul means when you walk into a room, people feel better when you leave than they felt before you came in. This is what he has. . . . I want you all to know the depth of love I have for this man. . . . More than a job well done. The definition of the job.[15]

Brian Michaud

Brian Michaud currently teaches grades K–4 and chorus in Dighton, Massachusetts. He holds a bachelor's degree from Berklee College of Music, a master's degree from the University of Connecticut, and a Doctor of Musical Arts from Boston University. Brian holds a Kodály teaching certificate from the Kodály Music Institute at New England Conservatory, has completed two levels of Orff training, is a certified Music Together teacher, and is versed in Dalcroze and Gordon's Music Learning Theory. Brian has been a finalist for Massachusetts Teacher of the Year and has presented at state and national conferences.

A performer at heart, Brian has played professionally as a vocalist, guitarist, bassist, pianist, and drummer in a wide variety of musical settings from classical and jazz to rock and country. Of all the genres he performs, Brian admits that he loves playing in rock bands most of all; there is an allure to being on stage and having the audience dance the night away, and he loves the exhilaration when the crowd cheers and begins to sing along as soon as the first couple of chords hit the air.

In addition to teaching and performing, Brian has published two young adult fiction books, The Road to Nyn *and* The Ring of Carnac; *his writing talents gained him a presenter's spot at the 2017 Massachusetts Readers Association Conference. Outside of his professional career, Brian takes pride in being a husband to his wife, Kim, and a father to his daughter, Faith. He enjoys*

Figure 2.3. Brian Michaud. Figure courtesy of Brian Michaud.

spending time with his family and traveling to new and exciting locations,
especially those with an interesting history to share. At home, he is constantly
working on one handyman project or another while his wife stands ready with
a steady supply of bandages.[16]

A rock music performer in his spare time and an elementary general music
teacher by day, Brian Michaud is a kid at heart—so much so that he reminds
his colleagues of Tom Hanks in the movie *Big*. Michaud's classes are highly
structured and well planned, yet clothed in fun and engaging activities that
feature ample opportunities for students to try out leadership roles. If you
were to walk into his elementary classroom, you might find him acting the
role of student, doing whatever the present student leader requested: singing,
dancing, jumping, crawling on the floor—anything, Michaud says, except
wiggling like a worm: "The only thing I won't do is the worm. When the
students want to do the worm, I go, 'You do that so I don't have to go to the
hospital.'"

I am a big kid, so for me it's very easy to connect with the kids. I enjoy what
I do. I enjoy playing the games, I enjoy singing the songs, so I don't have to fake
it. There are those moments where I'm thinking, "Oh my God, if I sing 'Doggie,
Doggie, Where's Your Bone' one more time I'm gonna cry," but for the most
part, I enjoy the songs that I do with them.

I enjoy seeing them learn, and seeing their progress, like when the child
who's in 2nd grade finally uses their singing voice after talking like a frog for
two years. I love what I do, so I think it's not a job for me. Somebody once said

to me, "You know you've found the right job if you could do it for 40 hours a week and not get paid." And if I was independently wealthy, I could still go to work every day and not worry about getting paid. I just enjoy it.

Michaud teaches in a small, rural community with a population of approximately 7,000 people. He has taught at Dighton Elementary for twenty-two years—the only teaching "gig" he has ever had. Like Steve Massey, Michaud has taught in the same community for so long that he is now teaching children of his former students. Over those two decades, he has learned through trial and error that genuine connection and active engagement with students pays off with countless dividends.

Michaud has spent many years designing and refining a grade-by-grade elementary music curriculum based on his background in Kodály and other well-known approaches. Although he has a definite lesson outline with specific standards and objectives for the students to meet, the day-to-day interactions and execution of his general plan are fueled by student-centered activities that engage and empower the students:

> I try and give the students decisions whenever possible. A lot of times we'll be doing an activity and I'll have them take over my job as leader. I try to put myself in the shoes of the kids when I'm designing a lesson. I'll say, "OK, if I were a ten-year-old boy or a six-year-old girl, what would I enjoy doing?"

Brian Michaud's student-centered approach involves strategies that include opportunities for student choice. He arranges the classroom to encourage movement and sharing of leadership roles, exercises empathy with students, and asks them about (and listens to) their needs and interests.

Marcus Santos

A contemporary percussionist and educator, Marcus Santos is a native of Bahia, Brazil. He commits his life to the study, teaching, and performance of his hometown's Afro-Brazilian music and heritage. Marcus has performed with several world-famous artists such as the Gypsy Kings (Spain), Daniela Mercury (Brazil), and the Brand New Heavies (England). He has also performed for the president of Brazil, TEDx, and with the "One World Band" produced by MTV. Marcus played at the Sony Pictures' Oscar-nominated movie Rachel's Getting Married *with Anne Hathaway. He has been honored with the 2013 KOSA Recognition Award, Outstanding Arts Performer Award by the Brazilian Immigrant Center (2008) as well as Outstanding Percussionist Award by Berklee College of Music in 2004.*

Marcus is the author of the DVD Modern Approach to Pandeiro *and performed in the DVD* Musically Speaking II *by BOSE. Marcus has led workshops on Afro-Brazilian percussion and music for social change in festivals, universities, and*

Figure 2.4.   Marcus Santos. Figure credit: Tom Schwartz.

conventions around the world such as Fiesta del Tambor (Cuba), Carnegie Hall (NYC), PASIC (USA), and Harvard University. He is currently the artist director of the Grooversity network project that includes twenty-four drumming groups from the United States, Canada, Germany, and France.[17]

I was first introduced to Marcus Santos while finding practicum placements for students in my secondary general music methods class at Boston University. I gave my students a large selection of secondary general music teachers in the Boston area from which to choose, allowing them to go where they were most interested and then to reflect about the experiences later with the rest of us. Over the course of the semester, I noticed that an increasingly larger number of students started to report visits at Somerville High School, where Santos taught world percussion and general music. Week after week, my students came back exhilarated, inspired, and amazed by the way that Santos could create excitement and energy in any and every student, with whatever resources he had.

Here are some of the ways my students described him:

"Marcus Santos is a master."
"Exciting and energetic"
"Palpable enthusiasm"
"Carefree yet controlled"
"Infectious attitude and passion"
"Super encouraging to all the kids"
"Relatable and warm and easygoing"
"Completely captivating"
"Charismatic and unflappably upbeat"
"Passionate and humorous."

Yet, with all of his enthusiasm, Santos is anything but a pushover or someone just letting kids bang on drums all day. Rather, he addresses his students by name, teaches them theoretical and historical principles, zooms fluently and effortlessly between detail and holism, and consistently exacts the highest standards of percussive techniques. As my students also described,

"He's not just a pretty face."
"He is that unique case where his passion for teaching seems directly channeled into its efficacy."
"Over the course of an hour, four out of five mornings a week, these students are transformed from sleepy, [apathetic] teenagers, to engaged musicians who actively create and communicate with each other through drumming."

Enthusiasm and energy are just the frosting on the cake, on top of lessons that are carefully strategized to surf the waves of adolescent energy and to engage a classroom of diverse learners with a breadth of different needs. Sequencing, pacing, scaffolding, choreographed movement, alternation of activities—and even the coordinated crescendo of sound and activity in each class period—all play a role in Santos's ability to transform a class of urban high school general music students with a variety of skill levels and cultural backgrounds into empowered, capable, and self-directed percussionists.

Renae Timbie

Renae Timbie currently serves full-time as worship director at Westminster Presbyterian Church in Muncie, Indiana. She has previously worked as visiting instructor of music at the American University in Cairo, Egypt, as well as held part-time positions at Taylor University, Ball State University, and Boston University. She has taught various choral ensembles in the collegiate and community settings, as well as academic courses primarily in music appreciation

Figure 2.5.   Renae Timbie. Figure courtesy of Renae Timbie.

*and world music. Dr. Timbie's teaching and research interests include the rela-
tionship of music and culture, music in social justice, and collaborative learning
in choral education.*

*Renae's upbringing as a third-cultural kid (TCK) in Egypt and France
has contributed to her passion to connect cultures and engage worldviews
through music. Renae enjoys collaborating with musicians and people of all
backgrounds to facilitate meaningful music making and create engaging performances. She holds a Doctor of Arts in Choral Conducting from Ball State
University, Master of Music in Choral Conducting from Ball State University,
and Bachelor of Arts in Voice Performance from Taylor University.*[18]

Interviewing Renae Timbie about empathy is like asking a fish about
water; she has a keen and instinctual ability to connect deeply with people no
matter who they are, and no matter their worldview. Timbie is a U.S. citizen
by passport and heritage, but she walks fluently between American and Arab
worlds. Her developmental years were spent living in Egypt, where her parents served as Christian missionaries, and her heart remains with the Egyptian

people. Her experience living in various parts of the world as a child, student, and most recently as a visiting professor at the American University in Cairo has allowed her to develop the background and understanding to view all people as human beings with feeling, dignity, and worth.

Timbie's sense of empathy, openness, and hospitality has propelled her work as a choral director in university, church, and community settings, and most recently in her teaching of Syrian refugee children during a visit to Greece. She regularly engages students in collaborative group work—even in standard choral rehearsals: She provides choir members with opportunities to engage in small groups to examine and challenge assumed rehearsal and performance practices, based on the cultural knowledge they glean together about the repertoire they perform.[19] Then, after students have studied a particular musical culture well enough to situate their performance in context, she provides an opportunity for them to challenge traditional performance approaches and design new ways to more empathically connect with that particular culture through performance. As a result, she cannot always predict how a performance might end up; however, she can count on it being meaningful.

Timbie's collaborative, student-driven approach to learning choral repertoire is intentionally subversive, as she has claimed that her approach "aims to shift the authority of knowledge from the teacher to the learners. It challenges the long-established hierarchy of teacher-to-student."[20] Her focus with collaborative learning—what one of her more traditional choral director colleagues called "terrifying" in the way that it usurps the authority of the baton—Timbie simply calls "compassion."

Timbie has found that her approach produces "opportunities for social interaction, for encountering other cultures through music, and for expanding the students' worldview."[21] And, based on her success and intrinsic rewards using such an approach, she sees no reason for any other choral director to be afraid. In fact, Timbie remarked that she "can't imagine teaching without collaborative learning" in any context.[22]

Recently, Timbie spent a week in a Syrian refugee camp in Greece, interacting with children and parents who, she said, had "seen hell." During this week, she made music with children, helping them gain a sense of self-worth and purpose after everything else in their life had been stripped away from them. Over the course of the week, she witnessed the situation of children in the refugee camp morph from a state of disarray and confusion to one with children who had a glimpse of peace, purpose, and musical healing. As of this writing, Timbie is working out the details to move to Greece full-time so she can continue to facilitate musical healing with those who have lost virtually everything.

CONCLUDING THOUGHTS

This chapter celebrates the successes of five CMTs, demonstrating how each inspires and engages with students in their care. However, before we move on to a discussion of specific qualities of compassion, I first add a caveat, to bring us all down to earth: These five teachers would be the first to remind us that they are far from perfect. In fact, each of the CMTs took the time in their interviews to mention that they make mistakes every day.

I have intentionally chosen the term *compassionate music teachers* for this book, resisting other more commonly used and inflated terms such as *superheroes* to remind us of two things: First, our strivings here are about human connection, not about accomplishment or superiority to anyone else (students, colleagues, or otherwise). Second, the potential to be compassionate is both approachable and universal—something I believe any of us can reach simply by paying attention to our actions and to the needs of others. As we move forward together to subsequent chapters, I invite us all (myself included) to keep an open mind to possibility, with a belief and understanding that each of the qualities of compassion is attainable by all of us.

Reflection Questions

1. Which one of these CMTs is most like you? Why?
2. Which of these CMTs would you strive to be more like when you teach? Why?
3. If you could choose particular aspects of each CMT to make your own teaching more compassionate, which would they be?
4. Who is someone in your own life whom you would consider a CMT? Why?

NOTES

1. Barbara Lourie Sand, *Teaching Genius: Dorothy DeLay and the Making of a Musician* (Portland, OR: Amadeus Press, 2000), 191.
2. This research was approved by the Boston University Institutional Review Board. I contacted each research participant initially by e-mail, providing each individual with a document explaining study procedures. I provided each individual with the choice to either (a) participate confidentially or (b) volunteer a name, a biography, and photos. All individuals I contacted consented to be interviewed, and all chose the latter option. Prior to our discussion, I provided the participants with a pre-interview prompt to help them reflect on five initial qualities of compassion (trust, empathy, patience, inclusion, and authenticity), which I derived from prior research literature

as preliminary theoretical ideas (see Hennie Boeije, "A Purposeful Approach to the Constant Comparative Method in the Analysis of Qualitative Interviews," *Quality & Quantity* 36 [2002]: 393). Interviews lasted approximately sixty to ninety minutes each and were conducted in person or via Skype. I coded written transcriptions of the interviews according to the aforementioned *a priori* themes, also noting an emergent theme of "community" through memo writing and conversations with research participants (see Barney G. Glaser, "The Constant Comparative Method of Qualitative Analysis," *Social Problems* 12, no. 4 [1965]: 440). Constant comparative data analysis, with comparisons both within and between interviewees as well as to existent literature, resulted in six final categories (trust, empathy, patience, inclusion, community, and authentic connection). Prior to the book's publication, I gave each research participant the opportunity to view the full book manuscript and offer additional insights or clarification. Each participant responded with only minor edits, all of which were incorporated into the final draft.

3. Ihas's research has resulted in two manuscripts: "Full Service Violin Teacher: Mentoring Practices of Miss Dorothy DeLay" (unpublished); and "Sculpting Musical Artists: A Tribute to Miss Dorothy DeLay" (American String Teacher 67, no. 4 (2017), 14–17).

4. Dijana Ihas is an associate professor of music education at Pacific University, in Forest Grove, Oregon. Prior to her university position, Ihas worked as a certified K–12 public school music teacher, and taught general music and elementary, middle, and high school string orchestra classes. In addition to serving as orchestra chair for Oregon Music Educators Association (OMEA) and as president elect for American String Teachers Association (ASTA) Oregon chapter, Ihas serves on the board of National String Project Consortium (NSPC). Ihas's publications have appeared in *American String Teacher* (AST) magazine, *Journal of String Research*, and *Council for Undergraduate Research (CUR) Quarterly*. Ihas has a PhD in music education from the University of Oregon, a Master of Music Education degree from the University of Arizona, a Master of Fine Arts in Viola Performance from the University of California in Irvine, and a bachelor's degree in viola performance from the University of Sarajevo, Bosnia and Herzegovina. She has trained in a variety of music education approaches, including Suzuki, Bornoff, Rolland, Havas, Kodály, Orff, and Gordon.

5. Anne Inglis, "Obituary: Dorothy DeLay: Unconventional Teacher behind the World's Greatest Violinists," *The Guardian,* last modified April 2, 2002, accessed July 28, 2017, https://www.theguardian.com/news/2002/apr/02/guardianobituaries. schools.

6. Sand, *Teaching Genius,* 51–52.

7. Sand, *Teaching Genius,* 57.

8. Sand, *Teaching Genius,* 58.

9. Sand, *Teaching Genius,* 214.

10. Ihas, "Full Service Violin Teacher"; Sand, *Teaching Genius.*

11. Dijana Ihas, personal interview, June 29, 2017.

12. Ihas, "Full Service Violin Teacher" and "Sculpting Musical Artists;" Barbara Lourie Sand, *Teaching Genius.*

13. Angella Ahn, personal communication with the author, August 29, 2017.

14. Biography provided by Steve Massey. Used with permission.

15. Wynton Marsalis, tribute to Steve Massey at the Foxborough High School Pops Concert, May 7, 2017, transcript from video "Wynton Marsalis Surprise Visit to Honor Steve Massey," last modified May 9, 2017, accessed July 28, 2017, https://www.youtube.com/watch?v=jf_lPe3U23w.

16. Biography provided by Brian Michaud. Used with permission.

17. Biography provided by Marcus Santos. Used with permission.

18. Biography provided by Renae Timbie. Used with permission.

19. Renae Timbie, "An Ethnographic Case Study of Collaborative Learning in a Higher Education Choral Ensemble" (doctoral diss., Ball State University, Muncie, IN, 2016).

20. Ibid., 10.

21. Ibid., 3.

22. Unless otherwise noted, all CMT quotes are from personal interviews with the author.

Chapter 3

Trust

Compassionate action, being there for others, . . . starts with seeing ourselves. . . . As we learn to have compassion for ourselves, the circle of
compassion for others—what and whom we can work with, and how—
becomes wider.

—Pema Chödrön[1]

Displaying true compassion is not as simple as merely crossing off a checklist
or dressing up in a particularly desirable persona when circumstances require
it. Compassion is both intentional and organic, both simple and complex.
Furthermore, as the preceding quote from Pema Chödrön suggests, the art of
genuinely reaching outward requires us first to reach inward—something that
can evoke feelings that run the gamut from uncomfortable to downright terrifying if we aren't in touch with what we might find when we go there. Yet,
by first coming to know and show compassion for ourselves, we open up the
possibility of showing genuine compassion to others.

In this and the following five chapters, I outline six qualities of compassion (trust, empathy, patience, inclusion, community, and authentic connection) to provide a framework for compassionate music teaching. By bringing
our awareness to these six qualities, we are inviting ourselves to walk into
a vulnerable state of being: We may open ourselves up to new feelings and
new experiences that may challenge us, our beliefs, our convictions, and
our pedagogical practices. Encountering this state of newness may require
that we ourselves transform in some way, which may be the scariest part of
all. Yet only by taking these kinds of risks can we experience the greatest
rewards. Since trust is critical when confronting our vulnerabilities, we start
there.

CHARACTERISTICS OF TRUST

One night as a teenager, while I was hanging out with my brother Brian over a box of pizza, he asked me a question:

"Do you know why I've never rebelled?"
"No—why?"
"Because Mom and Dad trust me. And I don't want to lose that trust."

Despite the incredulousness of Brian's assertion that he hadn't *ever* rebelled, this idea intrigued me. I hadn't ever thought about it before that moment, but I realized then—and in decades of reflection since that time—that Brian was on to something: Our parents had extremely high expectations for our behavior (and they further modeled what they taught), but they allowed us to make those choices without imposing threats or incessantly checking up on us. It was just a way of being for our family—a part of who we were. And because my family was very close and communicative, being a part of the family's modus operandi was something that we valued highly and strove to maintain.

Our family had a good dose of what researchers call "relational trust"—a kind of confidence in group membership that results from (a) shared group identity, (b) reinforcing of community through reciprocal exchanges among group members, and (c) understanding the intentions of others in the group.[2] Relational trust goes beyond mere reliance on contractual obligation or agreeing to follow a moral authority: It involves the interplay of organizational, interpersonal, and intrapersonal confidence.[3] Trust experts have clarified that trust does not refer to a warm and fuzzy emotional feeling but rather "the conscious regulation of one's dependence on another."[4]

Discernment of trust in a relational community takes place as group members interpret one another's actions in terms of *reciprocal respect*, for which balanced and open communication is essential; *competence*, or a person's ability to carry out roles and responsibilities that are valued by the group; *personal regard for others,* which might involve going beyond what is expected in a role for the benefit of other group members; and *integrity,* or consistency between what group members profess to do and what they actually do.[5]

A similar concept to that of relational trust is "collective trust," which refers to the overall level of trust experienced by a group.[6] Whereas relational trust involves the relationships and understandings that create a positive climate between individual people, collective trust represents the general perception of trust experienced by the group as a whole.[7] Multiple researchers have developed their own unique perspectives on what makes trust "tick" in various organizational settings, but scholars generally agree that trusting

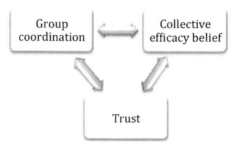

Figure 3.1. The interrelationship between group coordination, collective efficacy belief, and trust.

relationships can be recognized by the level of *vulnerability* to which group members are willing to submit; *positive expectation* in other group members' actions; *risk* that group members are willing to take; and *interdependence* among group members.[8]

Based on my brother Brian's own anecdotal evidence, he believed that trust in our family made his adolescence less dramatic than it otherwise might have been. Research backs him up: Trust has been found to be a powerful catalyst for good in various organizational settings, leading to positive outcomes in group member attitude, behavior, and performance.[9]

In school settings, trust has produced astounding effects on student achievement and test scores in reading and mathematics, even when controlling for variables such as family income, race, and student mobility.[10] Similarly, high-poverty schools with high collective trust have demonstrated significantly higher achievement levels in math and reading than similar socioeconomic status (SES) schools with low collective trust.[11] Collective trust leads to a further sense of collective efficacy (or a group's collective belief in its ability to accomplish specific tasks).[12] Finally, collective efficacy beliefs can lead to greater effort and resilience and are related to group coordination.[13] Therefore, as illustrated in figure 3.1, it is possible that groups with high levels of trust might enjoy a cyclical pattern in which trust, collective efficacy beliefs, and group coordination continually reinforce one another.

Trust and Teacher Credibility

Teacher credibility refers to the ways in which students perceive a teacher as being a credible source of information. Trust is a principal component of students' perceptions of a teacher's credibility, either in its own right or as a dimension of a teacher's character.[14] Researchers have highlighted three characteristics that make teachers credible in their students' eyes: competence, character, and caring.[15]

Countless writings in music education over the past century have focused on the first characteristic, *competence,* with the goal of helping teachers understand and perfect the craft of music performance and pedagogy. In this book, however, I shift the balance to be more inclusive of the other two characteristics, caring and character. *Caring*, which has been defined by scholars as "empathy and responsiveness,"[16] relates to the way in which we "care for" someone, rather than merely "caring about" someone or something.[17] In other words, "caring for" goes beyond a more distanced concern to a state of action. I discuss this difference further in chapter 4. *Character*, or "professional integrity,"[18] is discussed at length in the current chapter in terms of developing and maintaining trust.

THE NATURE OF RELATIONAL TRUST: SEVEN FACETS

Mere focus on competence without character and caring leaves music education dry and vacuous, like an empty container without soul. Yet, as we exercise trust and allow a wholly integrated version of ourselves to emerge in music learning settings, we can inspire students to likewise fully commit to the music they create—and even to their own sense of purpose—in deeply meaningful ways. Seven facets of trust include vulnerability, confidence, benevolence, reliability, competence, honesty, and openness.[19] Below, I consider how practicing each facet might lead to greater trust between music teachers and students.

Vulnerability

It makes sense that having others around us whom we know we can trust helps ease our anxiety of potential errors and other unknowns. In comparison to other kinds of trust, relational trust is most effective at relieving individuals from potentially oppressive power dynamics that exist in schools.[20] Since we know that fear impedes creativity and the ability to learn,[21] it is easy to envision on the flip side how relational trust could allow individuals to risk vulnerability, thereby setting the stage for deep, meaningful, and productive learning to take place.

Interdependence in groups naturally leads to vulnerability and risk. There is a potentially high level of vulnerability involved in authentic student-teacher exchange, yet many of our traditional education structures unfortunately keep us in a continual state of socio-emotional disconnect with students, administrators, and even other teachers. Much of this disconnect may have to do with the positions of relative superiority and inferiority between teacher and student that have existed in educational settings for centuries, and the consequential restraint from risk-taking that such power imbalances can produce. In his book *The Courage to Teach,* Parker Palmer explained:

> We are distanced by a grading system that separates teachers from students, by departments that fragment fields of knowledge, by competition that makes students and teachers alike wary of their peers, and by a bureaucracy that puts faculty and administration at odds.[22]

On the surface, we can easily recognize that teachers are placed in a position of authority over students, as teachers in traditional classrooms are the ones to control rules, grades, and even conditions for growth. Students are, therefore, aware of their position of vulnerability from the outset. Something that society often forgets, however, is that teachers also walk into a classroom with a tremendous awareness of their liabilities: They spend day after day attempting to meet standards imposed on them by others, putting on performances (both in the classroom and onstage) that they hope will be well received by those who would, in many cases, rather be elsewhere.

Parker Palmer revealed his own sense of inadequacy:

> After thirty years of teaching, my own fear remains close at hand. It is there when I enter a classroom and feel the undertow into which I have jumped. It is there when I ask a question—and my students keep a silence as stony as if I had asked them to betray their friends. It is there whenever it feels as if I have lost control: a mind-boggling question is asked, an irrational conflict emerges, or students get lost in my lecture because I myself am lost. When a class that has gone badly comes to a merciful end, I am fearful long after it is over—fearful that I am not just a bad teacher but a bad person, so closely is my sense of self tied to the work I do.[23]

Research suggests that new teachers develop a sense of "teacher identity" over time, yet in the early stages young teachers overwhelmingly focus their attention and energy on their own fears, their actions and words, and their need for basic day-to-day survival in the classroom and beyond.[24] Parker Palmer confessed that he, too, neglected to consider student fears and vulnerabilities in the beginning of his career:

> My own fear is matched by the fear within my students, though in my early years of teaching I conveniently forgot that fact. From where I stood, exposed and vulnerable at the front of the room, my students seemed enviously safe, hidden behind their notebooks, anonymous in the midst of the crowd.
>
> I should have remembered from my own experience that students, too, are afraid: afraid of failing, of not understanding, of being drawn into issues they would rather avoid, of having their ignorance exposed or their prejudices

challenged, of looking foolish in front of their peers. When my students' fears mix with mine, fear multiplies geometrically—and education is paralyzed.[25]

Embracing Vulnerability

On the other hand, when we allow ourselves (and our students) the space to be vulnerable, we can reap great rewards for trust and subsequent learning—especially where we add musical expression to the mix. As CMT Renae Timbie pointed out, we live in a culture that does not prize vulnerability:

> We're not taught vulnerability, especially in the United States. Vulnerability is seen as a scary and weak thing, actually. And as a teacher, you might think, "How are you going to get everything done, have authority in your classroom, have anyone follow you if you don't show strength?"
>
> But I think that authentic connection comes from vulnerability. To say, "I'm going to dare to be different and be vulnerable, and to show I'm just as broken, I'm human like you're human." For anybody—in or out of the classroom—anybody wants to be told that they are known, that they are safe, that they are valuable. So to have that power as a teacher to create that atmosphere requires you to kind of come to their level; to say, "Look, I'm invested in you, so let me show you I don't have all the answers either." I don't think that's typical. And I think that's where this ties into compassion.

How does one embrace vulnerability? The trick with this particular facet of trust is that its very essence lies in our willingness to give up control, to let down our guard.[26] Therefore, the moment one starts "doing" something to attain a certain state of being, vulnerability is lost. The best we can "do" might be to simply notice when we try to control a situation, and then realistically assess the safety we have (or don't have) in being able to trust others. If we feel safe enough to be open and vulnerable with another person, then we can be assured that we have relational trust.

After forty-six years of teaching, CMT Steve Massey has come to embrace and even consider "special" the vulnerability that he shares with his students as a music teacher, as they prepare for and create musical performances together:

> Unlike sports teams that perform, the coach in the music ensemble performs *with* the students, which is a whole other dynamic than the coach sending in a play and saying, "go run that play." So sports teams bond, and they like their coach, but a music team performs *with* their coach. And I'm as involved in their actual performance as they are. I think that has the potential to be special. . . . You're taking all the same risks that they are, so that builds a sense of trust and a sense of bonding that I don't want to say is unique to music, but it's clearly significant.[27]

Confidence

Confidence is viewed by scholars as a facet of trust related to the future: After someone makes a commitment to us to do something, we must then await the completion of that task and simply trust that everything will be accomplished in due time. Confidence is defined as "the degree to which a person can rest in that uncertainty"[28] until others in the group have fulfilled their obligations. Once those obligations are met, group members will then have demonstrated trust through other facets such as competence and reliability (as discussed later).

In terms of music teaching, we place trust in our students when we simply allow students the time and space they need to develop. On the other hand, when we over-function for students—including providing an overload of information and/or incessantly checking up on them—we demonstrate a lack of trust in their ability to learn and to work things out on their own. Lack of teacher confidence can lead to lack of student competence later on.

CMTs Marcus Santos and Steve Massey both demonstrate confidence in their students' abilities to lead themselves. They teach students leadership strategies in big and small ways—and then step out of the way and let their students mentor and support each other. I described Massey's approach in detail in the previous chapter. Marcus takes a day-by-day and group-by-group approach to leadership with his high school students as well as in his clinics across the world. As he described, in each new case he scans the space for students who show leadership potential on any particular song:

> I might go in and do the first 15 minutes or so, at which point I'm trying to survey the area and see who is getting it super quickly, and who has the personality that wouldn't mind being in front of everyone. And then we do the exact same thing that I just did, but with someone in the group who's leading or doing the leading part. And that gives room for me to walk around and pay closer attention to see who needs more help, and even walk toward that person and give special attention if it's needed. It adds to the dynamic of the classes too.

Marcus further explained his philosophy behind student leadership:

> As a teacher, you can't do everything, right? Of course, you wish, "Oh, I just want to make it as easy as possible for every student." But you can't do everything. And you won't even be as interesting for students if you do everything for them, because there is also that sense of ownership: "*We* did this!" Instead of, "The teacher did everything and we just got to deliver it."
>
> There is so much that we can learn from students. When they take this leadership role, it's our chance to learn from them and see what works, and what doesn't. So we can actually replicate sometimes what students did in other classes. I really think I am the best teacher I can be when students are leading

and being creative, and developing the music with respect, respecting other students' opinions and my opinion too. When we work together, that's when I feel like, yes, we're going to have a great semester or a great workshop.

Benevolence

People in trusting relationships believe that others have their best interest in mind and that they will not be taken advantage of, particularly when they are placed in situations where they might make mistakes or risk embarrassment. Just as teachers in general education settings "often must rely on the goodwill of principals as they experiment with new teaching strategies and make inevitable mistakes,"[29] music students must also trust in the benevolence of their teachers and fellow classmates as they try out new technical approaches or express themselves musically.

Perfectionism—when not balanced by benevolence in trusting relationships—has been shown to wreak havoc on music performance anxiety. Research suggests that "people with a history full of demanding authority figures . . . often apply similarly unreasonable expectations to their musical performances."[30] Furthermore, in my own research of adolescent musicians, I found that students in competitive auditions where they were ranked against one another minimized their emphasis on expressive performance and instead focused their attention on what others might think.[31]

Is it possible to have high standards for performance and still show benevolence? The CMTs in this book would say "absolutely yes." Much of our discussion in later chapters focuses on specific ways that this balance can be achieved. In benevolent music teaching settings, music teachers still exact the highest standards for performance while also offering unconditional support and positive regard as those students make an effort to attempt new things. Said differently, benevolent music teachers make perfectionism "about things, not people."[32]

According to a 2001 article in *Strad Magazine,* Dorothy DeLay was successful in mentoring and preparing numerous virtuosos who were both competent and confident, which she did through (a) inherent beliefs in their ability to succeed; (b) regular communication about what students were doing well; and (c) customized teaching strategies that allowed students to experience micro-moments of success at every step of the learning process.[33] Violinist Piet Koornhof described what we might call benevolence in DeLay:

> She gives her students confidence in their capabilities by structuring the learning process step by step. "You have to prove to them that they can do it . . . they have to succeed from the very beginning," she says. She breaks every area worked on into small steps, appropriate to each student; provides ways of measurement to increase awareness; makes the lessons fun and positively reinforces a student's successes, however small, with compliments.[34]

DeLay went a step further, however, by teaching students to be benevolent *with themselves*, thereby engendering a sense of intrapersonal trust:

> After having just played for DeLay, a student looks worried about his perfor-
> mance. DeLay immediately notices and says, "You know, the better you get, the
> more dissatisfied you are, because you can hear more." This is a wonderful
> example of how she changes a student's frame of reference, giving a negative
> experience a new, positive meaning. She takes his dissatisfaction and gives it
> the new meaning of being a sign of improvement. The student immediately
> feels better and consequently plays better, which in turn reinforces the truth of
> what DeLay has just said.[35]

Reliability

Reliability has to do with consistency and predictability. Statisticians often
refer to the reliability of a test to mean that the results would be virtually
the same in multiple iterations of the same test. However, trust scholars are
quick to point out that reliability from a merely statistical standpoint does not
necessarily relate to a positive or desirable act: "We can trust a person to be
invariably late [or] we can count on someone to be consistently malicious,
self-serving, or dishonest."[36] In terms of trust, then, reliability combines with
benevolence to represent the trust that we might have in someone to consistently act in a way that is advantageous to others.

Dorothy DeLay's students remarked that she lived up to her last name:
She was reliably late—not just a few minutes, but a few *hours* late. "If you
had a lesson scheduled at 3 p.m., you would need to schedule a block of time
until 8 p.m. and wait for your turn."[37] Decades worth of students endured
this consistent pattern of tardiness, because they understood what it meant:
On the other side of that studio door, Dorothy DeLay was reliably focused
on providing benevolent attention to whatever student happened to be in the
studio at that time.

Students were willing to make the investment of waiting for hours for lessons with DeLay because once their lesson began, they knew that they would
be the center of her world: "Inside that studio, nothing else existed, no one
else existed. Even though she was late, they waited. Because they trusted that
once they were with her, something magical was going to happen."[38]

Competence

Competence is critical for fostering teacher-student and student-student trust
in music learning settings. No matter how kind or emotionally supportive a
teacher might be, it is all for naught if that teacher is not competent in helping students achieve musically. As trust experts Megan Tschannen-Moran

and Wayne K. Hoy suggested, "There are times when good intentions are not enough."[39]

Student Competence

Students must be able to trust that teachers will be able to provide them with the skills they need to be quality musicians, and they also benefit from peers whose musical strengths challenge and sustain their own musical growth. Teachers will benefit from using pedagogical content knowledge (a healthy balance of both technical and teaching know-how)[40] in such a way that they encourage student self-efficacy and group collective efficacy among their students.[41] In chapter 5, I discuss specific ways in which teachers can help students develop musical competence.

Teacher Competence

It goes without saying that music teachers need to have prerequisite skills and knowledge about music to be effective teachers.[42] The CMTs in this book gained trust in their respective communities by creating a track record of musical success. In the case of new teachers—either new to the profession or new to a program—demonstrating musical and pedagogical competence may be the most effective means of establishing initial trust.

Teachers can foster trust from their students by demonstrating their own competence as a guide who is both capable and prepared to lead. However, it is also necessary for a teacher to lead with a plan that represents student needs. As Renae Timbie noted:

Teachers need to set the tone of trust in the relationship. I think that's expected of us as the teacher. So for me, if you were to go into a choir or a refugee camp and just say, "Hey guys, I'm here, I'm your buddy; you can trust me," you're going to get trampled on, first of all. We want a strong leader. This might sound completely against vulnerability, but it's not. Students want to be led. They want a guide.

So it's important to come in with a plan that says, "Look, you can trust me because this is what we are going to do." But the trust comes from saying, "We aren't just doing this because I have to check all these things off the list. It's not because it's for my own agenda, because I'm going to feel better about myself." I can identify with going into a situation where I felt like the professor was only there for their sake; you know, "I need you to do this so I can get tenure" or something. Nobody feels good about that.

But it builds trust to say, "Look, I'm here for you. I'm here with this agenda, but here's the reason. And I want to help keep us focused on why this matters to you. This is why it is important to listen to me. This is why it's worth trusting me; here's the plan. I'm here to help us make sense of it, and we all have different roles to play, but that doesn't mean that you're less valuable than me."

If teachers have built up an atmosphere of trust with their students, then students may be more likely to trust that any necessary changes to that plan are also in their best interest. Timbie explained:

> When I have done collaborative learning activities in choral rehearsals, there have been many different changes along the way. I think, because of the trust had already been built, and because the connection was already there, I could be honest and say, "Look, we're going to change," but again, "here's the reason why." The trust hasn't changed because I've helped them see the vision.

Honesty

Trust scholars equate honesty with concepts such as integrity and authenticity. Honesty is critical for a music teacher, particularly when providing feedback to students. Naturally, positive praise is critical for nurturing a student's sense of self-efficacy.[43] However, praise needs to be honest: If a student performance isn't truly good, then telling students so—even when simply saying "good" as a means of asking them to stop playing for a moment—could, from this perspective, be a breach of trust. On the other hand, praise can be both helpful and instructive when it is balanced, specific, genuine, and truly warranted.[44]

Furthermore, it is not necessarily helpful for music teachers to skirt around negative feedback, as students may read right through such awkward partial truths.[45] According to research, a primary feature of expert music teachers is the use of frequent, specific, and task-related feedback—both positive and negative.[46] Direct and *task*-related (note: not student-related) comments can be viewed by students as a means of proximal goal clarification[47] or a constructive means to help a student progress.

Dorothy DeLay understood the importance of providing direct, specific, and honest feedback to gain students' trust. In an interview with Sylvia A. Gholson, DeLay stated,

> If I lose the student's respect, then I lose the opportunity of being effective. . . .
> I believe that telling students the exact truth is necessary, and letting them know that I respect them and that I'm on their side is necessary, and giving them all the support I possibly can.[48]

DeLay's efforts were not in vain. Her students recalled how she was an expert at building students up emotionally, while also being extremely clear about how they had not yet met her expectations. According to her students, the directness, specificity, and honesty of DeLay's feedback led to "150 percent" trust in her abilities as a teacher, such that there was never anything they would question.[49]

Following are recommendations for balancing encouragement with honest feedback, from a book my colleagues and I wrote on promoting performance confidence:

> Some teacher educators speak about the "compliment sandwich," in which instruction is placed between two compliments, perhaps to lighten the blow of the impending critique. While we certainly encourage being positive, compliments need to be authentic and useful to the student.
>
> Merging compliments and instructions together can be the best use of teaching time. Examples include: "Increasing the bow speed really helped that crescendo! What are some other ways that you can raise the volume even more?" or "Listening to the flute soloist really improved the intonation and phrasing; now listen to the percussion section to make sure it holds together rhythmically.[50]

Openness

According to trust scholars, openness involves the extent to which we communicate freely with others. It relates to the facet of vulnerability, in that we might share personal or private information with others. Openness also relates to the facet of confidence, because we have an expectation that those personal expressions will not be taken advantage of.[51] While it is clearly inappropriate for teachers to share overly personal and/or private information with students, openness in a music learning setting might relate to the way in which we feel safe to express musically with one another.

Emotionally safe yet artistically challenging music learning settings can be ideal places for fostering students' sense of trust in others, as well as self-trust in their own musical performances. Music scholar Lee Higgins coined the phrase "*safety without safety*" to describe instances of musical risk-taking among trusted others in music improvisation settings.[52] In music-making settings that exude "safety without safety," a group music leader "promotes responsible facilitative practice, whilst making room for . . . unexpected [musical] inventions."[53] Thus, so-called "'failures' are celebrated. As moments of learning they are not understood as devastating but rather as an important aspect of the creative process."[54]

Higgins proposed that risk-taking is propelled forward by prior achievements and is further fostered as trusted others allow us a safe place to "fail." As we then have trust that we are safe in our risk-taking, we open up the possibility of innovation. On the other hand, a group setting that lacks "safety without safety" might lead either to performances that Higgins calls "dull and predictable" or to students who are expressively paralyzed.[55] Risk-taking among trusted others leads to balanced and increased creativity and confidence: "Safety without safety keeps the pathways open, always-already welcoming the unexpected."[56]

Marcus Santos's approach to encouraging students, while asking them to give their very best musically, resonates with this "safety without safety" idea:

> If it's a really rigid musical environment, and we are aiming for perfection, and mistakes are not accepted, the overall result might not be as excellent as if we look, on the other side of the spectrum, at a relaxed and fun and loving musical environment where people feel free to let their feelings show through the music.
>
> It's the middle ground: I love it when people tell me this, especially when I'm in a recording studio, and they go, "OK, this is the tenth take; it's great, but I know we can do better so let's start it again." I try to pass it to the students as well. We can push someone to the limit in a loving way, encouraging them to be better.

DISTRUST AND RECONCILIATION

As teachers, we would do well to foster a climate of trust from the beginning of any relationship, and then continually maintain those facets of trust that encourage mutual and reciprocal confidence in the teacher, other classmates, and the group as a whole. The alternative may result in undue or unnecessary fear, which can wreak havoc on learning and performance.[57] Trust scholars have warned that "engendering distrust can be costly."[58]

Distrust tends to provoke feelings of anxiety and insecurity, causing people to feel uncomfortable and ill at ease and to expend energy on monitoring the behavior and possible motives of others. When students feel unsafe, energy that could be devoted to learning is diverted to self-protection. People may use various means to protect themselves from the possible harm of the distrusted person and to minimize their vulnerability.[59]

This understanding of how distrust impedes a student's ability to concentrate is at odds with many old-school music teaching approaches (including that of imposing authority or threats upon students to motivate them to practice), particularly when those threats or impositions are inconsistent. As a student's sense of trust wanes, so does the ability for that student to give full energy and attention to learning and practicing musical skills which, as important as a teacher might view them, will eventually pale in comparison to a student's need for self-preservation.

Sarcasm is a technique often used by teachers attempting to bring levity or humor into the classroom. However, sarcasm creates a triple negative whammy with qualities of compassion: Not only does it put a teacher's authenticity and trust into question, but research suggests that it might send confusing emotional messages that can interfere with the promotion of empathy (especially in young children).[60] Distrust breeds further distrust, as people are less likely to seek information and clarification from others who have misled them in the past, thereby limiting future opportunities to develop confidence in that relationship.[61]

We often take for granted the trust that we experience in a good relationship until it starts to fade. As one scholar has suggested, "We inhabit a climate of trust as we inhabit an atmosphere and notice it as we notice air, only when it becomes scarce or polluted."[62] It is possible to regain trust when lost, but only when future conditions align with those of trusting relationships and highlight experiences of reciprocal respect, personal regard for others, and integrity. Those who desire the trust of others may need to open the door of vulnerability a bit wider and be the first to demonstrate facets of trust such as confidence in others, benevolence, reliability, competence, honesty, and openness—and then act consistently until such time that others feel safe enough to join in.

On the other hand, efforts at reconciliation may fall flat where serious oppression has taken place, especially when individuals who are invited to apologize have benefitted from an imbalance of power and may lack a sincere desire for that power to be redistributed out of their favor. Yet as long as we perceive education—or politics, or just about anything—as a power play with a winner and a loser, the most authentic kind of trust is not possible. I recommend instead that we re-envision the *entire* power game and consider, as Paulo Freire did, how the art of sincere dialogue might allow everyone in a relationship a means to be fully heard and fully human.[63] Then, as genuine trust subsumes fear of being hurt or taken advantage of by others, those who are freed from oppression can "liberate themselves and their oppressors as well."[64]

The Art of Apology

Sincere apologies from teachers and administrators lead to greater student trust, as students come to perceive their leader's behavior as predictable and honest. As one scholar put it, "Greater trustworthiness is perceived by subordinates when superiors share control."[65] Effective apologies may take up to four steps: clear and complete *acknowledgment* of offense, which includes avoiding conditional, vague, or passive language; *explanation* of what happened, particularly when demonstrating the unlikeliness of the offense to happen again; genuine *expressions of remorse*, shame, and/or humility; and *reparation or compensation* for damage done.[66]

While teachers are often very good at demanding an apology from students—either to us directly or to another offended student—we are not always as eager to apologize ourselves when circumstances warrant it. This reticence on our part may likely relate to a fear of losing our sense of authority, power, or control over students. However, considering the costs of distrust in a learning space (and particularly to one that involves the musical expression of emotions), a weak or incomplete apology might be much too great to risk.

Brian Michaud reminds himself of the importance of admitting his mistakes to his students, as well as to himself:

> I don't remember any of my teachers ever apologizing for anything when I was growing up. Maybe they did, but I don't remember that. I think that it's important to acknowledge when we make mistakes, that we're human beings and not perfect. There have been times when I've raised my voice louder than I should have. I don't like when that happens (and neither do my students), so I will apologize.
>
> I think that's important to acknowledge when we make mistakes. If we were all perfect then that would be so easy! Admit to the students when you've made a mistake. I think they respect that.

Marcus Santos described how he views mistakes as both universal and hospitable: "Everybody makes mistakes. And then I think the best part of making mistakes is the good laugh that we can have afterward. It lightens the room, right?"

A Personal Reflection

In my earlier years as an orchestra director, I often let the stress of the moment get to me, and I would sometimes forget that there were living, breathing, vulnerable students on the other side of my baton. In those harried moments, I often said hurtful things to students that I regretted afterward. Later in my career, I came to realize that stopping in those moments and saying "Whoa, I need to breathe"—and then doing so—not only helped me gain my composure, but it also sent my students a more positive message about how their musical capability was separate from my stress, or even my approval.

Just a few months ago, I found myself in a state of anxiety that had nothing to do with the university students who were waiting for me when I raced, heart pounding, into our student teaching seminar. "My frenzy has nothing to do with you," I said, quickly adding: "I need to meditate or something." Although I tried to carry on and limp through the lesson content, my student Marisa interrupted and said, "Well, why *don't* we meditate?"

I looked around the room to find six pairs of eyes looking at me, awaiting my response. "Why don't we?" I responded, and led the class in a guided meditation while teaching them some principles from the Alexander Technique.[67] Needless to say, the student teachers and I all relaxed after a long, hard day at our respective schools, and the lesson went much better than I could have ever imagined.

Building Trust by Reaching Out

Building trust also involves another quality of compassion—empathy—as it is necessary for us to understand how others may be experiencing a lack of trust so that we can make appropriate efforts to provide assurance. People in imbalanced power relationships (such as company employers versus employees, or school principals versus teachers) have different criteria by which they measure trust.[68] For example, superiors such as company presidents and school principals have been found to value competence, reliability, and commitment most of all, while employees of companies and schools equated trustworthiness of their superiors most with benevolence, kindness, and openness.[69] Rather than offering proverbial apples when someone needs oranges, therefore, it may be better to reach out with a sincere desire to understand what others might be experiencing (including their values and criteria for trust), and work from there.

Marcus Santos reaches out to his students to understand their interests, to get on the same page with them while planning for all aspects of his curriculum:

> I try to choose a curriculum that they will enjoy performing. And of course I will add technique and music theory once I have their trust. I will add what needs to be added to make sure that we achieve the goals of the curriculum. But I try to first ask them, "So what do you guys want to play?" I ask, "Tell me a song you like to hear," and then we all listen together. If they are passionate about playing, it will be easier to get to that music theory class later in the semester.

FOSTERING TRUST IN MUSIC LEARNING SETTINGS

So, when and how do music teachers develop conditions of trust? First, we can work on incorporating conditions and facets of trust immediately, consistently, and continually. Trust takes time to develop and may involve an initial period of trial and error in which people demonstrate willingness to be vulnerable and accept risks for one another. Meanwhile, relationship partners can demonstrate competence in being able to carry out roles that support mutual values.[70]

Finally, I offer a list of strategies from a publication by the Northwest Regional Educational Laboratory that was originally intended to help foster a trusting climate between principals and teachers in general education settings.[71] With a bit of tweaking, I have adapted the list to fit our purposes in developing a trusting climate for music teaching and learning.[72]

Demonstrate personal integrity. This point goes back to our discussion of honesty, openness, and authenticity. Owning mistakes, providing honest and specific feedback, and focusing on music as the goal all help students see a teacher as someone who can be trusted to have their best interests in mind.

Be accessible. It is of course important to students to know that they can rely on their teacher to be there when they need help. However, being accessible in a compassionate way also means being open, being human, and being fully present with students. In future chapters I provide examples of how the CMTs listen attentively, take note of individual student needs, and provide them with the resources they need in a variety of ways.

Facilitate and model effective communication. Part of building trust is simply being able to understand the needs of another. As I will show in later chapters, the act of reaching out and asking students questions about their progress, and even their understanding of their progress, helps students and teachers ensure that they are working toward the same goals.

Involve [students] in decision-making. The CMTs involve students in decision making at every possible level, from selection of songs and activities to taking on major leadership roles. Throughout the rest of the book, I describe the numerous and various ways that CMTs provide their students with opportunities for ownership over their own learning and music-making.

Express value for dissenting views. As I discuss in depth in the following chapter, empathy builds when we engage in dialogue with others, particularly when we honestly listen to those whose ideas or worldviews differ from our own. Honoring the voices of all students allows them a sense that their perspectives are important, even if they differ from the majority or from that of the teacher. Only then will students trust that they are safe and valued enough to commit to group goals.

Reduce [students'] sense of vulnerability. Relational trust is enhanced when we know we are safe around others and can let down our guard. Because student-teacher relationships are typically unequal in power, it is especially important for teachers to ensure that students' sense of vulnerability is not in excess. Fostering a sense of ease allows students to expend their energy and mental space on learning and musical expression.

Ensure that [students] have basic resources [or knowledge they need to be successful]. Because competence is an important facet of trust, it is critical for students to have what they need to thrive in any relationship. As students come to develop particular musical skills as a result of instruction, they will grow in confidence of themselves as well as their teacher. They will also develop trust in peers whom they see improving in similar or complementary ways.[73]

[Hold students accountable for meeting their obligations to the group]. Reliability leads to trust; on the other hand, trust is lost when standards are inconsistent. The rest of this book is sprinkled with examples of how CMTs provide consistency in group settings, whether regarding student behavior, technical skills, or leadership responsibilities, as a means of building trust.

Celebrate experimentation and support risk. No matter the style of music, there is always room for experimentation: Even classical music master Dorothy DeLay welcomed students to bring repertoire of their choice into her studio. Furthermore, as the "safety without safety" discussion above suggests, students can thrive expressively when they are provided room to experiment and safely "fail."

Show that you care. Caring is one of the three things that students look for when judging a teacher's credibility. When I asked Marcus Santos why he thought his students trusted him, his answer was simple: "Maybe because they think, "he cares, he wants to do what we want to do." In the chapters that follow, I share examples of how the CMTs care for their students, for music, for life beyond the music classroom, and for the ways in which music connects to life.

Reflection Questions

1. How have you come to know that you can trust certain people in your social and/or professional circles? Which facets of trust are most apparent in these instances?
2. Which facets of trust are easiest for you to experience with your students?
3. Which facets of trust can you further develop with your students?
4. Of the three components of teacher credibility (competence, character, and caring), which one(s) would your students be most likely to associate with you? Why do you think so?
5. Choose one of the strategies for fostering trust offered at the end of this chapter. What is a specific action that you can take right away to put this strategy in motion?

NOTES

1. Pema Chödrön, *When Things Fall Apart: Heart Advice for Difficult Times* (Boston, MA: Shambala, 2000), 84–85.

2. Anthony Bryk and Barbara Schneider, *Trust in Schools: A Core Resource for Improvement* (New York: Russell Sage, 2002), 22.

3. Ibid., 22–26.

4. Megan Tschannen-Moran and Wayne K. Hoy, "A Multidisciplinary Analysis of the Nature, Meaning, and Measurement of Trust," *Review of Educational Research* 70, no. 4 (2000): 549.

5. Ibid.

6. Patrick B. Forsyth, Curt M. Adams, and Wayne K. Hoy, *Collective Trust: Why Schools Can't Improve without It* (New York: Teachers College Press, 2011). See also David Carl Casper, "The Relationship between Collective Student Trust and Student Achievement" (EdD diss., University of Oklahoma, Norman, OK, 2012).

7. Casper, "Collective Student Trust and Student Achievement," 20.

8. Dimitri van Maele, Mieke Van Houtte, and Patrick B. Forsyth, "Introduction: Trust as a Matter of Equity and Excellence in Education," in *Trust and School Life,* ed. Dimitri van Maele, Mieke Van Houtte, and Patrick B. Forsyth (Dordrecht: Springer, 2014), 5.

9. Dimitri van Maele, Mieke Van Houtte, and Patrick B. Forsyth, "Trust as a Matter of Equity and Excellence," 1–36. These authors cite a number of studies to support this argument, including: Holly H. Brower, Scott W. Lester, M. Audrey Korsgaard, and Brian R. Dineen, "A Closer Look at Trust between Managers and Subordinates: Understanding the Effect of Both Trusting and Being Trusted on Subordinate Outcomes." *Journal of Management* 35, no. 2 (2009): 327–47; Li-Fang Chou, An-Chih Wang, Ting-Yu Wang, Min-Ping Huang, and Bor-Shiuan Cheng, "Shared Work Values and Team Member Effectiveness: The Mediation of Trustfulness and Trustworthiness." *Human Relations* 61, no. 12 (2008): 1713–42; Ana Cristina Costa, "Work Team Trust and Effectiveness," *Personnel Review* 32, no. 5 (2003): 605–22; J. B. Cunningham, and J. MacGregor, "Trust and the Design of Work: Complementary Constructs in Satisfaction and Performance," *Human Relations* 53, no. 12 (2000): 1575–91. Dale E. Zand, "Trust and Managerial Problem Solving," *Administrative Science Quarterly* 17, no. 2 (1972): 229–39.

10. Bryk and Schneider, *Trust in Schools*.

11. Casper, "Collective Student Trust and Student Achievement."

12. Tschannen-Moran and Hoy, "Multidisciplinary Analysis of Trust, 584.

13. Albert Bandura, *Self-Efficacy: The Exercise of Control* (New York: Macmillan, 1997); James Ray and Karin S. Hendricks, "Collective Efficacy Belief, Within-Group Agreement, and Performance Quality among Instrumental Chamber Ensembles," unpublished manuscript, under review.

14. See Nicole P. M. Freeman, "Credibility and the Professor: The Juxtaposition of Student Perceptions and Instructor Beliefs" (PhD diss., University of Central Missouri, Warrensburg, MO, 2011); Chanthika Pornpitakpan, "The Persuasiveness of Source Credibility: A Critical Review of Five Decades' Evidence," *Journal of Applied Social Psychology* 34, no. 2 (2004): 243–81; Soo Young Rieh and David R. Danielson, "Credibility: A Multidisciplinary Framework," *Annual Review of Information Science and Technology* 41, no. 1 (2007): 307–64.

15. James C. McCroskey and Thomas J. Young, "Ethos and Credibility: The Construct and Its Measurement after Three Decades," *Communication Studies* 32,

no. 1 (1981): 24–34; Jason J. Teven and James C. McCroskey, "The Relationship of Perceived Teacher Caring with Student Learning and Teacher Evaluation," *Communication Education* 46, no. 1 (1997): 1–9; Carl Obermiller, Bryan Ruppert, and April Atwood, "Instructor Credibility across Disciplines: Identifying Students' Differentiated Expectations of Instructor Behaviors," *Business Communication Quarterly* 75, no. 2 (2012): 154.

16. Obermiller, Ruppert, and Atwood, "Instructor Credibility across Disciplines," 154.

17. See Nel Noddings, *A Richer, Brighter Vision for American High Schools* (New York: Cambridge University Press, 2015), 123.

18. Obermiller, Ruppert, and Atwood, "Instructor Credibility across Disciplines," 154.

19. Wayne K. Hoy and Megan Tschannen-Moran, "Five Faces of Trust: An Empirical Confirmation in Urban Elementary Schools," *Journal of School Leadership* 9, no. 3 (1999): 184–208; Tschannen-Moran and Hoy, "A Multidisciplinary Analysis of Trust," 556–58.

20. Bryk and Schneider, *Trust in Schools,* 20.

21. Eric E. Jensen, *Teaching with the Brain in Mind* (Alexandria, VA: Association for Supervision and Curriculum Development, 1998); Casey McGrath, Karin S. Hendricks, and Tawnya D. Smith, *Performance Anxiety Strategies: A Musician's Guide to Managing Stage Fright* (Lanham, MD: Rowman & Littlefield, 2017).

22. Parker J. Palmer, *The Courage to Teach: Exploring the Inner Landscape of a Teacher's Life* (San Francisco, CA: Jossey-Bass, 2007), 36.

23. Ibid., 36–37.

24. Margaret H. Berg and Peter Miksza, "An Investigation of Preservice Music Teacher Development and Concerns," *Journal of Music Teacher Education* 20 (2010): 39–55; Karin S. Hendricks and Ann M. Hicks, "Socio-Musical Connections and Teacher Identity Development in a University Methods Course and Community Youth Symphony Partnership," *String Research Journal* 7 (2017): 99–116.

25. Palmer, *The Courage to Teach,* 37.

26. According to Brené Brown, the term derives from the Latin *vulnerare,* or "wound," meaning that when we are vulnerable we leave ourselves open to potential attack or damage. See Brené Brown, "Shame Resilience Theory: A Grounded Theory Study on Women and Shame," *Families in Society* 87, no. 1 (2006): 48.

27. All CMT quotes are from interviews with the author, unless otherwise cited.

28. Tschannen-Moran and Hoy, "Multidisciplinary Analysis of Trust," 557.

29. Tschannen-Moran and Hoy, "Multidisciplinary Analysis of Trust," 557; see also Wayne K. Hoy and Dennis J. Sabo, *Quality Middle Schools: Open and Healthy* (Thousand Oaks, CA: Corwin Press, Inc., 1998).

30. Casey McGrath, Karin S. Hendricks, and Tawnya D. Smith, *Performance Anxiety Strategies: A Musician's Guide to Managing Stage Fright* (Lanham, MD: Rowman & Littlefield, 2016), 22.

31. Karin S. Hendricks, "Relationships between the Sources of Self-Efficacy and Changes in Competence Perceptions of Music Students during an All-State Orchestra Event" (PhD diss., University of Illinois at Urbana-Champaign, 2009).

32. McGrath, Hendricks, and Smith, *Performance Anxiety Strategies,* 129.

33. Piet Koornhof, "The Secrets of Violinist Dorothy DeLay's Teaching Methods," *Strad Magazine,* July 13, 2015, para. 9, accessed March 7, 2017, http://www.thestrad.com/the-secrets-of-violinist-dorothy-delays-teaching-methods/.

34. Ibid., para. 9.

35. Ibid., para. 23.

36. Tschannen-Moran and Hoy, "Multidisciplinary Analysis of Trust," 557.

37. Dijana Ihas, personal interview, June 29, 2017.

38. Ibid.

39. Tschannen-Moran and Hoy, "Multidisciplinary Analysis of Trust."

40. J. Si. Millican, "Describing Instrumental Music Teachers' Thinking: Implications for Understanding Pedagogical Content Knowledge," *Update: Applications of Research in Music Education* 31, no. 2 (2013): 45–53; J. Si. Millican, "Describing Preservice Instrumental Music Educators' Pedagogical Content Knowledge," *Update: Applications of Research in Music Education* 34, no. 2 (2016): 61–68; S. M. Wilson, L. S. Shulman, and A. E. Richert. "'150 Different Ways' of Knowing: Representations of Knowledge in Teaching," in *Exploring Teachers' Thinking*, ed. J. Calderhead (London: Cassell, 1987), 104–24.

41. See Diane R. Grieser and Karin S. Hendricks (unpublished manuscript), Pedagogical Content Knowledge and Preparation of String Teachers; Karin S. Hendricks, "The Sources of Self-Efficacy: Educational Research and Implications for Music," *Update: Applications of Research in Music Education* 35, no. 1 (2016): 32–38.

42. Dijana Ihas, personal interview with the author, June 29, 2017.

43. See Bandura, *Self-Efficacy.*

44. Frank Pajares, "Self-Efficacy during Childhood and Adolescence: Implications for Teachers and Parents," in *Self-Efficacy Beliefs of Adolescents*, ed. Frank Pajares and Tim Urdan (Greenwich, CT: Information Age Publishing, 2006), 339–67; Stephanie E. Pitts, Jane W. Davidson and Gary E. McPherson, "Models of Success and Failure in Instrumental Learning: Case Studies of Young Players in the First 20 Months of Learning," *Bulletin of the Council for Research in Music Education* 146 (Fall 2000): 51–69.

45. Robert A. Duke and Jacqueline C. Henninger, "Effects of Verbal Corrections on Student Attitude and Performance," *Journal of Research in Music Education* 46, no. 4 (1998): 482–95; Robert A. Duke and Jacqueline C. Henninger, "Teachers' Verbal Corrections and Observers' Perceptions of Teaching and Learning," *Journal of Research in Music Education* 50, no. 1 (2002): 75–87.

46. Duke and Henninger, "Effects of Verbal Corrections."

47. I provide a full discussion of proximal goal setting and adjustment in chapter 5.

48. Sylvia A. Gholson, "Proximal Positioning: A Strategy of Practice in Violin Pedagogy," *Journal of Research in Music Education* 46, no. 4 (1998): 542.

49. Dijana Ihas, unpublished research; used with permission.

50. McGrath, Hendricks, and Smith, *Performance Anxiety Strategies* 130.

51. Tschannen-Moran and Hoy, "Multidisciplinary Analysis of Trust," 558.

52. Lee Higgins, "Safety without Safety: Participation, the Workshop, and the Welcome," *Musiké: The International Journal of Ethnomusicological Studies* 3 (2008): 65–84.

53. Ibid., 77.

54. Ibid., 79.

55. Ibid., 79; see also McGrath, Hendricks, and Smith, *Performance Anxiety Strategies.*

56. Ibid., 79.

57. McGrath, Hendricks, and Smith, *Performance Anxiety Strategies.*

58. Tschannen-Moran and Hoy, "Multidisciplinary Analysis of Trust," 550.

59. Ibid.

60. Robert Rosenthal, Judith A. Hall, M. Robin DiMatteo, Peter L. Rogers, and Dane Archer, *Sensitivity to Nonverbal Communication: The PONS Test* (Baltimore, MD: The Johns Hopkins University Press, 1979); Janet Strayer, "Current Research in Affective Development," *Journal of Children in Contemporary Society* 17, no. 4 (1986): 37–55; Ross A. Thompson, "Empathy and Emotional Understanding," in *Empathy and Its Development,* ed. Nancy Eisenberg and Janet Strayer (New York: Cambridge University Press, 1987), 119–45.

61. Trudy Govier, "Distrust as a Practical Problem," *Journal of Social Philosophy* 23, no. 1 (1992): 52–63.

62. Annette Baier, "Trust and Antitrust," *Ethics* 96, no. 2 (1986): 234.

63. Paulo Freire, *Pedagogy of the Oppressed, 30th Anniversary Edition* (New York: Continuum, 2007).

64. Ibid., 44.

65. Casper, "Collective Student Trust and Student Achievement," 20.

66. Aaron Lazare, "Making Peace through Apology," in *The Compassionate Instinct,* ed. Dacher Keltner, Jason Marsh, and Jeremy Adam Smith (New York: W. W. Norton, 2010), 246–54.

67. See McGrath, Hendricks, and Smith, *Performance Anxiety Strategies.*

68. Tschannen-Moran and Hoy, "Multidisciplinary Analysis of Trust," 573.

69. As cited in Tschannen-Moran and Hoy, "Multidisciplinary Analysis of Trust," 573; M. Blake and A. J. MacNeil, "Trust: The Quality Required for Successful Management," *Creating High Functioning Schools: Practice and Research,* ed. Yvonne Cano, Fred H. Wood, and Jan C. Simmons (Springfield, IL: Charles C. Thomas, 1998): 29–37; John J. Gabarro, "The Development of Trust, Influence, and Expectations," *Interpersonal Behavior: Communication and Understanding in Relationships* (Englewood Cliffs, NJ: Prentice Hall, 1978): 290–303.

70. Robert L. Swinth, "The Establishment of the Trust Relationship," *Journal of Conflict Resolution* 11, no. 3 (1967): 335–44; see also Bryk and Schneider, *Trust in Schools.*

71. Cori Brewster and Jennifer Railsback, *Building Trusting Relationships for School Improvement: Implications for Principals and Teachers* (Northwest Regional Educational Laboratory, 2003), 13–14. Accessed March 7, 2017, at educationnorthwest.org/sites/default/files/trust.pdf.

72. The italicized words are verbatim from the document, with the exception of bracketed words that I have changed in order to suit an audience of music teachers.

73. See Bandura, *Self-Efficacy.*

Chapter 4

Empathy

What we are contemplating has much more importance than it seems . . .
how wonderful [it] is to see that the grown-up people think of the small-
est like this as to teach them to begin with the noble feelings, with the
noble deeds. And one of [these is] music. To . . . make them understand
that music is not only sound to have to dance or to have small pleasure,
but such a high thing in life that perhaps it is music that will save the
world.

—Attributed to Pablo Casals[1]

Empathy is perhaps one of the most misunderstood human characteristics
that we all seem to want (especially in other people). "If only so-and-so had
more empathy," we say. But then what? What would an increase in empathy
actually get us? Empathy is a trait that people possess or develop, but not a
positive act in and of itself. It is possible to be empathetic and still do nothing
to serve others—or in some extreme circumstances, we might even use our
understandings about how others feel to hurt or manipulate them. Conversely,
it is possible to have zero empathy and do perceptibly kind or generous acts
for a completely self-serving purpose, or to behave well simply because there
are rules to follow.[2]

What empathy *can* do—and why we perceive it as a worthy quality—is
that it helps us take on the perspective of another person, so much so that we
can imagine or even feel what it would be like to be that person or to live that
person's life. In a general sense, then, empathy has the *potential* to motivate
us to treat others as we would want to be treated ourselves—but only if we
choose to act upon those empathetic thoughts and feelings in kind and noble
ways.

DEFINING EMPATHY

The word *empathy* stems from the Greek *empatheia, empathies, and em- + pathos*, representing feelings and emotion. Although certainly related to the broader concept of compassion, *empathy* describes more specifically the experience of understanding or "getting into" the emotions and feelings of others. Empathy came into use in the early 20th century as a means of expressing the German notion of *Einfühlung*, or a way of "feeling into" or "feeling within."[3]

Over time, empathy has come to represent "putting oneself in the place of" another.[4] The idea goes beyond mere sympathy, where we might "feel for" someone but not experience the same emotions as that person in an identical or more complete way. As empathy scholar David Howe has explained, "Whereas empathy puts me in your emotional shoes, sympathy simply tells you that I've walked there too. Sympathy is me-oriented; empathy is you-oriented."[5]

Cognitive and Affective Empathy

Most empathy scholars agree that humans manifest two general kinds of empathy: *cognitive empathy*, or the ability to consider in our minds what someone else might be experiencing and *affective empathy*, or the ability to actually feel in our bodies and emotions what others are feeling.[6] Cognitive empathy involves understandings of others' feelings that take place within our own minds, such as the detection of emotional cues that may be verbal or nonverbal, or by placing ourselves hypothetically in situations that we observe others experiencing.[7] Affective empathy, on the other hand, is involuntary and involves an imitative or mirrored response to someone else's emotional or physical experiences.[8] Anyone who has manifested physical symptoms of anxiety when watching someone else perform, for instance, will understand how affective empathy works.

Cognitive empathy is important for being able to take the perspective of other people and then understand, in our forethought, how our actions might affect them in certain ways. But as mentioned in the introduction to this chapter, we might mistakenly assume that all who possess cognitive empathy would utilize this trait for good. Unfortunately, positive actions cannot be taken for granted when one steps into the mind of another, as history is wrought with examples of narcissistic and sociopathic leaders who have strategized ways to torture and manipulate others for their own gain.[9]

Affective empathy isn't all roses either, as some people may be unable to manage the emotions they are feeling, including even being able to separate out what emotions are their own from those of others. Such confusion may leave people anything but able to help others in need.[10] Therefore, those of us in service-oriented professions need to be mindful of our own emotional states, to prevent ineffective teaching, exhaustion, and burnout.

Compassionate Empathy

While researchers have for decades regarded empathy as a process of detecting emotional cues, taking the perspective of another person, and/or responding emotionally to the experiences of others,[11] these empathic experiences are insufficient in and of themselves for making the world a better place. What is needed is to exercise what scholars have called *compassionate* or *motivational* empathy, in which a person not only understands and feels for (and with) others but also feels compelled to make things better for people in need.[12] The difference is "caring for" versus merely "caring about," as briefly discussed in the previous chapter.[13] This additional step involves making a moral choice and acting upon those thoughts and feelings in an altruistic way.

MATURE EMPATHY AND ALTRUISM

People who are more socially mature will, understandably, have a more refined level of empathy—a deeper and more insightful ability to view the world from another's vantage point, including an awareness for and acceptance of values and beliefs that might differ from their own. Author Alfie Kohn has described this more developed level of empathy as one that far surpasses the Golden Rule:

> There are different levels of perspective taking, of course, and more sophisticated versions may elude very young children. The best we may be able to hope for in the case of a 4-year-old is the rather primitive ethics of the Golden Rule. We might say (in a tone that sounds like an invitation to reflect, rather than a reprimand), "I notice you finished all the juice and didn't leave any for Amy. How do you think you would feel if Amy did that?" The premise of this question, probably correct, is that both kids like juice and would be disappointed to find [no juice] available.
>
> But George Bernard Shaw reminded us that this sort of assumption doesn't always make sense. "Do not do unto others as you expect they should do unto you," he advised. "Their tastes may not be the same." And, we might add, their needs or values or backgrounds might not be the same either. Older children and adults can realize that it's not enough to imagine ourselves in someone else's situation: we have to imagine what they're feeling in that situation. We have to see with their eyes rather than just with our own. We have to—if I may switch metaphors—ask not just what it's like to be in their shoes, but what it's like to have their feet.[14]

People with more advanced levels of empathy are those who will be more likely to engage in helpful behavior. As empathy expert Martin Hoffman described it, "Mature empathy reflects a sensitivity to subtle differences in the severity and quality of the consequences that different actions might have for different people."[15] It is not surprising, then, that the link between empathy and altruism is stronger in adults than in children,[16] as they have had more time to practice refining their behavior.

Moving from Empathy to Positive Action

Empathy and moral principles work together to promote positive social action.[17] Individuals with more mature empathy (as a result of socialization and self-awareness) will have a better sense of how and when to effectively respond to the thoughts and feelings they share with others. For empathy to lead to action, therefore, it is imperative that we both refine the sensitivities we have toward others, and also learn to make sense of those empathic thoughts and feelings in helpful and productive ways.

I often read the news and grieve in my heart for the misfortunes of others. Sometimes the extent of my response, however, is simply to share something on my Facebook feed, or merely make a comment to the person sitting next to me. On the other hand, Renae Timbie's work with Syrian refugees demonstrates the extent of her capacity to move from empathy to positive action—and to use music as a means of bringing hope, peace, and healing to others.

While speaking with Syrian parents in the refugee camp, Timbie came to understand four sources of grief that they had experienced: watching family and friends dying right in front of their eyes; the loss of their homes and valuable property; tragic passage from home to Greece; and loss of their home culture, including their children's education in that culture. She explained:

I was sitting there and my heart's being tugged, saying, "This is a place where music can have impact." This is where I can come in and say, "What if we can preserve your culture?" What if we can learn and use their music rather than coming in with a Latin piece or something and saying, "Here, sing this," but instead to say, "You teach me. Let's get your music and teach it to other people. Let's preserve your culture."

For me the dream is to do that with adults. The kids are going to school, but the adults are sitting around the camp feeling hopeless, and being told over and over again that their lives are worthless: "You can be bombed at any time, you're in this holding pattern now, nobody wants you. Your lives are worthless." So to be able to go to the camps, to work toward something with music that gives them meaning, but it also gives them a voice. And then to have them teach us their music says to them, "Your voices are valuable. Your voices are more than just the violence." And that's the connection of culture to music that I think is so vital. Especially in music.

In my work with refugees, I hope to say, "Here's this Syrian music. Please teach me about this. I will be your guide, but you're the expert on this. Even if you're not the expert, you know more than I do." So if we have a choir of immigrant and refugee singers, from Syria, Iran, Iraq, Afghanistan, Kurdistan, and we're using their music, to let them speak to one another. They're the ones who want to give voice, and for the world to hear their music, their culture. This is something that meets a need: They have a voice.[18]

Refining Empathy through Disagreement with Others

Just as Timbie envisions music as a means of bringing disparate cultures together, we should also never underestimate the power of disagreement itself in helping to refine our sensitivities to one another. People are more satisfied in relationships where they are able to discern the thoughts and feelings of another during moments of discord.[19] Empathic relationships are not fostered by merely choosing to be more sensitive, but by practicing interactions with others and resolving conflicts as they arise.[20]

This point is important to those of us who tend to avoid conflict at all costs (and even for those who carefully select lunch associates or friends on social media, for that matter): It is not in avoiding disagreements that we come to be kind and understanding people, but through the successful, continual, and honest negotiation of differing views. Marcus Santos noted how he tries to understand other people no matter their worldview, in order to help his own personal development:

It's extremely important to try to learn from everyone. I try to learn from teachers and from students, trying to pick every brain I can, and then incorporate it into my own understanding and my development as a human being. And to help my development of moral values. I see it as accepting every single opinion out there and trying to not judge too, and just listen even if I disagree—because you also want people to do the same for you, to respect your opinion. I'm not a conservative person, but I watch conservative news because I want to see what they are thinking, and how they're perceiving reality. Understanding the worldviews of others is very important for human development.

In settings as different as university choral rehearsals and refugee camps, Timbie's goal is the same: to use music to help people foster empathy for those with different worldviews. Here she describes the philosophy behind collaborative learning activities in her choral rehearsals, in which students work together to understand (and more authentically represent) the cultures of the pieces they are singing:

I think music-making in which we emphasize cultural literacy is really what we're talking about: How do you see the world, how do you see people, how do they see the world? So I think it helps expand and confront others' worldviews,

Figure 4.1.   Renae Timbie working with a university choir. Figure courtesy of Renae Timbie.

and my own. It adds to the idea that all voices are valid. It's just recognizing that their voices might be different than ours!

We see the world from what we have experienced, what we know, and what we're comfortable with. And then you're confronted with someone who comes from a very different neighborhood, who has seen the world differently, and from a different comfort zone. And that can look scary sometimes—you know, for me especially, with my heart being with Arabs—Arabs are scary people to a lot of Americans, you know? All we see is the terror happening in Syria or in Iraq.

I had an American friend tell me recently, "I remember a time, I looked at the news and there was a father weeping for his child. This child was dying or sick or something, it was an Arab man weeping, and"—and my friend was horrified by this thought, but the thought was, "Oh! That father is grieving just like I would grieve. Oh, that father has emotions!" I think we think that someone who is so different doesn't even have emotions, or doesn't feel deeply.

Whether we want it that way or not, when we are confronted with someone else's worldview and are caused to look at it, it causes us to look at it and say, "OK, maybe it's more than what I thought it was." When Arab Spring had just started, my [university] choir students and I spent four or five weeks just on Arabic music. And I was able to say, "Look! Arabs are more than just what you see on the news. Let's look at their pop music. Let's look at where this war actually came from instead of just assuming things." And then that brings compassion because we're understanding, We're expanding upon what that worldview is, and we can appreciate that we are different.

RESEARCH IN MUSIC AND EMPATHY

Musicians work in a field that lives, breathes, and dances in emotional states. Music learning offers fertile ground for empathetic experiences; in fact, the concept of empathy stems from aesthetics, where philosophers have suggested that art allows us to feel or take the perspective of something outside of ourselves (e.g., a painting, a play, a musical performance) and experience it as if it were a part of our own life.[21] Aesthetic experience is parallel in many ways to that of empathy, where we either perceive what it must be like to be someone else, or—in some cases—actually feel someone else's feelings as if they are our own.

Music and Prosocial Behavior

Researchers from all over the world have been interested in the connections among music-making, empathy, and positive social dispositions. Two Finnish studies revealed significant increases in children's empathy, self-esteem, and prosocial behaviors after children participated in a twelve-hour program in which they sang, played instruments, and talked about lyrics with a positive social message.[22] Music also seemed to make a difference for four-year-olds in a German study: Children who engaged in music-making with others displayed more cooperative and helpful behavior than those who had the same amount of social interaction minus the music.[23]

Music is related to prosocial behavior even in infants. Canadian researchers found that infants who were actively involved in music-making activities showed greater development of social behaviors than infants who only listened to music passively,[24] and in another study found that infants who were bounced by an adult to a musical beat showed more helpful behaviors toward that adult than infants who were bounced in a random way, without a musical beat.[25]

Music and Empathy

Research relating music and pro-social skills is much more abundant than that of music and empathy specifically. However, a small amount of research suggests that there may be a direct connection here as well: Researchers from the United Kingdom recently discovered that children (ages 8–11) who participated for a year in a music group interaction program had significantly higher empathy scores than they did before beginning the program, as well as significantly higher scores than control group children at the end of the year.[26]

But music may simply be an important pastime for those who are already sensitive to others. In research that I conducted with colleagues from the United States and Canada, we discovered that children with higher empathy scores were more likely to persist in long-term group music lessons than those with lower empathy.[27] Furthermore, we found that children's empathy correlated with parents' disposition toward music: Parents who reported the highest value on music in their household also reported the highest empathy scores for their children.[28] Our findings are consistent with other research suggesting that parent and child personality can predict whether a child will persist in music lessons.[29]

Researchers have used all sorts of tests to better understand the relationships among music-making, empathy, and social skills. Meanwhile, countless music teachers who have experienced an ineffable connection with others while making music might simply roll their eyes at the research findings and say, "Well, that was obvious." Even empathy experts outside of music such as David Howe recognize this age-old relationship: "Making music is famous for its ability to bring people together and to increase their feelings of care and warmth."[30]

Which comes first, the empathy or the music? Or does it matter? I place a caution here against using any of the research cited earlier to allegedly "prove" the importance of music, and instead recommend getting to work to utilize music and music learning spaces as a means of encouraging connection, sensitivity, and kindness. That is what teachers *can* control, and that is what we do best. It may be that the connection between music and human goodness is more direct and less tangible than scientists can measure, and certainly philosophers over the ages have suggested as much.[31] Yet compassionate music teachers simply take it as truth and live the reality every day.

EMPATHY AND EDUCATION

Although the world is becoming increasingly connected through various forms of technology, we seem increasingly more divided and territorial. As a result, some of our baser human instincts seem to be emerging in very ugly ways as we attempt to protect ourselves from any number of unknown fears. "This is the challenge of our time," empathy expert Frans B. M. de Waal wrote: "globalization by a tribal species."[32] As we come more frequently in contact with people who look or act differently than we do, those who lack the ability to take the perspective of others are more likely to view the "other" as an enemy; hence why Alfie Kohn, quoting Franz Kafka, has suggested that war is nothing but "a monstrous failure of imagination."[33] Empathy becomes all the more important, then, as de Waal considers it "the one weapon in the human repertoire that can rid us of the curse of xenophobia."[34]

Unfortunately, our current educational climate does not leave a lot of room for the fostering of empathy in today's youth. With an extreme emphasis on assessment, standards, and competition, we are often asked to reduce students and their experiences to scores, categories, and labels. This focus on quantifiable outcomes scarcely leaves time or space for awareness of students' feelings about their *own* learning, let alone helping them develop sensitivity to the experiences of others who share that same learning space.

It is likely not coincidental that, as we (and subsequently our schools) have shifted our sights to a microscopic focus on things—achievements, merits, test scores—rather than on people and experiences, we have simultaneously become a society that is statistically less trusting of others.[35] As administrators and policymakers focus on "racing to the top" or attempt to motivate by pitting schools, programs, and students against one another (for fear of failing or having funds taken away and given to others), we naturally move away from the very essence of trust, or an "expectation that other people's future actions will safeguard our interests."[36] These outdated approaches of fear-based motivation scarcely help, as we know that such an atmosphere actually interferes with motivation and productivity.[37]

Yet empathy and related social skills should be at the core of what we practice in social settings such as schools to as empathy expert Frans B. M. de Waal has stated, "Effective cooperation requires being exquisitely in tune with the emotional states and goals of others."[38] Music education may provide a particularly promising backdrop for the nurturing of empathy: Our practice of becoming more sensitive to sound can transfer to myriad other ways in which we cultivate sensitivity to other people.[39]

Some experts have recognized the need for more of a humanizing element in education. Efforts to develop human sensitivities have been put into motion in such programs as socioemotional learning, which emphasizes empathy as a critical step to promoting positive social behavior.[40] In my own experience, however, I have noticed that support for these programs often shows up in elite and/or high-income school districts, but not equally in other lower-income schools where students would similarly benefit. As Gloria Ladson-Billings has asserted, "In far too many urban schools, we . . . think the big task is how to get students to behave . . . how to sit quietly, listen to and obey adults, and comply with rules."[41]

While there is nothing inherently wrong with listening to adults or following rules, there is an inherent injustice with some students having opportunities to practice social skills that will help them better understand others (and, subsequently, learn to cooperate and interact with people in meaningful and productive ways)—while other less-privileged students are taught simply to stay out of trouble and even to fear authority. This dissonance in various educational philosophies highlights other problems of trust and inclusion, and is further addressed in chapter 6.

As music teachers, then, we might go further than simply using whatever discipline or socioemotional programs are practiced in our respective schools or communities, and focus on our *individual* responsibility to ensure that we are teaching and modeling empathy—and the positive actions in response to that empathy—in ways that inspire and teach our students how to be genuinely thoughtful and kind to one another. In words attributed to Pablo Casals, "Perhaps it is music that will save the world."[42] No matter whether we believe Casals's audacious claim, isn't it possible that we could at least foster empathy in music learning settings to help make the world a little kinder, one child at a time? The rest of this chapter is devoted to a discussion of the ways that we, as music teachers, might work toward that aim.

TEACHING WITH EMPATHY

In the case of teaching, empathy can of course be a simple "be kind" impulse or a reminder to consider how your words might affect students. However, empathy can go much further as a means of helping teachers to perceive, predict, and address student learning needs in ways that we might otherwise overlook if we did not take a virtual leap into their worlds. Some of the best teachers in the business are not necessarily great because of their musical ability or pedagogical prowess; rather, they are most effective because they "get" what students "get" and can figure out how to translate what they don't.

Teaching with Cognitive and Affective Empathy

The skills associated with empathic teaching in a *cognitive* sense involve being sensitive to verbal, nonverbal, and situational cues. Practicing cognitive empathy also involves an honest attempt to understand the perspective of our students, both in terms of (a) what they don't yet understand and where they got lost in the process of learning, and (b) what they care about and how they see the world. Music curriculum scholar Tawnya Smith has argued that perspective-taking can and should extend to understanding students' values and worldviews, and adapting our instructional content, pedagogical approaches, and even the way we present material to fit with the needs and interests of students in ways that will truly resonate.[43]

The *affective* empathy that we feel with students can serve as a means of tapping into student needs. Sometimes our "gut" will tell us when to push a student a bit harder, or it may tell us to back off and allow students space to process on their own terms and timetable. The trick here lies in practicing personal composure and self-awareness of our own emotions and potentially conflicting inner voices, so that we are in a state in which we can make appropriate decisions based on what we sense students may need.[44]

"Reading" Students: A Type of Literacy?

As I analyzed the CMT interviews, it was notable to me how each of them talked about the importance of "reading" their students, in a sense of being able to determine student needs and understandings in any given moment. Their frequent and universal use of the word *read* caused me to consider how empathetic teaching is, in a sense, a kind of literacy. Steve Massey described it this way: "I read them. I do auditions, and I hear them individually, and I chat with them periodically when I can to find out how things are going."

Marcus Santos and Renae Timbie used the word *assess* rather than *read*, but the point is the same. To Marcus, "having students play leadership roles is good for assessing. It is good to have myself as a teacher step out and then assess the room." For Renae, her hope for her work in the classroom, community choirs, and refugee camps is the same: It is about "assessing the needs; being able to say, 'How do we meet these people where they are? How do I meet the needs of the people in front of me? How can I make this experience have meaning?'"

"I try and read the kids as much as possible," Brian Michaud said:

Sometimes I'll throw my lesson plan out if I see that the kids are getting bored with something. We do request days where they can pick their favorite activities, and that really helps me because then I can sit down and say, "OK, these are favorites, . . . oh, that was a surprise; I didn't realize they enjoyed that so much." And I give surveys at the end of the year.

Dorothy DeLay's students remarked that her background studies in psychology, as well as her work with thousands of different personality types over the years, helped her to understand people so well that she could

shift her teaching so that they could better understand her, rather than simply asking, "Why don't you understand me? I am the expert here." She had the ability to really get into people, to read them, to know how to bring them along.[45]

DeLay herself described the way she would "read" students:

Well, just watching people's faces and getting some kind of visual feedback to things you say to them. You can often read what their reaction is, and here's this student who is very bright and in some ways different from the other kids.

Who still, although she's got a fine emotional gift, has not done the necessary technical work. If she had done the necessary technical work she would be having a fine career at this moment. So, I was trying to figure out what it is in her background that had kept her from doing this.[46]

The Art of Translation

Much of the work that Renae Timbie does involves literal translation from English to Arabic and vice versa. Marcus Santos similarly switches fluently between languages as he visits various countries and greets new immigrant students who show up at school. However, Timbie, Santos, and the other CMTs are also experts at translating a variety of *musical and technical ideas* in ways that individual students can better understand. Their approaches might involve analogies, metaphors, or changing of goals—as one might expect of any good teacher—but the notable difference is that those analogies, metaphors, or goals are presented in the conceptual *language of the student*. In a way, we could say that each CMT has learned to "speak" countless languages, as each student and each class they teach has a different and unique way of viewing the world.

Understanding Our Audience

Marcus Santos's strategy is this: "First, before you say anything, notice who you're talking to. And then translate." During his interview, I was impressed by the way he even made an effort to understand *my* world, so that he could better explain his ideas to me. The following is a transcript of our conversation about how making music gives him energy:

Santos:	So I think it comes down to enjoying it. Because we forget we're tired, right? I'm trying to think of an analogy of when we—you know—Are you a runner?
Hendricks:	I hike.
Santos:	Oh, cool, cool! So, imagine you're hiking, right? And then all of a sudden, you just feel that energy, it's like, "Oh, I'm tired . . . I don't know if I can make it." And you walk another three minutes and you see something beautiful. Or something very inspirational. And your entire body seems to get a second wind that came out of that energy and all of a sudden you feel like you just started hiking. Right?

With only the slightest pause (long enough to say "Oh, cool, cool!"), Santos was able to shift the running analogy he had intended to share with me to one of hiking, maintaining the words *walk* and *hiking* and discussing the sights that a hiker might see along the way so that it fit with my frame of reference. Then, at the end of the analogy, his "right?" signaled his intention to ensure that I had understood.

When I commented to Santos about this remarkably rapid and fluent translation to my point of view, he added:

> So I can see something like that as a teacher, who says, "I need to understand my students, what they're interested in, how they learn, so I can adapt what I'm teaching them in a way that they will be able to comprehend." It's to make it about them, and to adapt to the needs of the classroom, but always having the goals in mind and trying to get to those goals. But there are several ways of taking of getting there. It is about trying to choose a path that will resonate more with them. They'll remember.

Understanding Understanding

Dorothy DeLay is remembered for her ability to "translate" instruction based on her understanding of how *students* were understanding *her*.[47] DeLay would first focus on understanding a student—typically by asking the student questions—and then provide customized or "translated" feedback to each student. Using what has been termed "proximal positioning,"[48] DeLay first sought to understand her students' needs before working with the student to establish goals and subgoals that would change over time.

DeLay's consistent questioning allowed her to navigate any number of ways a student might grasp a concept. She maintained the highest standards for performance but remained open to the needs—and understandings—of individual students to guide them to their uniquely most profitable path.[49] As one of her students described,

> That is part of Miss DeLay's genius—to put people in the frame of mind where they can do their best. . . . Very few teachers can actually get you to your ultimate potential. Miss DeLay has that gift. She challenges you at the same time that you feel you are being nurtured. . . . It is like putting a plant with just the right amount of light and the right amount of water with the right amount of frequency. If you put it in the sun all day long, it burns out. Maybe other teachers overfeed you with too much information, too much nurturing, too much water, or whatever, but she understands precisely what each student needs, and when.[50]

Understanding Worldview

When Renae Timbie works with adults, the translation comes through "getting inside" a student's worldview—attempting to understand the way that any student perceives life, philosophy, politics, and how the world functions.

In a group setting, she can use that understanding to ensure that everyone's concerns are heard, honored, and respected:

> To me, when we're teaching we're actually saying, "I'm here for you." We're celebrating diversity in our togetherness. We're looking at different worldviews. That means every worldview. That means every person. When I teach, I recognize I'm probably teaching to the majority, thinking, "Where can I find the most common?" And sometimes the student who's too cool for school, he's an outlier. So how do I connect with him in a way—what is it that's making him respond this way? Have I really represented every voice here?

Two Notes of Caution

Teachers who are already highly sensitive to the feelings of others might heed two notes of caution. First, people who experience a high level of affective empathy might need to keep their own emotions in check to provide better consistency in student discipline: Long-term damage might occur when adults experience excessive empathy for children and neglect to provide the necessary boundaries or consequences children need to mature socially or psychologically—simply out of fear of the pain they might experience at witnessing someone else's discomfort.[51]

Second, teachers also run the risk of overreaching on the cognitive side of empathy and at times might do better to stay out of the business of detecting students' nonverbal cues and simply take them on their word. Some people can get so caught up in the needs of others that they tend to "overfunction" in relationships, thereby neglecting their own needs and demonstrating a latent lack of trust in another person's ability to communicate.[52] Similarly, "destructive compassion" takes place when our concerns for another lead to overcontrolling behaviors in a relationship.[53] When students' verbal and nonverbal cues don't add up, an example of an appropriate and professional response might be to simply comment once on what we see ("you're saying that you want to play the solo but you're not smiling about it"); ask for clarification ("would you like to play the solo?"); trust and respect the student's response; and move on.

While some individuals seem more naturally disposed to either cognitive or affective empathy (or both) than others, fostering person-to-person understanding may simply be a question of slowing down and paying attention. Once these cognitive and affective sensitivities are refined, then "compassionate" empathy, or the desire to act upon those perceptions and feelings to help others in need, will likely follow. But just like any musical skill, the art of empathic attentiveness takes practice.

FOSTERING COMPASSIONATE EMPATHY
IN MUSIC LEARNING SETTINGS

In this chapter, I have described just how complex and multifaceted empathy can be. However, it is still possible to compile this research and make it meaningful in our daily practice. In the remainder of the chapter, I offer a list of habits and dispositions based on previously discussed research that we, as music teachers, might try on for size in our own teaching and lives. If we view empathy from a developmental perspective, these steps might help us become more thoughtful in our own actions and possibly help us encourage positive, empathy-motivated behavior among our students, colleagues, administrators—and just about anyone with whom we interact.

1. *Model empathy and action.* Beyond simply listening and being kind, modeling empathy might include speaking, out loud, about how we are perceiving the needs of others. We might discuss with students specifically what we are feeling or thinking, and how it relates to what we perceive others might need. Then, to demonstrate how empathy moves to action, we can model positive behavior in response to those feelings.

For example, in an intense rehearsal a conductor might mention awareness of students' nonverbal cues of fatigue, and ask them for their opinion about whether they think another round of rehearsal on that same spot might help a passage get better or make it worse. Then, of course, follow-through on the students' requests is critical, either in meeting their request or explaining clearly why another approach might be better. As students recognize that their needs are noticed and genuinely considered, they gain relational trust, which could potentially motivate students to practice on their own for the good of the group.

2. *Provide artistic experiences for perspective taking.* Opportunities to practice perspective taking can occur through exposure to stories, fictional or real, written by someone else, or written by the children themselves.[54] These stories might also be historical ones, in which important moral lessons from the past are shared with the next generation of citizens, who can learn from previous mistakes and take the perspective of those who have been disadvantaged.[55] Not only can we use music to help students understand the viewpoints of fictional characters whose themes might show up in various parts of a musical work, but we can also help them understand the perspectives of actual people who made the music possible.

For example, I found that high school students were more motivated to practice and learn Schubert's "Death and the Maiden" Quartet—and performed it more expressively—after they learned about Schubert's life and the personal connections he had with the music he wrote.[56] We might, therefore, help students connect to the composer, previous performers who have toiled over the same difficult passages, and even the copy editor whose bad day may have led to a typo in the music that slowed down our rehearsal or led to the embarrassment of a player who came in strong with a sour note.

3. *Be sensitive to the nonverbal messages that students may be giving.* Compassionate music teachers include those who, after a long rehearsal, take the time to comment on how tired the players look, and thank them for their efforts. Yet empathetic teachers also note when students' nonverbal messages do not match their words. As teachers communicate clearly about what they see versus what they hear, they invite students to also communicate openly. We can both model this sensitivity and point out to students when others might need a bit more thoughtfulness on their behalf.

4. *Engage students in dialogue with one another.* Providing student voice and choice can be motivational for musical engagement.[57] However, opening up ideas for conversation may also lead to unexpected conflict when student opinions differ. In order to help students mature and refine their empathic awareness, we can talk openly with them about the subtleties of social interaction.

Because empathy is still maturing in young minds and emotions, adult intervention or scaffolding in disagreements can be key.[58] We can encourage cognitive empathy now and in the future by taking the time to talk through differences of opinion in positive and productive ways, and helping students understand how they can better relate to others. Notably, taking time for these kinds of discussions may have a side benefit of helping students discover and come to value a number of musical approaches, styles, and possibilities that they otherwise may not have imagined. Such discussions allow the teacher to learn new approaches as well.

5. *Minimize the focus on competitiveness and increase a sense of community.* Empathy, cooperation, and music belong together. Meanwhile, setting our sights on performing better than others may steer us away from relationships of trust. Furthermore, a spirit of competitiveness not only sets us apart from one another, but it has also been shown to interfere with students' propensity to express themselves.[59] Instead, we might consider the approach taken by Suzuki, whose words "cooperation, not competition"[60] and "first character, then ability"[61] resonate with his emphasis on developing a beautiful music *and* a beautiful heart. As noted by Steve Massey, when music itself is the motivation, "that's going to be enough."

6. *Provide a safe learning culture where mutual caring and concern is the norm.* According to David Howe, "Learning to be socially competent can only take place in classroom settings that feel safe and supportive, ordered and predictable."[62] Teachers who exercise cognitive, affective, and compassionate empathy will likely create and model an environment where students

are considerate of one another. Order and predictability are still possible—and should take place—in flexible learning environments when teachers exercise a healthy and balanced amount of empathy. As teachers practice sensitivity to student needs, they will be able to recognize and enforce appropriate boundaries and consequences to foster a long-term sense of safety and security. I discuss some of these approaches further in chapter 5.

7. *Stay attuned to your own emotional and physical needs.* Self-understanding and self-care is critical for teachers, or for anyone in a serving profession. Individuals with more refined empathy, as well as those who are more in touch with their own needs, will likely be more effective at responding to the thoughts and feelings they share with others. As the old "sharpen the axe" adage suggests, we will likely be much more effective at helping others when our own needs have been met, and we are in a state of personal health and well-being.

Reflection Questions

1. How and in what ways can you utilize *cognitive* empathy to motivate and engage students, and to improve your own instruction?
2. How and in what ways can you utilize *affective* empathy to motivate and engage students, and to improve your own instruction?
3. How and in what ways might empathy be used ineffectively, inappropriately, or in ways that are harmful?
4. What can you do to practice self-care and refine self-awareness, thereby enhancing the way you respond to the thoughts and feelings of others?
5. Choose one of the strategies for fostering compassionate empathy provided at the end of this chapter. What is a specific action that you can take right away to put this strategy in motion?

NOTES

1. Shinichi Suzuki, *Nurtured by Love: A New Approach to Talent Education,* trans. Waltraud Suzuki (Miami, FL: Summy-Birchard, [1969] 1983), 102.

2. Simon Baron-Cohen, *Zero Degrees of Empathy: A New Theory of Human Cruelty* (London: Penguin UK, 2011).

3. For a detailed description of the evolution of this term over time, see Lauren Wispé, "History of the Concept of Empathy," in *Empathy and Its Development,* ed. Nancy Eisenberg and Janet Strayer (New York: Cambridge University Press, 1987), 17–37.

4. Ibid., 27.

5. David Howe, *Empathy: What It Is and Why It Matters* (London: Palgrave Macmillan, 2013), 12.

6. Mark R. Dadds, Kirsten Hunter, David J. Hawes, Aaron D. J. Frost, Shane Vassallo, Paul Bunn, Sabine Merz, and Yasmeen El Masry, "A Measure of Cognitive and Affective Empathy in Children Using Parent Ratings," *Child Psychiatry and Human Development* 39, no. 2 (2008): 111–22; Kathleen M. Einarson, Karin S. Hendricks, Nancy Mitchell, Elizabeth Guerriero, and Patricia D'Ercole, "Empathy Level in Young Children Is Associated with Persistence in Group Music Training and with Parental Beliefs and Values," unpublished manuscript; Janet Strayer, "Affective and Cognitive Perspectives on Empathy," in *Empathy and Its Development,* ed. Nancy Eisenberg and Janet Strayer (New York: Cambridge University Press, 1990), 218–44.

7. Ibid.

8. Ibid.

9. See Daniel Goleman, "Hot to Help," in *The Compassionate Instinct,* ed. Dacher Keltner, Jason Marsh, and Jeremy Adam Smith (New York: W. W. Norton, 2010), 173; Daniel Goleman, *Emotional Intelligence* (New York: Bantam, 1995).

10. Strayer, "Affective and Cognitive Perspectives"; Howe, *Empathy: What It Is and Why It Matters;* Goleman, "Hot to Help."

11. Norma Deitch Feshbach, "Parental Empathy and Child (Mal)adjustment," in *Empathy and Its Development,* ed. Nancy Eisenberg and Janet Strayer (New York: Cambridge University Press, 1987), 271–91; Martin L. Hoffman, "Empathy: Justice and Moral Judgment," in *Empathy and Its Development,* ed. Nancy Eisenberg and Janet Strayer (New York: Cambridge University Press, 1987), 47–80.

12. Paul Ekman, *Emotional Awareness: Overcoming the Obstacles to Psychological Balance and Compassion* (New York: Henry Holt, 2008); Goleman, "Hot to Help"; Martin L. Hoffman, *Empathy and Moral Development: Implications for Caring and Justice* (New York: Cambridge University Press, 2001); Hoffman, "Empathy: Justice and Moral Judgment."

13. See Nel Noddings, *A Richer, Brighter Vision for American High Schools* (New York: Cambridge University Press, 2015), 123.

14. Alfie Kohn, "A Different View," in *The Compassionate Instinct,* ed. Dacher Keltner, Jason Marsh, and Jeremy Adam Smith (New York: W. W. Norton, 2010), 157–60.

15. Hoffman, "Empathy: Justice and Moral Judgment," 65.

16. Nancy Eisenberg and Paul Miller, "Empathy, Sympathy, and Altruism," in *Empathy and Its Development,* ed. Nancy Eisenberg and Janet Strayer (New York: Cambridge University Press, 1987), 292–316.

17. Martin L. Hoffman, "Empathy: Justice and Moral Judgment."

18. All CMT quotes are from interviews with the author, unless otherwise cited.

19. Philip A. Cowan, Carolyn Pape Cowan, and Neera Mehta, "Feeling Like Partners," in *The Compassionate Instinct,* ed. Dacher Keltner, Jason Marsh, and Jeremy Adam Smith (New York: W. W. Norton, 2010), 103.

20. Ibid., 108.

21. Howe, *Empathy,* 6–8; Wispé, "History of the Concept of Empathy."

22. Merja Hietolahti-Ansten and Mirja Kalliopuska, "Self-Esteem and Empathy among Children Actively Involved in Music," *Perceptual and Motor Skills* 71, no. 3 (1990): 1364–66; Mirja Kalliopuska and Inkeri Ruokonen, "A Study with a

Follow-Up of the Effects of Music Education on Holistic Development of Empathy," *Perceptual and Motor Skills* 76, no. 1 (1993): 131–37.

23. Sebastian Kirschner and Michael Tomasello, "Joint Music Making Promotes Prosocial Behavior in 4-Year-Old Children," *Evolution and Human Behavior* 31, no. 5 (2010): 354–64.

24. David Gerry, Andrea Unrau, and Laurel J. Trainor, "Active Music Classes in Infancy Enhance Musical, Communicative and Social Development," *Developmental Science* 15, no. 3 (2012): 398–407.

25. Laura K. Cirelli, Kathleen M. Einarson, and Laurel J. Trainor, "Interpersonal Synchrony Increases Prosocial Behavior in Infants," *Developmental Science* 17, no. 6 (2014): 1003–11.

26. Tal-Chen Rabinowitch, Ian Cross, and Pamela Burnard, "Long-Term Musical Group Interaction Has a Positive Influence on Empathy in Children," *Psychology of Music* 41, no. 4 (2013): 484–98.

27. Kathleen M. Einarson, Karin S. Hendricks, Nancy Mitchell, Elizabeth Guerriero, and Patricia D'Ercole, "Empathy Level in Young Children Is Associated with Persistence in Group Music Training and with Parental Beliefs and Values," unpublished manuscript, under review.

28. Ibid.

29. Kathleen A. Corrigall and E. Glenn Schellenberg, "Predicting Who Takes Music Lessons: Parent and Child Characteristics," *Frontiers in Psychology* 6 (2015): 282; Kathleen A. Corrigall, E. Glenn Schellenberg, and Nicole M. Misura, "Music Training, Cognition, and Personality," *Frontiers in Psychology* 4 (2013): 222.

30. Howe, *Empathy*, 170.

31. See, for example, Wayne Bowman, *Philosophical Perspectives on Music* (New York: Oxford University Press, 1998).

32. Frans B. M. de Waal, "The Evolution of Empathy," in *The Compassionate Instinct,* ed. Dacher Keltner, Jason Marsh, and Jeremy Adam Smith (New York: W. W. Norton, 2010), 24.

33. Kohn, "A Different View," 157.

34. Frans B. M. de Waal, "The Evolution of Empathy," 23.

35. Jeremy Adam Smith and Pamela Paxton, "America's Trust Fall," in *The Compassionate Instinct,* ed. Dacher Keltner, Jason Marsh, and Jeremy Adam Smith (New York: W. W. Norton, 2010), 203–12.

36. Ibid., 205.

37. Ibid.

38. de Waal, "The Evolution of Empathy," 22.

39. See chapter 8 for a more complete discussion on this topic.

40. See, for example, Scott N. Edgar, *Music Education and Social Emotional Learning: The Heart of Teaching Music* (Chicago, IL: GIA Publications, 2017).

41. Gloria Ladson-Billings, "You Gotta Fight the Power: The Place of Music in Social Justice Education," in *The Oxford Handbook of Social Justice in Music Education,* ed. Cathy Benedict, Patrick Schmidt, Gary Spruce, and Paul Woodford (New York: Oxford University Press, 2015), 417.

42. Shinichi Suzuki, *Nurtured by Love,* 102.

74 Chapter 4

43. Tawnya D. Smith, *Using the Expressive Arts to Facilitate Group Music Improvisation and Individual Reflection: Expanding Consciousness in Music Learning for Self-Development* (PhD diss., University of Illinois at Urbana-Champaign, 2014); Tawnya D. Smith, "Multiple Worldviews in the Classroom: Scaffolding for Differentiated Instruction and Social Justice Learning," unpublished manuscript.

44. Ibid.

45. Dijana Ihas, personal interview, June 29, 2017.

46. Sylvia A. Gholson, "Proximal Positioning: A Strategy of Practice in Violin Pedagogy," *Journal of Research in Music Education* 46, no. 4 (1996): 542 (italics added).

47. Gholson, "Proximal Positioning."

48. Gholson, "Proximal Positioning." This term was coined after the "zone of proximal development" concept; see Lev Vygotsky, "Interaction between Learning and Development," *Readings on the Development of Children* 23, no. 3 (1978): 34–41; L. S. Vygotsky, *Mind in Society: The Development of Higher Psychological Process*, ed. Michael Cole, Vera John-Steiner, Sylvia Scribner, and Ellen Souberman (Cambridge, MA: Harvard University Press, 1978).

49. Gholson, "Proximal Positioning"; Barbara Lourie Sand, *Teaching Genius: Dorothy DeLay and the Making of a Musician* (Portland, OR: Amadeus Press, 2000),

50. Sand, *Teaching Genius,* 219.

51. Feshbach, "Parental Empathy and Child (Mal)adjustment."

52. Harriet Lerner, *The Dance of Anger: A Woman's Guide to Changing the Patterns of Intimate Relationships*, 4th ed. (New York: HarperCollins, 2014).

53. Jason Marsh, "Can I Trust You? A Conversation between Paul Ekman and His Daughter Eve," in *The Compassionate Instinct,* ed. Dacher Keltner, Jason Marsh, and Jeremy Adam Smith (New York: W. W. Norton), 165.

54. Howe, *Empathy*; see also Lesley Roessing, "Creating Empathetic Connections to Literature," *Quarterly-National Writing Project* 27, no. 2 (2005). Retrieved December 14, 2017, https://www.nwp.org/cs/public/print/resource/2229

55. See Mark A. Barnett, "Empathy and Related Responses in Children," in *Empathy and Its Development*, ed. Nancy Eisenberg and Janet Strayer (New York: Cambridge University Press, 1987), 146–62.

56. Karin S. Hendricks, "Investing Time: Teacher Research Observing the Influence of Music History and Theory Lessons upon Student Engagement and Expressive Performance of an Advanced High School String Quartet," *Bulletin of the Council for Research in Music Education* 184 (Spring 2010): 65–78.

57. See Randall Everett Allsup, "Mutual Learning and Democratic Action in Instrumental Music Education," *Journal of Research in Music Education* 51, no. 1 (2003): 24–37; Gary E. McPherson, Jane W. Davidson, and Paul Evans, "Playing an Instrument," in *The Child as Musician: A Handbook of Musical Development* (New York: Oxford University Press, 2006), 331–51; James M. Renwick and Gary E. McPherson, "Interest and Choice: Student-Selected Repertoire and Its Effect on Practising Behaviour," *British Journal of Music Education* 19, no. 2 (2002): 173–88.

58. Karen L. Bierman and Stephen A. Erath, "Promoting Social Competence in Early Childhood: Classroom Curricula and Social Skills Coaching Programs," in *Blackwell Handbook of Early Childhood Development,* ed. Kathleen McCartney and Deborah Phillips (Malden, MA: Blackwell, 2006), 595–615.

59. See Casey McGrath, Karin S. Hendricks, and Tawnya D. Smith, *Performance Anxiety Strategies: A Musician's Guide to Managing Stage Fright* (Lanham, MD: Rowman & Littlefield, 2016); Karin S. Hendricks, "Relationships between the Sources of Self-Efficacy and Changes in Competence Perceptions of Music Students during an All-State Orchestra Event" (PhD diss., University of Illinois at Urbana-Champaign, 2009).

60. Tanya Carey, "President's Message," *American Suzuki Journal* 18, no.7 (Winter 1990): 3.

61. Shinichi Suzuki, *Nurtured by Love*, 66.

62. Howe, *Empathy*, 167.

Chapter 5

Patience

Compassion doesn't always call for grand or heroic gestures. . . . A word of kindness, a loving touch, a patient presence, a willingness to step beyond your fears and reactions are all gestures of compassion that can transform a moment of fear and pain.

—Christina Feldman[1]

The preceding quote by author Christina Feldman illustrates how easy it can be to demonstrate compassion toward others: simply by being there with a kind word, a gentle touch, or being a "patient presence." I would simultaneously celebrate and challenge this notion of simplicity. While it is true that we don't need to be the Dalai Lama or Mother Teresa to demonstrate small gestures of kindness, coming from a place of patience is not always simple to do. CMT Brian Michaud put in in statistical terms:

I was doing the math the other day, and I figured, "Let's see, I've been teaching 22 years, average at least 20 kids in the classroom. I see about 1,000 classes a year, so that's 440,000 opportunities for somebody to get under my skin." You're going to slip at some point![2]

On the other hand, patience can result when we exercise the thoughtfulness and self-discipline to step beyond those initial reactions that Feldman speaks of—as well as the fearful assumptions that may drive them. The CMTs in this book demonstrate how such simple acts, when consistent and multiplied over time, can reap a long-term pattern of success.

DEFINING PATIENCE

When I asked each of the CMTs to define "patience," I received remarkably different responses. All of them—like every one of us—face daily challenges to test their patience. However, depending on the particulars of the job, those challenges are unique. For Steve Massey, patience comes in constantly striving toward perfection, when he refuses to settle for a musical product that is of a lesser quality than he knows his students are capable of. Brian Michaud defines patience in terms of classroom management, including not taking personally the misbehaviors of his students. For Marcus Santos, patience also involves being gentle with yourself, no matter how badly your day might be going. For Renae Timbie, patience is about taking the time to genuinely listen to students—something that Dorothy DeLay exemplified through her continual questioning and attentiveness to individual student needs.

It is said that Shinichi Suzuki defined patience as "controlled frustration."[3] In a way, this definition fits with Suzuki's belief that every child was capable of learning music, without exception; and that it was up to the *teacher* to find a way to help each individual child develop musically.[4] While I agree wholeheartedly with much of Suzuki's philosophy, I wonder if we might choose different words besides *controlled* and *frustration* to explain the phenomenon of compassionate patience: *Control* disallows room for flexibility, and *frustration* might better be replaced with "curiosity."

No matter the choice of words, patience in a compassionate sense might be defined as looking beyond the present moment and considering a long-term trajectory for our students, in which we ask these questions:

- Where would we like them to be?
- Where would *they* like to be?
- Where are they now?
- What steps are missing, and how do they get there?

As we separate student needs and/or actions from our own emotions and expectations, we may be better able to consider any student situation simply as a problem to figure out—no different than solving a puzzle or riddle. In this case, the act of patience becomes less about frustration or disappointment and more about sleuthing out the particular and individual needs of our students—whatever the issue might be.

In this chapter, I offer several ideas based on theories from cognitive and developmental psychology, complemented with insights from CMT interviews and observations. Some readers might suggest that psychological theories are just that—theories—and that it is impossible to project what any one student will do in any given situation, particularly when we add cultural differences to the mix.[5] I agree wholeheartedly. In fact, this argument only further underlines the importance of patience: Students are neither monolithic nor clones of their teachers, and any unexpected delay or bump in the road of learning may simply require a shift in vantage point to figure out where the disconnect lies. With this in mind, I address patience as a quality of compassionate music teaching in four ways: understanding student potential, assisting with student development, managing classroom dynamics, and fostering student empowerment.

PATIENCE IN POTENTIAL

Compassionate patience involves the willingness to envision the potential for growth in others. When we truly believe that other people can change or improve, then we are more likely to stay by their side when they fail, and even offer more assistance to help them. In the case of music education, a misunderstanding of what musical "talent" is—and how students can attain it—can possibly limit our ability to envision student potential, and thereby limit our own patience when working with certain students. On the other hand, keeping an open mind about the ways in which students can develop their musical abilities can help us stay open to the possibility that all students are capable of learning and expressing themselves musically.

When I teach, I firmly reject students' or parents' self-diagnoses of natural talent, or lack thereof. As a researcher, I understand that we are born with certain physical, emotional, and cognitive characteristics that give us certain advantages over others (we'll talk more about that later). But as a teacher, I tire easily of people overusing stories of talent or genius to celebrate an elite crop of musicians, rather than recognizing the capacity for anyone to learn and grow—and especially the potential for all humans to be musical.

Varying Views of Talent

One extreme position on the subject of talent was held by Shinichi Suzuki, who dared to suggest that musical talent didn't exist at all:

> "I have no talents"—what sadness and despair are occasioned by this nonsensical belief! For years, people everywhere have succumbed to this false way of thinking, which is really only an excuse for avoiding work. . . . Every child can be educated; it is only a matter of the method of education. Anyone can train himself [or herself]; it is only a question of using the right kind of effort.[6]

A more middle-of-the-road position was taken by music learning theorist Edwin Gordon, who firmly believed in the existence of musical aptitude but recognized the importance of good education and practice:

> A person is born with a particular level of music aptitude. The level of music aptitude with which a person is born, however, fluctuates in accordance with his

[or her] informal and formal music environment. . . . Thus, the basis of his or her music aptitude is both innate and environmental. . . . Many students with exceptionally high music aptitude have not achieved in music because they have not had appropriate music instruction, and thus have not been motivated to learn music.[7]

Music psychologists have debated the nature of musical talent for some time. After conducting a review of hundreds of studies examining the nature of talent, researchers Michael Howe and Jane Davidson concluded that the true determinants of excellence in any area stem from a variety of sources, including "early experiences, preferences, opportunities, habits, training, and practice."[8] They concluded that categorizing some children as innately talented is

discriminatory . . . [,] unfair, and wasteful, preventing young people from pursuing a goal because of the unjustified conviction of teachers or parents that certain children would not benefit from the superior opportunities given to those who are deemed to be talented.[9]

The Complexity of Talent

Other psychologists have made room for theory of talent that mixes innate potential for music with environmental and personal influences. Figure 5.1 shows a model of music ability development that music professors Gary McPherson and Aaron Williamon adapted for music from Gagné's Differentiated Model of Giftedness and Talent.[10] McPherson and Williamon presented this model as a part of their effort to "scrutinize much of the folklore that typically accompanies remarkable achievement,"[11] and have shown in this structure how the development of musical abilities is a highly complex and dynamic process that no one can predict.

As the model shows, we may start out on Earth with a certain amount of musical potential, based on a wide array of mental and physical abilities. However, our musical ability is influenced by a great number of things, from the community into which we are born to the connections we make with others along the way. Certain intrapersonal factors, environmental catalysts, developmental processes, and even chance (the people we meet, being in the right place at the right time, etc.) all play a part in the musicians we become.[12] Many of these influences are in our control, yet many are not. This is why students who we initially think are going to "make it big" sometimes drop out or fizzle, while others who initially show no promise at all end up persisting and surprising us—sometimes even surprising themselves.

In short, research tells us that the notion of "talent" is too complex an issue for us to make a premature judgment on the potential of a student. It would behoove us, therefore, to give everyone the benefit of the doubt and put our

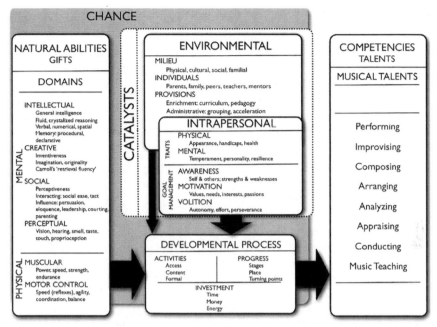

Figure 5.1. Gary E. McPherson and Aaron Williamon, "Building Gifts into Musical Talents," in *The Child as Musician: A Handbook of Musical Development*, 2nd ed., ed. Gary E. McPherson (Oxford, UK: Oxford University Press, 2016), 342. Used with permission.

best into facilitating the growth of every student according to individual needs. This was the philosophy held by Dorothy DeLay. She stated:

> Is musical sensitivity innate? I think it is too easy for a teacher to say, "Oh, this child wasn't born with it, so I won't waste my time. Too many teachers hide their own lack of ability behind that statement. I don't like that statement. It gets my back up. I don't want it to be true that a quality like that is inherited, because you can't do anything about it. I want it to be true that we can all learn anything.[13]

Marcus Santos takes a similar position to that of DeLay:

> It's understanding that we learn at different paces. Right? And you have to have patience: If it's taking a little longer for a student to learn something, we have to repeat and find different ways to teach. But then that can also be inverted to the teacher, when you can point your finger at yourself: If the student does not understand the message, you might not be doing a good job expressing it. So then that is not really about being patient, but looking at yourself and how you can do a better job.

Mindset: Riley's Story

One time, when I started beginning private cello lessons for three-year-old Danny, I asked his mother Riley if she would also like to take lessons. She responded by telling me that no, she wasn't, because she wasn't musical. I spontaneously laughed out loud and told her that was ridiculous—and that I would find a cello for her to use. I told her that if her son could learn, so could she, although perhaps not as quickly. I was a bit taken aback when Riley immediately bowed her head and started to sob. "Oh, no, what have I done?" I thought, and later spoke with Riley's husband Eric about Riley's unexpected burst of emotion. He explained the reason behind her tears:

> There are a lot of things that she never got to try when she was a kid. In high school, she was on the tennis team, but I don't think that she had any kind of lessons or joined any leagues or anything. And I think a part of her has felt like if she had shown enough talent in something her parents would make that a priority, because her younger sister took piano lessons, because her sister had some musical talent. And so to have somebody say, "You can do this" was an affirmation that I think she had never had.[14]

At first, Riley lacked what Stanford psychologist Carol Dweck calls a "growth mindset," in which people believe in their abilities to develop and grow.[15] Riley's "fixed mindset," in which she (and her parents, apparently) believed she had no musical potential, initially stopped her from having as much as a willingness to try. The good news is that Riley eventually took me up on the offer of lessons and developed quickly, and we had a whole lot of fun making music together. But this happened only after she was able to let go of a belief that she had no talent, develop a growth mindset instead, and then tap into her own potential.

PATIENCE IN DEVELOPMENT

Once we recognize the potential in every child to learn, we can then recognize the need to help students develop according to their own needs and individual timetables. When we use only one approach with every student or class, it is easy to blame failure on the students themselves if they don't excel as quickly as others. However, once we recognize the myriad ways that musical talent develops, we are compelled to think differently—to stop considering *whether* a student or class will "get it," and instead consider *how* a student or class might "get it." The answer to this question is as unique and varied as the students themselves. However, I offer a brief description of several psychology-based approaches to musical development, which can be applied and customized to individual and group needs.

The Self-Efficacy Equation: Goals Plus Belief

Our students' abilities to accomplish a specific musical task are influenced by their understanding of:

1. a specific goal;
2. the steps necessary to accomplish that goal; and
3. belief in the ability to carry out those steps.[16]

Often impatience comes on the part of students and/or teachers when either steps 2 or 3 are out of alignment with reality. For example, a horn student who expects to be able to perform the Glière concerto without sufficient knowledge of embouchure strength, breathing efficiency, or the amount of time and specific technique required to develop those skills may become exasperated (and exhausted), yet not understand why. As we help students more accurately come to terms with where they are now, in comparison to where their future goals lie, we empower them to act in task-specific ways that will promote their future success.

The successful accomplishment of goals leads to a more accurate perception of our self-efficacy.[17] Self-efficacy belief, a concept coined by psychologist Albert Bandura, differs from self-esteem because of its specific focus on one task rather than a general view of one's worth as a person. An increase in self-efficacy belief can, however, help to increase general self-esteem.[18] The good news for music teachers, then, is that we can exercise patience with our students by focusing our attention on helping them develop confidence in music-related tasks—what we do best—without concerning ourselves with the much more complex task of boosting up a student's entire sense of self-worth.

Self-efficacy belief is developed over time in tandem with actual competence, as students have a series of *enactive mastery experiences,* or opportunities to actively demonstrate their abilities:

> Because efficacy beliefs develop as habits, music teachers can help students develop mastery over time by helping them prepare for and perform increasingly challenging tasks. This [preparation] might include coaching them toward self-initiated and self-regulative activities that develop independence and academic self-sufficiency, and help students feel a sense of control over their own learning.[19]

Setting and Adjusting Goals

A teacher who is impatient with a student's progress may likewise have an inaccurate sense of the steps that a particular student (or class) needs to accomplish the task at hand. Simply restating "you just need to practice!" or even affirmations such as "you can do this!" may not help—and can in fact be hurtful—if the student's understanding of the steps to get there in the first place is insufficient.[20] Compassionate music teachers can recognize when their own blood pressure starts to rise and take a moment to revisit the student goal and its corresponding steps to determine whether additional or different steps might be required.

As shown in figure 5.2, a teacher and student might work together to develop a long-term (distal) goal and then devise a set of short-term (proximal) steps to attain that larger goal over time. However, if frustration arises, the student and teacher can work together to revisit the proximal steps and insert additional smaller steps as necessary, or to replace steps that turned out to be ineffective with other, more productive techniques. On the other hand, if a student is becoming bored with steps that are too easy, several proximal steps might be condensed or combined.

Steve Massey described how he maintains high standards by adjusting goals as needed, rather than giving up on a student, class, or piece of music:

> If you're working on a phrase, and you run down the practice routine, and the phrase is still not accurate, then students haven't practiced a particular technique. And patience involves the willingness to keep coming back to that phrase and not allowing it to be inaccurate. I will spend months on a piece if I have to. Once we commit to learning a piece, we're not going to give up on it because it's not going well. And I think the life lesson is that there are many elements in music-making that require thousands of repetitions for excellence. Depending on the technique you start with, if you have flawed technique to start with and now you're trying to play very complex music, then you have to not just learn the complex music; you have to rebuild the flawed technique.

Setting and adjusting proximal goals can relieve the stress of both student *and* teacher. For example, a band director might scaffold student learning and set small, manageable benchmarks throughout a performance cycle to keep students interested and avoid the frenzied rush as the concert approaches, as well as the subsequent crash of momentum that follows once the concert is over. Consider figure 5.3, in which I have shown two hypothetical levels of

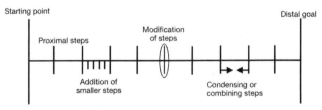

Figure 5.2.   Setting and adjusting proximal goals

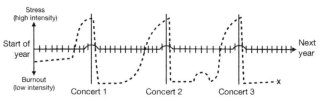

Figure 5.3. Two examples of relative rehearsal intensity, stress, and burnout over the course of a school year

intensity and stress leading up to three respective concerts over the course of a year. The solid line represents a scope and sequence that have been carefully mapped with proximal goals and that are revisited according to student needs.

The dotted line, however, represents a more haphazard rehearsal approach in which the ensuing concert becomes a type of fear-based motivation for students to "kick it into gear." While the carefully mapped approach shows a slight peak in intensity as the concert approaches, it is likely an optimal amount of energy that can be fueled into expressive performance. On the other hand, the high-stress spike of the haphazard approach may lead to anxiety in the concert, followed by burnout afterward.

When I discussed the aforementioned diagrams with Steve Massey, he offered the following in agreement:

> Every rehearsal is a performance. And if you approach it that way with intent, and with energy, then there's no reason the rehearsal after a concert should be any different than any other. It's the programs that take the day off after a concert and sit around and talk about the concert or have a party and have food and cookies that make the concert something that it is not. A performance is not a culmination; it is an experience. It's a performance for an audience, but we can perform for each other, and do perform in every rehearsal, and we should treat that as an opportunity to perform at a performance level.

Marcus Santos similarly attains the highest musical standards with his world-drumming students by focusing on the gradual attainment of distal goals. He also takes note of the students' level of attentiveness, adapting and changing course as necessary when "things start to get dull or we lose that focus." Although he will return again and again to important skills or theoretical concepts that students eventually need to grasp, he maintains student interest in each class by "alternating activities so we're never stuck too long on one thing."

Questions as Diagnosis Tools

Asking students questions (such as those presented in chapter 1) can be particularly helpful for diagnosing where a developmental or mental disconnect may be occurring. Dorothy DeLay was legendary in her patient use of questioning to narrow down not just the minutest details of a performance but also the minutest details of a *student's understanding* of that performance. Her students recalled that she had the presence of mind to concentrate for long periods of time, and simultaneously on multiple diverse details such as technique, intonation, and a student's psychological needs.[21]

By asking questions as focused and detailed as "what is your concept of F-sharp?"[22] DeLay could assist students in higher-level thinking but also better comprehend how well students comprehended their own placement on a spectrum of proximal goals. Then, by using cognitive empathy to place herself in their position of awareness, she was able to interpret students' musical, technical, and even psychological needs and help them refine their focus.[23]

Not only did DeLay exercise the compassionate qualities of patience and empathy in these moments, but she embodied trust as well: She gave students the onus of responsibility for their own learning, and for the regulation of their own progress. DeLay was remembered for not always being able to physically perform the pieces that her students played;[24] however, because she was such an expert at coaching students toward self-regulation, those students developed the ability to master the most challenging repertoire at some of the highest levels of virtuosity known in history.

In sum, high standards are attainable with an effective plan, and with an honest awareness of the time and effort required to attain them.[25] The issue, then, becomes less about telling students to "go practice." Instead, it becomes an issue of helping students set goals and recognize what steps those goals will require to accomplish, and encouraging them to revisit and adjust those steps as they become more authentically aware of their capabilities.

PATIENCE IN CLASSROOM MANAGEMENT

The theories and approaches discussed thus far demonstrate that it is possible to be patient with students who make mistakes, and still hold high standards for learning and performance. In fact, it is likely that our efforts to step back and sleuth out a problem may lead to more effective teaching and a higher level of accomplishment, because the intricacies of learning will be carefully considered and individual progress more refined. The same can be said for classroom management: A truly compassionate teacher is not a pushover or "softie" who loses control of a classroom, nor any sense of stability in a private studio. Rather, a compassionate teacher is one who establishes trust through order, predictability, and consistent adherence to policies that are fair.

Disconnecting Our Emotions from Student Behavior

Brian Michaud explained that he is able to find that balance with his elementary students by first disconnecting his own emotions from any unruly behavior:

> It all comes back to not taking things personally. When you're upset, it's a very selfish kind of feeling. You're thinking about yourself and your own emotions. I remind myself to not take it personally. Patience is understanding that you have 20 different personalities in the room, and that children are better behaved than most adults in a crowd situation (if you've ever been in a faculty, meeting, right?).
>
> And you also have to be able to overlook the small stuff. For example, if you're teaching a lesson and a kid whispers to another kid, there are some teachers who might say, "What are you whispering about?" I just let it ride. Because adults do that all the time in meetings; they turn, they have something in their craw. But it's also knowing where the line is.
>
> That being said, patience is not allowing yourself to be walked over and taken advantage of. There's a point when you can be too patient. When that happens you're only hurting the children in the room who are ready and willing to learn. So when you let too many things go, when you're too patient and you let too many things slide, that's not fair to the other children.

Exercising Empathy

Marcus Santos also used the word *selfish* concerning teachers' harsh treatment of students; however, with a bit of humor he turned the idea on its head:

> I'm the most selfish person you've ever met in your life. You know why? Because all I want is for people to treat me the way that I treat them. So if I'm a jerk to someone, then people should treat me in a jerk-like way, you know? And that's a common phrase [the Golden Rule], but I'm giving people the opportunity to treat me badly if I treat them with a harsh attitude. Like with empathy, I think it's about listening to them, trying to connect with them, and treating them the way you want to be treated.

Renae Timbie also noted the importance of seeking to understand others, recognizing that she also is in need of compassion:

> I want to be empathetic. It's hard sometimes. I strive to see something through someone else's eyes. I want people to be that to me because I get a lot of things not right, even things I'm supposed to get right. I want somebody to come

alongside and strive with whatever that is that I offer; to strive to know me. I want to be seen. And so do my students.

Envisioning Long-Term Potential

As discussed in the previous chapter, a healthy balance of empathy involves understanding and relating to student needs and concerns, but not getting so swept up in students' emotions that we lose our ability to allow natural consequences to occur out of fear of the empathic pain we might experience in watching someone else suffer. The same can be said for the way we address differences and fluctuations in student behavior: As we keep our eyes on long-term behavioral goals and potential, we allow ourselves the mental and emotional space to patiently reflect and strategically act on present and proximal concerns.

In effect, figure 5.2 can work as a model for addressing student behavior as well as for the development of musical goals. As we envision character development as just that—development—we can more patiently respond to unruly student behavior by recognizing where students lie on the continuum of behavior and by adjusting goals and approaches as necessary. Sometimes these adjustments might entail consequences and corrections on the part of the student; however, in many cases the adjustment might be on the part of the teacher, such as changes in pacing, approach, or content of a lesson.

"Discipline with Dignity"

The point here is that it may be wise to assume goodness rather than malice in our students, and when disruptive behavior occurs, to handle it with curiosity, interest, and flexibility rather than taking personal offense. Brian Michaud described the approach this way:

It's discipline with dignity.[26] You don't call a student out, yell, get upset with them; you treat them the way you would want to be treated. I think that falls into that compassion umbrella too: realizing that there are children who are trying their best to learn and want to soak up everything you've got. If a child doesn't follow instructions, I don't get upset, I just calmly explain that they have to sit out of the next activity because their behavior's not fair to the others in the room.

Where you've got a lot of personalities, you don't know their background. They might have had a bad day, and they're acting out as a result. Patience is just asking them to keep improving. I find that I'll ask a child to sit out and they want to come back in. It's music, it's fun, it's activities, it's games, and they want to be part of the group. If it's unusual for a child to act out, I will pull him or her aside and ask the child privately if anything is wrong. It's important to try to delve into the root of the problem rather than simply reacting to disruptive behavior.

It is, perhaps, especially critical to maintain student dignity in music-making settings, where expressions of emotion and self-identity are at the forefront. Plenty of scholars and teachers alike have noted the relationship between music learning and character development.[27] As Renae Timbic remarked, "Music teaching is such an easy tool to bring dignity, to bring value to people." She continued,

> Compassion in teaching is working out of the understanding that every human has dignity, no matter what their background or situation is. We all come with different baggage; we come with different filters. We are different in how we see the world. But each human being has dignity, and so to operate out of that understanding, that is compassion in our teaching. No matter what it is that you are, and what you represent, you are no less important than I am. You are no less valuable than I am even though you may be different. I think there's a dignity element to that.

Keeping a Sense of Humor

Brian Michaud also noted how he tries not to make mountains out of molehills, for everyone's sake:

> Sometimes you make a joke out of it too. If you're lighthearted about it when it's a small infraction, they will be better behaved for you in the long term than if you get upset with them and yell. Of course, if you get upset with them and raise your voice, they're going to behave for that one minute because they're scared; not because they want to please you. So I think the whole thing is that when you're teaching children, you're hoping that they're going to be behaving and doing the right thing and making the right choices when your back is turned and when you're not in the room, not just when you're staring at them. The most important thing that we teach kids is basically to be good people.
>
> What's surprising is that I'll meet the parents and they'll say, "My child loves your class!" And I'll think, "Oh my God, I have to talk to your child just about every single day!" But I'm glad they love my class. And those are the things you must keep in the back of your mind: Even though the child is misbehaving and you need to discipline them, it might be their favorite place they are all day.

Building a Culture of Trust and Excellence

As Brian's words suggest (and as discussed in chapter 3), fostering a culture of trust and excellence can go a much longer way than can punishment or disciplining through fear. Establishing culture is also critical to the musical and classroom management success of both Marcus Santos and Steve Massey. Although their classrooms and students are vastly different, their approach is the same: Develop a culture where the highest level of excellence and participation is expected, teach key student leaders to help other students embrace that culture, and let the students govern themselves.

A Culture of Music

Steve Massey has taught for thirty-seven years in a suburban community with exceptional parent support. Over the past few decades, Steve has gradually built up a program that incorporates student leadership (with weekly leadership classes), parent involvement, a private lesson program, and a large music faculty with assistant directors in each class. He did not simply inherit or move into such a program; he built it over decades of thoughtful vision and in cooperation with other community members. Now, as he reached his final year before retirement, he led a program where almost 100 percent of his students take private lessons, students lead one another, and parents and faculty work together toward common goals.

Despite that Steve Massey's hair is grayer than when he arrived nearly four decades ago—a sign of a life well lived—the work is sustainable and life-giving to him, because he is not doing more than his share of the workload. Instead, he shares the work (and the joy) with a community of other people who have similarly caught the vision. He described it this way:

> Maybe the most important success is that, besides producing an outstanding band, I think we've produced outstanding people. And we've done it within a framework of an outstanding culture, which includes faculty, parents, everybody. So that, to me, is how I measure success. But it's the whole idea of getting the teacher to understand: It's not about *you* explaining. It's about *them* discovering, with your guidance. That's a whole different way of seeing the world. It's your job to guide them, to help them discover the score. It's not your job to direct them and tell them how to interpret the score completely.

Steve Massey's student-directed approach to music learning debunks the myth of any need for authoritarian control in a band rehearsal. He explained:

> It's hard for a lot of directors to give up that power. They don't want to ask the kids, "What's wrong with that?" I think they feel that they are going to lose control of the rehearsal. They're worried about class management. And I can understand that, in the early stages of a teacher's career. But if you have a culture of excellence, you have no class management issues.
>
> Every time I say to band directors, "You ever try sitting in a circle?" They get very nervous because they're afraid the kids are going see each other and

they're going to fool around. I don't know what they're afraid of. I don't know how musicians can really make music together if they can't see each other. It's visual.

I watch all the great jazz rhythm sections: The bass player and drummer, they're staring at each other. And there's so much that they're saying nonverbally, all the time! And so we can all sit around and say, "What do you think . . .?" and I can also stand on the podium, and they'll follow me. I'm not saying we want to give up our authority. We want to share it.

A Culture of Trust

Marcus Santos teaches on the other side of Boston from Steve Massey, and, in many ways, on the other side of the educational spectrum. Santos reported that his general music classes consist of approximately 95 percent immigrants, with a significantly high percentage of English language learners. Santos teaches students who, in his words, "might not have a pampered household." He does not have the benefit of a decades-long school music tradition in the community, nor can his students' parents—many of whom are working two or three jobs to make ends meet—spare the time and resources to help his school music program thrive.

Yet, despite the stark differences in their communities, programs, and repertoire, Santos's approach to working with students is remarkably similar to that of Massey: Santos also situates his students in a circle and empowers them to lead and mentor one another. He scans the room with every new song to find a new set of leaders so he can be free to walk around the room and assist students with particular needs. Not only does this practice establish a sense of trust within the ensemble, but it also allows him to help the students understand the importance of focused behavior during rehearsal.

Santos described his approach to behavior management:

I actually pull them aside sometimes if they are having a bad day—because, you know, they are teenagers; they will have bad days. I'll pull them aside and ask, "Hey, what's going on? You have been great, and today you were fooling around too much; is everything okay with you?" And then I say, "You're a leader here, and other students look at you. So if you misbehave, they're going to misbehave too." And then I know we've got each other's back.

"Love and Logic"

For those who are still working to develop a culture of excellence in both musical performance and classroom management, it can be critical to use a classroom management approach that incorporates empathy, patience, and trust. One such approach is the "Love and Logic" program established by former school principal Jim Fay and psychiatrist Foster W. Cline.[28] The "Love and Logic" approach is grounded in the philosophy that empathy and consistent consequences are much more effective than teacher-imposed punishment for wrongdoing, in part because students and teachers are both able to maintain a sense of control.[29]

In contrast to an authoritarian punishment model (where the teacher may demonstrate signs of frustration and anger while punishing the student for making a mistake—either innocently or from poor choices), the "Love and Logic" model invites teachers to remain calm and controlled, exercising empathy about a consequence the student will necessarily face. The crux of the difference is in the point of focus: Misbehavior is not viewed as an attack on the teacher, but rather as a choice with a necessary outcome.

In this approach the teacher is merely a bystander and a support, while the consequence is viewed as an independent result of behavior that does not exist within or from the teacher. The teacher then becomes a kind of consultant or coach for students as they learn how to manage choices and consequences: The teacher cheers from the sidelines when students make positive choices, and expresses empathetic disappointment when choices lead to consequences that may be less than desirable for the student.

Jim Fay suggested that motivation through the exercise of domination or unequal power is dangerous because it does not allow students to learn important life lessons, such as that:

> Control really comes from within [not from external imposing of power]; Most undesirable behaviors in the real world have natural consequences attached to them; In the real world, our mistakes become our own responsibility; Children are capable of making good decisions and working out problems . . . when adults provide both guidance and the opportunity to do so.[30]

As teachers allow students to make their own choices and face natural consequences, they are then, according to Fay, more "available to students to help them with decision-making and problem-solving rather than acting as armed guards."[31]

The following are four basic principles of "Love and Logic,"[32] with interpretations I have added based on research in student motivation and in the context of music education:

1. *"The student's self-concept is always a prime consideration."* The Love and Logic approach is intended to promote student self-concept, because students exercise agency over their own lives and learn through trial and error how to navigate in a world that is consistent and fair. As students gain a sense of control over their own choices, they are then encouraged to take responsibility for their own choices in the future.

2. *"The child is always left with a feeling that he/she has some control."*
Research in self-efficacy supports the Love and Logic model: As students
are given opportunities to recognize the power they have over their own
decisions (what self-efficacy researchers call "enactive mastery experiences"),[33] they become increasingly more confident in making choices
that will lead to positive outcomes. On the other hand, teacher-controlled
punishment takes the exercise of control away from students and thereby
reduces the sense of mastery and confidence that students might have
developed to help them navigate their own lives.

3. *"An equal balance of consequences and empathy replaces punishment
whenever possible."* There is no power play involved in the Love and
Logic model, because consequences exist externally, outside of the identity of either student or teacher. Teachers and students then both maintain
a sense of control: Teachers maintain control over their own emotions
(and subsequent stress level) by not taking student choices personally, and
students maintain control over their own actions, making choices based
on real-life consequences rather than avoiding certain behaviors simply
because they are afraid of making the teacher upset (as alluded to in an
earlier quote from Brian Michaud).

4. *"The student is required to do more thinking than the adult."* Invitations
for students to work out their own consequences and plans for improved
behavior—even taking time overnight or over the weekend to do so—
relieves teachers of any extra burden and provides students with an opportunity to genuinely consider their actions and associated outcomes.

The Love and Logic model also provides four steps to responsibility,[34]
which are framed here to fit with the context of music teaching:

1. *"Give the student a task that he/she can handle."* No different than the
musical tasks addressed previously, behavior can be plotted according to
distal and proximal goals. Then, as Brian Michaud suggested, we can "just
ask them to keep improving" according to a manageable plan.

2. *"Hope that the student makes a mistake."* What a liberating thought—
actually letting go of our need to control another's journey toward perfection! By hoping that students make errors, the focus becomes on awaiting
and anticipating learning opportunities. On the contrary, modeling a fear
of failure can wreak havoc on a students' budding sense of priorities and
general level of anxiety. As music teachers, we would also do well to
take this advice into music instruction, to similarly view musical errors as
opportunities for student growth.[35]

3. *"Let equal parts of consequences and empathy do the teaching."* A healthy
amount of empathy allows us to take on the role of consultant or coach,
rather than viewing ourselves as one who was personally insulted or

defied. As Brian Michaud and Marcus Santos mentioned in their interviews, a large part of maintaining composure in a classroom is remembering not to take the behaviors of children or teenagers personally. As we remove ourselves from the equation, we make space for natural consequences to provide meaningful life lessons.

4. *"Give the same task again."* This final step allows the teacher to demonstrate trust, and also shows that trial and error are a natural part of learning in real life.

Balanced-Responsibility Statements

When I first started practicing Love and Logic techniques in my own teaching, I was delighted by how much energy was freed up when I was no longer taking responsibility for students' actions as well as my own. New words and phrases started to replace angry and sarcastic ones, and the language became natural with some thought and practice. Here are some examples of statements that help to balance the responsibility between student and teacher:

"I will begin when everyone is listening." (Using an "I" statement rather than a "you" statement, only talking about what *I* will do, since that is all I can really control)

"I will know everyone is ready when I see your eyes looking at my hand." (I don't ask for them to look in my eyes; that could invite a potential power play that I neither need, want, nor intend)

"In this class, we start tuning when the bell rings." (Setting a clear boundary and expectation without putting anyone on the spot)

"Would you like to pick up that paper airplane now, or help me clean the room after school?" (Providing choices about behavior and consequences)

"Would you like to play music with us today, or do a written assignment by yourself?" (Never making music—such as singing a solo in front of the class—a punishment; music should always be the reward)

The aforementioned examples may work particularly well in teacher-led classrooms or director-led ensembles. Small-group and other situations where students are given considerable voice and control over their learning might allow even more room for flexibility, negotiation, and subsequent motivation.[36]

The Orchestra Room Couch

In a high school where I once taught, the orchestra room was home to four or five couches at a time, all hand-me-downs from various student homes. The couches provided a tangible welcome to students, inviting them to hang out and call our room a home away from home. The orchestra room was abuzz with excitement and energy whenever class was not in session: before school, after school, during lunch, and even between classes.

One day, a group of students decided to see how many people they could fit on one loveseat, as if they were reenacting a Volkswagen Beetle experiment. I listened to their chatter from my office, raising one eyebrow as the student count rose from 12 to 13, then from 14 to 15. I then heard a creak followed by a WHAM!—The couch had fallen apart under the students' collective weight. The burst of sound was followed by dead silence as the students sat in shock on the floor.

Taking a deep breath (and pausing a bit longer than usual, just for effect), I walked toward them. With a voice of empathy, I simply asked: "Oh, no. What are you going to do?"

"We didn't mean to! It was his fault!"

"That's too bad," I responded. "What are you going to do?"

After some additional silence and an exchange of looks, one student responded, "We'll take care of it, Ms. Hen."

The next week a new hand-me-down couch appeared in the orchestra room, compliments of the senior orchestra president's grandmother. Thanks to a hands-off approach that I learned through Love and Logic courses, I was able to practice keeping my cool, give up the need to unnecessarily lecture anyone, and turn the responsibility over to those who rightfully should have had it. The broken couch cost me absolutely zero energy and provided a good amount of teenage-produced entertainment.

Individual Differences

I add a caveat here: The approach I have just described may work very well with students who are used to negotiating with adults in this way. It should be clear, however, that in some cases other more serious measures may be necessary, such as when dealing with life-or-death situations, drug abuse, or weapons. For example, although Marcus Santos thrives in settings where he can turn the ownership of the musical experience over to his students, he recognizes that, with certain at-risk students, "the last thing you want is to ask their opinions, because it might start a fight."

Students will, of course, respond to adults differently depending on their individual background and experiences, thereby requiring different approaches to develop student-teacher trust. For example, a very peaceful and gentle colleague of mine (who has been described by her other colleagues as "having the patience of Job") has often spoken about the necessity of being stern and forceful with a particular student who was the son of militaristic parents; otherwise he would not take her seriously. By meeting him at a place and approach he understood, he trusted her and worked very hard in music lessons.

In travel across the United States, I have visited some of the wealthiest schools and some of the lowest-income schools in the country. I have spent time in suburban schools where students' cars were worth three times those of faculty members, and also in urban schools where the students could not drink out of the water fountains because of lead contamination and where bathrooms were on continuous lockdown. I taught in a school where gang fights were more common than school assemblies, and I taught in another school where students were entrusted with their own keys to the school so that they could produce a musical theater production entirely on their own. I have observed students in high-drug, high-crime areas thrive in music classes, with nearly 100 percent of the students fully engaged and stating that their music teacher was their lifeline. Meanwhile, I have seen students whose parents spent a fortune on cotillion and other etiquette-boosting activities show disinterest and downright disrespect in music classes that they deemed frustrating or irrelevant.

My research and professional experience in various school settings has led me to assert that, although the *types* of music that we teach and *approaches* to music learning will certainly differ according to student needs, backgrounds, and interests, the general principle of musical engagement is the same: Students share a nearly universal desire and ability to cooperate and participate when they are respected, valued, and engaged in an activity that they value and in which they feel competent.[37] Patience, then, comes in working together with students as they engage in activities that are both personally meaningful and possible for them to achieve.

PATIENCE IN EMPOWERMENT

Finally, compassion involves exercising the patience to step out of the way and empower students with agency over their own learning. In this case, patience might involve listening to students, demonstrating an interest in their perspectives, and valuing their unique contributions. Patience may also mean setting our own egos and desires aside so that we can more fully serve the interests and needs of our students.

According to Renae Timbie, patience comes when we recognize that our needs are not the most important: "In any given teaching moment, students' needs are more important than mine." Brian Michaud shared similar sentiments, noting that "it all comes back to not taking things personally." This is not to say that teachers should be doormats; rather, Timbie and Michaud are suggesting that a simple focus of priorities can help a teacher let go of preconceived notions and more effectively tap into the needs and concerns of students.

Giving Students a Voice

Preservice teachers are often taught to limit the amount of talk time in rehearsal. They are encouraged, instead, to emphasize opportunities for playing, with only brief comments of instruction between longer playing periods in order to maintain student attentiveness.[38] Might it be, however, that one of the reasons novice teachers are told so often to "zip their lips" is because they are the ones doing all the talking?

Students have come to music lessons to make music, not to hear someone else chatter on like the adults in a *Peanuts* cartoon. Certainly, classroom management issues may be a result of slow pacing, transitions, and loss of student interest, as teachers take longer than a child's attention span to figure themselves out.[39] On the other hand, students might welcome a more relaxed pace in any classroom if they are invited to participate more in the conversation. In Renae Timbie's perspective,

> So much about music and compassion is to say, "You are valuable. You do have a voice." And music is an easy way to give you voice. In any setting I have, not only when it comes to repertoire choice, but when it comes to owning and understanding the music, I think finding a way—or many ways—for students to have voice and meaning of music is really important. And so that's why, for me, collaborative learning has worked really well.

Timbie's perspective resonates with Steve Massey's and Marcus Santos's previous comments about involving students in building a culture of trust: When students' voices and contributions are valued, there is no need to fear anarchy or chaos in a classroom. Instead, we may find that our own workload is more manageable and the reaching of curricular goals is far more enjoyable. More importantly, we will likely find that music learning and expression is much richer and more meaningful for everyone.

Taking the Time to Listen

Listening to our students is critical, but our need to hear ourselves speak or to control the direction of an activity often gets in the way. Brian Michaud described how he has learned over the years the value of listening to what his elementary students have to say:

> I try to listen to the kids' stories whenever they want to tell them. Sometimes it takes a little while to realize this. You know, at first, you're teaching your

lessons, and you're thinking, "I've got these concepts I've got to cover," and this and that, but it comes down to this: You're really teaching kids.

It's a cliché, but it's so true that the kids don't care what you teach until they know you care. And once they know that you care and you're actually listening to what they have to say, then they're so much more jubilant because music class should be fun. It should be exciting, and it should be a place of joy, not just robotic instruction, not, "Okay, here's what I want you to do, and you do it and now we're going to go onto the next activity." It should be that the kids are there because it's fun.

Every time a second-grade class comes into the room, there are at least a few kids who step out of line to tell me something about their week. I listen, and that helps me know them better. For instance, when I know a student plays a musical instrument, but he or she has never brought it to school, I'll say, "If you ever want, feel free to bring it in, I'm sure the other kids would love to hear you play." Or if they take gymnastics and want to perform in front of the class, I always say, "Yes. Absolutely, come on up!" So allowing them to share that piece of themselves is important.

Renae Timbie expressed how she practices patience when she allows time and space for students to express their opinions and needs:

When it comes to teaching, patience is acting on the idea that others are more important than you are right now. Patience is saying, "You're different than I am, in whatever way. But in this moment, I'm going to choose to believe that your rights, your opinion, your need to be heard, are more important in this moment than mine." So in action, what that means is listening. I invite student-centered and student-directed learning so I can I invite students' voices.

Often there are voices and opinions that feel so off base, and that can be very distracting for me. But to say, "Okay, there's something that's being said here." But [patience is] to say, "Okay, there's something that's being said here." [I think] patience in that moment is to say, "I need to listen and hear what [it is] that you are desiring. Are you desiring to be heard? Are you desiring to be known?" and to help them get to the depth of what it is that they are trying to say.

I find, especially with college students, that there's something they want to say but they're not entirely sure how to say it. But once you've invited their voice, it helps them to think. But it requires me to say, "I'm going to be patient. I'm going to walk this through with you," and to listen and say, "I've invited your input, so I'm going to be patient and help you to draw that out. And even possibly be an advocate for you. Even if I didn't first see it, or even if I don't even agree, I hope to say, "Okay, this is what I've asked for. I'm going to be patient. I'm going to believe that allowing your voice to be heard is more important than me needing to get something done, or me needing to be right."

Lest we be afraid of looming deadlines and time crunches, we might consider how involving students more in the learning process can empower them to be agents of their own learning—thereby buying us rehearsal time, better assurance of home practice, and less need for repeated explanations in the unforeseeable future.[40] Brian Michaud described the benefits of stopping to listen:

> Sometimes compassion means taking time. It's taking the time out of your lesson to take care of the student. To get them back to that comfortable level. And if you don't get to all your activities, so be it. It goes back to teaching the kids rather than the subject. And if you do take that time, you might find in the long run that you get to more things in your subject than you had planned because you took the time in the beginning to be empathetic to the students, and you understand their feelings and needs.

Empowering our students may seem like a frightening proposition to some (and so I have been told by many well-meaning teachers). However, decades of research aligns with the voices of the CMTs in this book to suggest that it is certainly worth the risk.

CONCLUSION

The essence of patience is as unique to each of us as are our own identities, needs, and values. While definitions of patience may vary considerably, in this chapter I have presented the concept of patience as the ability to view students from a long-term perspective. Whether in terms of musical ability, developmental progress, behavior, or empowerment, the practice of patience is the same: Providing students with a distal vision and proximal support that can help both students and teachers reach beyond the present moment and create a much brighter and more promising future.

Reflection Questions

1. Which of the various definitions of "patience" in this chapter most resonates with you? Why?
2. As you consider the various influences on ability development shown in figure 5.1, which ones might you be able to further cultivate with your students? With yourself?
3. Choose one piece of music that you are teaching to a student or class. How might you take distal goals for that piece and break them into more

manageable proximal goals? How might your student(s) help with that process?

4. Which of the approaches to classroom management mentioned in this chapter resonates most with you? Why?

5. What are some specific ways that you can provide opportunities for student empowerment?

NOTES

1. Christina Feldman, *Compassion: Listening to the Cries of the World* (Berkeley, CA: Rodmell Press, 2005), 8–9.

2. All CMT quotes are from interviews with the author, unless otherwise cited.

3. Patricia D'Ercole, personal communication with the author, March 7, 2017.

4. Suzuki Association of the Americas, *Every Child Can: An Introduction to Suzuki Education* (Boulder, CO: Suzuki Association of the Americas, 2003); Shinichi Suzuki, *Ability Development from Age Zero,* trans. Mary Louise Nagata (Miami, FL: Summy-Birchard, 1981); Shinichi Suzuki, *Nurtured by Love: A New Approach to Talent Education,* trans. Waltraud Suzuki (Miami, FL: Summy-Birchard, [1969] 1983).

5. See, for example, Barbara Rogoff, *The Cultural Nature of Human Development* (New York: Oxford University Press, 2003).

6. Shinichi Suzuki, *Nurtured by Love,* 37.

7. Edwin E. Gordon, *Learning Sequences in Music: Skill, Content, and Patterns* (Chicago, IL: GIA 2007), 2.

8. Michael J. A. Howe, Jane W. Davidson, and John A. Sloboda, "Innate Talents: Reality or Myth?" *Behavioral and Brain Sciences* 21, no. 03 (1998): 399.

9. Ibid., 407.

10. Gary E. McPherson and Aaron Williamon, "Building Gifts into Musical Talents," in *The Child as Musician: A Handbook of Musical Development*, 2nd ed., ed. Gary E. McPherson (Oxford, UK: Oxford University Press, 2016), 342; used with permission. See also Françoys Gagné, "Transforming Gifts into Talents: The DMGT as a Developmental Theory," *High Ability Studies* 15, no. 2 (2004) 119–47; Françoys Gagné and Gary E. McPherson, "Analyzing Musical Prodigiousness Using Gagné's Integrative Model of Talent Development," in *Music Prodigies: Interpretations from Psychology, Education, Musicology and Ethnomusicology*, ed. Gary E. McPherson (Oxford, UK: Oxford University Press, 2016), 3–114.

11. McPherson and Williamon, "Building Gifts into Musical Talents," 340.

12. See, for example, my article with Gary McPherson on the particular predispositions and musical influences of a three-year-old boy with acute sound sensitivity: Karin S. Hendricks and Gary E. McPherson, "Early Stages of Musical Development: Relationships between Sensory Integration Dysfunction, Parental Influence, and Musical Disposition of a Three-Year-Old 'Maestro,'" *International Journal of Music Education* 28, no. 1 (2010): 88–103.

13. Barbara Lourie Sand, *Teaching Genius: Dorothy DeLay and the Making of a Musician* (Portland, OR: Amadeus Press, 2000), 70.

14. Karin S. Hendricks, "Songs My Student Taught Me: Narrative of an Early Childhood Cello Teacher," *International Journal of Education & the Arts* 14, no. Special Issue 1.4 (2013): 13, accessed August 27, 2017, http://www.ijea.org/v14si1.

15. Carol S. Dweck, *Mindset: The New Psychology of Success* (New York: Random House, 2006).

16. Albert Bandura, *Self-Efficacy: The Exercise of Control* (New York: Macmillan, 1997); Karin S. Hendricks, "Relationships between the Sources of Self-Efficacy and Changes in Competence Perceptions of Music Students during an All-State Orchestra Event" (PhD diss., University of Illinois at Urbana-Champaign, 2009); Karin S. Hendricks, "The Sources of Self-Efficacy: Educational Research and Implications For Music," *Update: Applications of Research in Music Education* 35, no. 1 (2016): 32–38.

17. Ibid.

18. Bandura, *Self-Efficacy*.

19. Hendricks, "The Sources of Self-Efficacy," 33.

20. See Casey McGrath, Karin S. Hendricks, and Tawnya D. Smith, *Performance Anxiety Strategies: A Musician's Guide to Managing Stage Fright* (Lanham, MD: Rowman & Littlefield, 2017).

21. Unpublished research data from Dijana Ihas; used with permission.

22. Dijana Ihas, interview with the author, June 29, 2017.

23. Sylvia A. Gholson, "Proximal Positioning: A Strategy of Practice in Violin Pedagogy," *Journal of Research in Music Education* 46, no. 4 (1998): 535–45.

24. Dijana Ihas, interview with the author, June 29, 2017.

25. Hendricks, "The Sources of Self-Efficacy;" Gary E., McPherson and Barry J. Zimmerman, "Self-Regulation of Musical Learning: A Social Cognitive Perspective," in *The New Handbook of Research on Music Teaching and Learning*, ed. Richard Colwell and Carol Richardson (New York: Oxford University Press, 2002), 327–47.

26. There is a published approach using this title as well. See Richard L. Curwin and Allen N. Mendler, *Discipline with Dignity* (Alexandria, VA: ASCD, 1988).

27. For a review of literature, see Karin S. Hendricks, "Music Education, Character Development, and Advocacy: The Philosophy of Shinichi Suzuki," in *Pedagogies of Kindness and Respect: On the Lives and Education of Children,* ed. Paul L. Thomas, Julie A. Gorlewski, and Brad J. Porfilio (New York: Peter Lang, 2015), 171–84.

28. Jim Fay and Foster W. Cline, *Discipline with Love and Logic: Resource Guide* (Golden, CO: Love and Logic Press, 1997). See also Jim Fay and Charles Fay, *Teaching with Love and Logic*, 2nd ed. (Golden, CO: Love and Logic Press, 2016).

29. Ibid., 10.

30. Ibid., 14.

31. Ibid.

32. All italicized quotes are from page 10 of the *Discipline with Love and Logic* text.

33. Bandura, *Self-Efficacy*; see also Karin S. Hendricks, "The Sources of Self-Efficacy: Educational Research and Implications for Music," *Update: Applications of Research in Music Education* 35, no. 1 (2016): 32–38.

34. All italicized quotes are from Fay and Cline, *Discipline with Love and Logic,* 11.

35. See McGrath, Hendricks, and Smith, *Performance Anxiety Strategies.*

36. See, for example, Ruth Debrot, "Social Constructionism in the Middle School Chorus: A Collaborative Approach" (DMA diss., Boston University, 2016); Lucy Green, *How Popular Musicians Learn: A Way Ahead for Music Education* (Burlington, VT: Ashgate, 2002); Lucy Green, *Music, Informal Learning and the School: A New Classroom Pedagogy* (Burlington, VT: Ashgate, 2008).

37. Edward L. Deci and Richard M. Ryan, *Intrinsic Motivation and Self-Determination in Human Behavior* (New York: Plenum Press, 1985); Paul Evans, "Self-Determination Theory: An Approach to Motivation in Music Education," *Musicae Scientiae* 19, no. 1 (2015): 65–83; Gary E. McPherson and Karin S. Hendricks, "Students' Motivation to Study Music: The United States of America," *Research Studies in Music Education* 32, no. 2 (2010): 201–13; Richard M. Ryan and Edward L. Deci, "Intrinsic and Extrinsic Motivations: Classic Definitions and New Directions," *Contemporary Educational Psychology* 25, no. 1 (2000): 54–67.

38. Thomas W. Goolsby, "Time Use in Instrumental Rehearsals: A Comparison of Experienced, Novice, and Student Teachers," *Journal of Research in Music Education* 44, no. 4 (1996): 286–303; Anne C. Witt, "Use of Class Time and Student Attentiveness in Secondary Instrumental Music Rehearsals," *Journal of Research in Music Education* 34, no. 1 (1986): 34–42.

39. Ibid.

40. Hendricks, "The Sources of Self-Efficacy;" McPherson and Zimmerman, "Self-Regulation of Musical Learning." See also Karin S. Hendricks, "Investing Time: Teacher Research Observing the Influence of Music History and Theory Lessons upon Student Engagement and Expressive Performance of an Advanced High School String Quartet," *Bulletin of the Council for Research in Music Education* 184 (Spring 2010): 65–78.

Chapter 6

Inclusion

True compassion . . . is based on the simple recognition that others, just like myself, naturally aspire to be happy and to overcome suffering, and that others, just like myself, have the natural right to fulfill that basic aspiration. The empathy you develop toward a person based on recognition of this basic fact is universal compassion. There is no element of prejudice, no element of discrimination.

—The Dalai Lama[1]

STORY OF A POLICYMAKER

During my thirteen years as a public school orchestra teacher, I was fortunate to work with dozens of tremendously supportive administrators. In multiple schools and in different communities, I was gifted with time, resources, and professional and emotional support from principals and superintendents who made it clear that they strongly wished for my programs to succeed. To this day, I am very grateful for that backing and encouragement.

Kristi Brasch[2] was an enigmatic exception. During her first two years as our high school principal, I tried to figure out why she gave lip service at best to my requests for support, never visited my room, and never once attended a concert. (Actually, I think I might have caught a glimpse of her jet-black leather jacket as it flickered in and out the door at one particular high-profile event, but it happened so quickly that I can't be sure.) Jumping to conclusions and assuming the worst about her as a person, I responded to her with a cold shoulder and went about my business as much as I could.

Then, one January morning, I nearly dropped my baton as I watched Mrs. Brasch walk into the orchestra room with the vice principal, who had asked me earlier if he could make a visit to "show the kids something." The vice principal—a tall, muscular man with a history of coaching behind him—asked to borrow a cello. He sat down, lengthened the endpin, and proceeded to serenade us with "Jolly Old Saint Nicholas." I don't even remember how it sounded because I was in a bit of shock, but after he finished he explained to us that his fourth-grade daughter was in a beginning strings class and she had taught him how to play.

After some cheerful applause from the students, Kristi Brasch stepped forward. Just as I began to imagine she might surprise us by picking up a viola, instead she sat down in the midst of the students and told us this story:

> *When I was in the third grade, I remember practicing for a school choir concert. The teacher looked at me and said, "Kristi, you mouth the words tonight."*
> *I've hated music ever since.*

Mrs. Brasch responded immediately to my dropped jaw and angry gasps from students, adding quickly:

> *I mean, I don't hate it, I just . . .*

I interrupted her before she said another word, doing my best to reassure her that she didn't need to apologize for what she said or how she felt. Instead I told her that we would welcome her to our music learning space any time. Even in that moment, I recognized that she felt unwelcome and unappreciated for expressing herself honestly, because her expression didn't appear to fit with what she thought was expected. I couldn't help but imagine the scene that took place several decades earlier, when a choir teacher was trying to impress an audience (and, ironically, maybe a principal) by making the music sound a certain way, and in so doing silenced one girl not just for a concert but for a lifetime.

I can't judge that teacher too harshly. Instead I need to first check myself. At the same time that I was assuring Mrs. Brasch, I was also scanning my memory to recall any moments where I might have similarly said something to a student and, in an instant, altered someone's musical life. With a tendency to lose myself in the passion of the moment, especially as concerts get closer, it might have been altogether possible. Words come so easy out of our lips, yet can have such a deep and lasting impact.

In that moment, my thoughts centered on this obviously wounded soul in front of us, and how her words might have affected my students. In later reflections, however, I considered how music teachers might waste copious amounts of time and money in music advocacy efforts if we turn individuals off to music, one by one, by giving them the impression that they're not good enough to engage in it with us. Why should music belong in public education if it doesn't really belong to everyone?

As my colleagues and I have written elsewhere, "One must wonder how often music educators 'save' performances at the expense of the emotional and educational needs of their students, thus losing support for music education when those children grow up and become influential members of society."[3] I trust that there is a better way. I believe we may find it as we open up music education circles and create a place for everyone.

MUSIC EDUCATION IN THE 21st CENTURY

It is impossible to write a book about compassion in the 21st century without a discussion of diversity and inclusion. The demographics of the United States are changing rapidly: We have recently witnessed an important milestone in history where we have estimated that nonwhite students now outnumber white children in our nation's public schools.[4] This shift in demographics is a result of an increase primarily in U.S.-born Hispanic and Asian children, with white births decreasing and black births staying relatively steady. Immigrants to the United States, while not a principal cause of this demographic shift, nevertheless provide a particular need for teacher attention: Schools have increased English language instruction to meet the needs of the seven in ten immigrant students who do not speak English at home.[5]

Isolation of Minority Musicians

Research suggests that general music instruction based on principles of Western classical music can lead to a sense of isolation among immigrants from non-European backgrounds and may inherently place other musics in an inferior position.[6] The increasing richness of our demographic landscape requires a matching richness in musical experience at school. Otherwise, our repertoire and approaches will quickly and sorely lose the race of relevance, leaving school music out to dry while the rest of the world sings on, loud and strong, without us.[7]

At the high school where Marcus Santos teaches, approximately 95 percent of the students are from immigrant families: "If I have a class of twenty kids, probably one of them is [a native-born] American."[8] Santos understands that his immigrant students enter his classroom with little to no interest in Mozart, so he meets them where they are—with music of their own cultures. Then, after piquing their interest in his class, he provides them with a well-rounded education from a variety of genres:

> Let's say you were a kid who just moved here from Colombia, and you speak very little English. The first class in the morning that you would have is my

drumming class. So I might see the new kid from Colombia and say, "Okay, today we're going to study cumbia." And then I'll ask you, "Do you like cumbia? Do you dance cumbia? Do you remember when you were in Colombia, how was it when you saw a concert?" How did that make you feel?"

And it's all to make them feel like, "Look, I'm here in school and I'm welcome. They want to hear about my background and my culture." And I hope that has moved with them into later classes, when they step into the English class, and the teacher might not have the opportunity to have a conversation like I had. Hopefully by the English class, the student will feel welcomed and feel more comfortable being there.

Isolation of Low-Income Students

Our country and world are also witnessing an increasing divide between rich and poor.[9] Music learning opportunities for some students are vastly different from those for others, whether in the diversity of school music curricula, private lessons, or even in community offerings. Those who can afford to move into neighborhoods with strong school music programs have already provided their children with an advantage beyond those who have less financially. Nearly a decade ago, music education researchers predicted an increase in the disparity of musical experiences between differing socioeconomic classes:

> Unfortunately, the benefits of instrumental music instruction are not equally available to all. Even participation in a public school music program, where no special transportation is needed and instruction is provided at limited or no additional cost, requires the availability of an instrument. Not all students have access to the necessary financial support required to purchase an instrument of any kind, much less an instrument of choice. As a result, the benefits of instrumental music study could increasingly become the province of the more affluent members of society.[10]

Although many school music programs contain instruments for student use, the inventories and quality of instruments can vary greatly from school to school. These disparities affect the learning experience of fledgling students, as well as their subsequent decisions to drop or persist in music class. Furthermore, opportunities for private lessons, transportation, and any other number of "extras" that schoolteachers request provide certain advantages to some students over others in the same class.

When it comes to music, we often assume that those who have achieved at the highest level are "talented;" however, other students who may not have achieved at the same standard may have worked just as hard and have just as capable a musical ear, but lacked the resources to arrive at the same place.

The "myth of meritocracy"—the notion that success is merely a result of hard work—is alive and well in our country.[11] However well intended this concept may seem at first glance, we have a duty to dispel the simplicity of this idea and ensure that all students have access to the same opportunities so that hard work can rightfully be held up as the means to success.

One music teacher who grew up in a low-income family expressed how, as a marching band student, she found refuge from a world of economic disadvantage:

> Band was a great social leveler. We all wore the same uniform, had the same responsibilities to the greater whole. My income no longer mattered. We had fundraisers that could make band free, or at least affordable. As a director now myself, my greatest priority is the person behind the instrument, hoping to elevate them to their highest potential.[12]

Steve Massey has similarly provided "equalizing" strategies for the students in his ensemble by raising funds and making space in his building to make private lessons accessible to *every* student in the program. Not being willing to slack on musical quality, he has instead reached out to the community for financial help to ensure that all students are prepared with the unique and individual attention they need to be successful.

Making "Visible Minorities" Truly Visible

According to the demographic data presented earlier in the chapter, the number of black students does not appear to be changing in the United States. I nevertheless ask a question: Have we sufficiently served the needs of black students in American public schools? Black students, teachers, and scholars would be the first to respond to this question with an emphatic "no."[13] People of color are also shockingly underrepresented in our school music programs. Despite the statistics of white students becoming a "majority minority" in our public schools, music ensembles in the United States are nearly 66 percent white. Furthermore, those students who make it through our music programs and eventually apply for music teacher licensure are more than 86 percent white, with current NAfME membership approximately 90 percent white.[14]

What is happening? Where are all the nonwhite musicians going? Is there what researcher Kenneth Elpus has called a "leaky pipeline" in our system that biases some students over others?[15] It is laughable to think that black and Latino/a students are any less musical than white, Asian, or any other students, although some of our music education leaders have unfortunately attempted to suggest as much.[16] Considering the large number of black and Latino/a artists who are making it big in the music industry, it is more likely that the types of music and approaches that primarily white teachers are presenting are simply reinforcing a particular white-centric musical experiences at the expense of others.

Black music teacher Deejay Robinson described the disconnect between the music he grew up singing at church and at home, and the music he encountered in school:

> I grew up in a big Southern city where church was the center of life. Gospel music was always around me. I sang in the church Gospel Choir on the first Sunday, the Young Adult Choir on the second Sunday, the Youth Choir on the third Sunday, and the Mass or Combined Choir on the fourth Sunday. . . . I had always wondered through all of the singing that was around me what was it about music that caused eyes to well up with tears and people to jump up and shout as if there was fire shut-up in their bones. . . . I believe I wanted to study music in order to understand what was it about singing that could transport one from the natural world to a supernatural world.
>
> After the audition [for the high school musical], the choral director, Mr. Abrams, asked me to audition for a coveted spot in the elite Chamber Chorus. I remember Mr. Abrams asking me about my background and commenting on the power of my voice, for he believed my tenor voice would be an asset to the chorus. . . . Mr. Abrams informed me that I should come prepared with a song to sing, classical preferred, and [expect] to sight-read rhythms and a melody. I was horrified.
>
> I was terrified and intimidated . . . because everything that was familiar was now unfamiliar. Except for me, no one auditioning for the chorus was Black. . . . I was an anomaly because my upbringing required me to learn music in a different manner than the White students I observed auditioning. In one fell swoop, the Chamber Choir audition brought into consciousness the innate difference between learning music in the Western European classical tradition of studying music theory, and the Southern Gospel tradition of learning songs through call-response, rote, and being immersed in the feeling of music. Moreover, the audition highlighted the advantage afforded to my White counterparts simply because White European culture and traditions were expected as the standard. Any deviation from those teachings was considered inferior purely based on racialized negativity that determines what is and is not music.[17]

Another black music teacher described her experiences in a primarily white undergraduate music education program, as she struggled to relate the musics and approaches she was taught to the needs and interests she knew her future black students would have:

> If I felt the educational practices that were taught to me by my professors would not work for the students I hope to teach, I deemed [them] irrelevant. I would think, that's all fine and dandy for the students I teach here, but that wouldn't work for the students I will teach at home. They would never sing those songs. Or, how can I make this music relate to their everyday lives where the students

are listening for hope from rappers, some of the only black successful people they see, but don't experience success in music class because they can't relate to "Jimmy Crack Corn" or Sousa's "Nobles of the Mystic Shrine?" Teaching these things would make me irrelevant to my students.[18]

Providing a Balance

As a fierce lover of classical music myself, I would not argue in any way that we should get rid of the artistry of European composers in our music curricula. However, a compassionate approach to music teaching involves opening ourselves up to the inherent greatness of other music as well and resisting the notion of superiority in any particular music, person, or approach. Lest we become nervous about the loss of musical quality in spreading ourselves too thin musically (or perhaps risking vulnerability as we try out approaches that are foreign to us personally), we can look for inspiration at classical music teaching artist Dorothy DeLay, whose willingness to learn new things and new repertoire along with students of diverse ability levels was one of the strengths that made her—and her students—true masters of their craft.

Brian Michaud described how he purposely provides a variety of musics and approaches in his classroom so that he can reach the unique interests of each student:

> There are so many different components of music. If the students are not interested in your lesson, do not take it personally. Because there are so many different facets of music, I try and touch on several different facets in each class. We play instruments, we move, we do folk dances, we sing songs, we do singing games, we read music, and we play musical games. For instance, my room has a 12' × 12' tiled grand staff in the center of the room. So we'll play musical twister: Put you left foot on D, put your right foot on G. It's just another way to learn music and to impart that knowledge, but in a fun way.
>
> So I guess compassion is just understanding that there are so many different aspects of music and there are so many different things that kids will be interested in; and you have to try and reach those different facets so that you can touch each child during each class. Touch their heart, and touch their mind, and make them feel comfortable. And have them walk out of the room and say, "Wow, that was fun," or "That was interesting," or "I enjoyed that."

Differentiated Instruction for Special (All) Learners

Anyone reading this text will likely be familiar with the increase in number of students with special needs who are becoming a part of our everyday educational conversation. Changes in special education laws, as well as improvements in identification and diagnosis, have helped to improve the educational landscape for many children over the past few decades. Many would say, however, that we have a long way to go. For example, racial and ethnic minority children are statistically less likely than similarly achieving white children to receive special education identification and services in the United States.[19]

Musical opportunities for special-needs students have been tragically limited in our history. As professor Judith Jellison has reported, "Children with disabilities, particularly those with more severe disabilities, typically have few opportunities for a genuine music education experience."[20] In a recent survey of music teachers in the United States, just over half (53 percent) of respondents reported that individual needs of students with special needs were being met in their music classrooms.[21] Furthermore, approximately half of music teachers reported that special-needs students were difficult to work with (44 percent) or that they "hindered the progress" of other students in the classroom (56 percent).[22] Although these numbers show improvement in comparison to a regional survey conducted twenty years earlier, still only around half (53 percent) of the teachers expressed confidence in their ability to effectively modify their music curriculum to meet the needs of exceptional students, with slightly more (62 percent) expressing comfort in providing needs-based adaptations.

It is safe to assume that compassionate music teachers want enriching musical experiences for everyone. As Jellison proposed, "Individuals who have experienced personal pleasure from music are often those who advocate quality music experiences for others."[23] However, considering the aforementioned statistics, I would ask: Are music teachers sufficiently prepared to meet the challenges of differentiated instruction for all learners?

It seems that we could improve: In a survey of teacher preparation programs throughout the United States, music education scholar Karen Salvador discovered that less than a third (29.6 percent) of those music teacher education programs required a course in differentiation for exceptional learners, and only 59.8 percent of programs integrated content regarding special learners in their other coursework.[24] Although many music teachers may receive support and education on these topics from other sources (e.g., general education classes and professional development), these courses tend not to focus on the *musical* needs of children with various exceptionalities.

Moving Beyond Labels

As the quantity and scope of issues under the "special needs" umbrella broaden and increase in the 21st century, scholars have begun to see a need to break away from assigning labels and categories that neither completely fit any child nor truly promote inclusion. In fact, many would argue that these labels actually do just the opposite by marginalizing particular students. Music educators Alice Hammel and Ryan Hourigan have, therefore, proposed a "label-free" approach that avoids placing students in potentially hurtful categories and that are likely inadequate in facilitating the individual needs of every student.[25] Instead, they advocate for individualized instruction that treats each child and classroom as a unique entity, requiring and deserving a unique learning experience.

In their "Winding It Back" framework, Hammel, Hickox, and Hourigan propose that teachers use a scope and sequence of instruction that can be "wound back" or "wound forward" according to individual needs, to meet students wherever they are.[26] Similar to the discussion of distal and proximal goals in chapter 5, the "winding" approach allows for incremental adjustments in instruction according to particular student strengths. The Winding It Back framework is based on three principles:

1. *"Honoring the individual learning needs of all students,"* which involves an awareness of students' self-esteem, finding ways to help them find success wherever possible, and honoring all forms of music learning.
2. Providing *"multiple access points and learning levels,"* or designing curricula based on individual needs rather than age or grade level, and ensuring that any one lesson allows for multiple levels of involvement according to individual student needs.
3. *"Adequate conditions for simultaneous learning,"* which include research-based criteria for special needs such as clear instruction, repetition, student choice and self-advocacy, a positive atmosphere, ample response time, and a positive behavior plan.[27]

The aforementioned principles are important and life-giving for all students, not just those with a particular diagnosis or individualized education plan (IEP). Because they highlight the effectiveness of looking beyond a label or category, they invite us instead to see all of our students as human beings who have a fundamental and innate need for music in their lives. Karen Salvador has similarly recommended that music teacher preparation programs respond to various needs of music teachers and their students by considering ways to focus on differentiated instruction for *all* students, noting that every one of us has unique and individual needs:

> Perhaps, by integrating content-specific strategies for differentiation of instruction throughout music education coursework and incorporating practica with diverse populations, music teacher preparation programs could help future music teachers adapt their instruction not only for special education populations

but also for students who are English learners, those who are considered at risk, and gifted students. Maybe an appropriate goal for music teacher preparation programs would be to help music teachers become increasingly adept at reaching each of their students as individuals. In the words of one [music teacher], "Who isn't a 'special learner'?"[28]

Accommodating for Various Ability Levels

Brian Michaud described how he accommodates for the needs of students of various ability levels in his classroom:

> We've had students who have had limited mobility or who used wheelchairs. To me the most important thing is for them to be able to take part in the classroom as best they can. Take a folk dance, for instance. That's an activity where you've got the whole group moving, and the whole group is supposed to be in sync. So I'll say to myself, "You know what? Today it's not going to be in sync. And that's okay." It's about the child being able to be part of the activity more than the activity being perfect. Is it going to take a little longer to do things? Yep. And that's okay.
>
> You also want to be thinking about those kids, though, who want to try and do it the authentic way. So a lot of the times, I'll split the class into two groups. One group might be moving a little bit slower, and the other group is moving up to speed. That way the kids who can do it up to speed don't have to do it at half speed all the time. Later, I'll switch the groups and do different activities, without it being obvious why I'm switching.

Marcus Santos similarly described the way that he adapts his lessons—even on the fly when necessary—to make it work for everyone: "If it doesn't work out, we adapt. We'll come up with a rhythm that will fit in." He also tries to give students with small disabilities manageable leadership roles so they can feel both competent and needed in the ensemble:

> They may want to be more involved but maybe they're not as involved because they know they are a little bit different. So I give them a simple task that doesn't put them too much in the spotlight, but will make other students have reason to go to them to talk to them; that can mean a lot to them.

Both Santos and Michaud mentioned how they involve students in the decision-making process regarding their own accommodations. Michaud noted:

> They might be included in a way that's more comfortable for them. We have a student who doesn't like to perform a variety of motions, but she loves to clap her hands and she loves to play instruments. So, "Okay! Here's a pair of

cymbals. Here's a drum. Here's a tambourine." And she's happy as a clam, playing her drum or tambourine along while the kids are doing the movement piece.

We had a boy who had some emotional issues. We were playing London Bridge, and he got caught in the bridge. He got upset and ran away from the group and hid in the corner. The kids could play London Bridge on their own, so I went over to him, and I handed him a drum. He played along on the drum for the rest of the song, and that's how he contributed to the group. He was not emotionally ready to take part in it in one way, but he was ready to take part in it in his own way.

I think that some people feel inclusion means that you have to somehow get everybody to do the same thing, but sometimes it's not in the best interest of the children with disabilities to try and make them. But I always give them the choice if they want to try it. Or sometimes they'll say, "Can I play an instrument [instead of singing or dancing]?" "Sure, go right ahead." Then they might change their mind halfway through: "Can I join in?" "Sure, you can join in!" It's about being flexible.

Recognizing Our Limitations and Seeking Help

Sometimes the best way we can be supportive of all learners—no matter their ability level—is to recognize our own limitations in helping them, and to reach out to others who are better suited to give them the support they need. As Renae Timbie stated,

> Sometimes inclusion in music teaching means you have to draw on someone else's resources. That is being compassionate, I think, to say, "You are valuable enough to me to figure out how I can connect to you." And that could very likely be beyond me.

Such is the case as Timbie prepares to work with refugees, knowing that her classical music training is insufficient to teach Arab music in refugee camps: She recognizes her own need to reach out to others who have the training and resources she lacks.

Steve Massey recognized his limitations in helping an autistic clarinet student who couldn't read music, and whose clarinet squeaked noticeably above the rest of the band. Because Massey made regular visits to the middle school, he noticed this student's needs before the student entered high school. He was, therefore, able to set the student up with a private teacher who spent all summer teaching him the fall marching band songs by ear. Whereas Massey lacked the time or specific skills to help this student, he found an ideal private teacher who ended up working one-on-one with the student for years. By his junior year, the student was a fully functioning member of the group.

JUSTICE AND EQUITY: EACH DOING OUR PART

When faced with the realities of inequity in our present society, many of us (myself included) can become overwhelmed by just how much there is to do. It is impossible for one person—no matter how compassionate—to erase or eradicate current inequities that have been built on centuries of colonization, imperialism, and xenophobia. All we can do is the work of one person (whatever work we each feel compelled to do), and slowly but confidently shift the tides to make a safe, welcoming, and inclusive educational community for everyone.

Examining Our Language and Actions

Taking the lead of music educator Deb Bradley, we might begin by examining the discourse that we take for granted—or even strive for with good intentions—that might actually be hurtful to others.[29] Although white teachers in the United States are (thankfully) removed from the imperialism that was practiced by our ancestors, Bradley suggested that the structures and habits of mind that reinforce our notion of superiority over others "continue to wield influence in many of the ways that we think and express ourselves."[30] According to Bradley, even the term *social justice*, a present-day buzzword in education circles, can often be misused and misrepresented

> as an act of charity: classes study and perform music from another culture, viewed through a lens that suggests the people of that culture somehow need "rescuing," and resulting in a perceived need to "do something" that leads in turn to the donation of concert proceeds to some related cause.
>
> While the educational process that leads to such motivation may raise student and audience awareness of social justice issues, the status quo remains intact, and the participants often come away feeling self-satisfied, even pleased about their sense of social responsibility. . . . They often leave students, teachers, and audiences feeling good by affirming individual and collective capacities for compassion. But these capacities and feelings often stem from, and reinforce, an unacknowledged and deeply problematic sense of moral superiority.[31]

Grooversity

Marcus Santos, a naturalized American citizen who was once an immigrant himself, understands the importance of seeing everyone on a level-playing field: "Being in that position, I think it makes you want to get to a point of accepting everyone because you were there too." Perhaps for this reason, his nonprofit organization "Grooversity"—which combines "groove" and "diversity"—emphasizes drumming for social change. However, in resonance with the same concerns mentioned in the quote by Deb Bradley above, Santos does not dictate or even suggest what "social change" will mean in various communities:

> It's up to you! It's not up to me. Grooversity will give tools to empower communities for drumming, yes. But we hope that people will get involved with Grooversity because they believe in the mission of using drumming to put people together. And once that particular community is gathered, *they* decide how they can make that community better. So the social change aspect is not really anything Grooversity imposes on anybody, because I don't know what people need and what is resonant for them. So the social change aspect is different for every community, and they make the decision.

Changing Microaggressions to Microaffirmations

The language and nonverbal behavior that we have learned from those who came before us may be wrought with *microaggressions*, which are certain words or actions that reinforce certain hurtful stereotypes, or that continue to balance perceptions in favor of some people over others.[32] Microaggressions have been defined as "brief, everyday exchanges that send denigrating messages to certain individuals because of their group membership."[33] They can

Figure 6.1.   Marcus Santos at the Montreal Drum Fest. Figure credit: Claude Dufresne.

be either overt or subtle, intentional, or taken for granted.[34] However, when compounded over time and with regularity, small acts of unkindness can cause great distress and damage to our sense of self and our ability to navigate the world around us.[35]

Music education professor Juliet Hess understood the principle of micro-aggressions as a child, long before she had a term for it: She grew up in a Jewish family in a primarily Protestant community and found herself having to continually "translate" the language and educational structures around her to fit with her own—different—identity. As she described it, "My experience of schooling was one of continual translation—translating classroom discourse to apply to my life, recoding discussions of holidays to substitute my young understandings of what it meant to be me."[36] Although Hess did not mention being blatantly mistreated by others because of her religion, she stressed that, in her own experience (and for others of any minority race, ethnicity, sexual orientation, or ability level), the need to continually translate can be an exhausting and demeaning exercise: "The necessity of engaging in translation is a microaggression continually encountered by individuals who embody difference."[37]

We can take a positive, gentle, and life-giving approach to changing our language and actions. For example, at the third symposium on LGBTQ issues in music education (while Juliet Hess was presenting her aforementioned talk), audience member Louis Bergonzi proposed the term *microaffirmations* to describe those small words or actions that sustain and honor the unique identity of another person. Bergonzi initially viewed "microaffirmations" in terms of specific ways to support LGBTQ individuals (e.g., using a gender-queer individual's preferred pronouns, or recognizing a student's two gay fathers as both being "dads"). However, we might expand this term more broadly to include the ways in which we affirm all individuals and their respective needs, concerns, and identities. Simply noting our language and actions can have a great effect on others, no matter who they are.

Bringing the "Hidden Curriculum" to Light

Finally—and as uncomfortable as it may be—it is critical for us to recognize that we live in a culture enmeshed in discourse that either subconsciously or blatantly reinforces hurtful notions of superiority. Our educational system was originally set up to maintain societal norms[38] and is embedded with many values and structures that pit people against one another, and/or unfairly privilege some at the expense of others, all in the name of "opportunity" or "success."[39] The problem is that "opportunities" for success are neither equal nor always fair.

Scholars use the term *hidden curriculum* to refer to "those systematic side effects of schooling that we sense but which cannot be adequately accounted for by reference to the explicit curriculum."[40] These "hidden" elements of daily life and school structure can teach students more about life than the actual textbooks or lectures they study. The quote from Deejay Robinson earlier in this chapter is one example of how the audition structure at Deejay's high school taught him to consider his Southern Gospel upbringing as inferior to that of his classically-trained classmates.

More specifically, the term *hidden curriculum* has been used to denote educational structures that reinforce inequality by providing additional cultural capital to those who are already advantaged.[41] A closer look at the hidden curriculum in our own educational structures can help us identify ways in which we might make things more equitable for everyone.

Let me start with myself: I look back in hindsight at the practice chart system I had in place in my own orchestra classroom, where students could waive the requirement to report practice hours by bringing in a grade from a private teacher. Other than placing a list of private teachers in the orchestra handbook, I provided zero resources to help students get those lessons. Albeit unintentionally, I reinforced inequality among own my students by giving "A" grades to students who simply showed up with a letter requesting such— whether or not they actually practiced—while, on the other hand, I calculated hour-by-hour practice grades for those who did not take private lessons, no matter the reason. Time spent practicing affects grades in all classes, grades affect scholarships, and so the cycle of financial inequality for my students likely continued, regrettably, under my watch.

Recognizing Our Role

Many critical theorists have gone as far as to argue that "the hidden curriculum is not unintended, accidental, or simply intrinsic,"[42] but that curricula are in many cases designed to reinforce the notions of one group's superiority over another. However, many of us (myself included) have innocently and unintentionally taken such unequalizing structures for granted, simply striving to do our best in school, in the ways we were taught, without even recognizing the disparity around us. Music educator and scholar Brent C. Talbot described his internal struggle as he came to recognize the "hidden curriculum" that he had unconsciously learned, and as he came to terms with his own place in the societal scheme of oppressor and oppressed:

> I [am] a product of a colonial past, as an extension and beneficiary of White European colonization. . . . This historic reality is an ironic hypocrisy of people

fleeing religious persecution from Europe only to participate in developing a social, political, and economic system built upon the persecution and oppression of others. Or to borrow from Freire,[43] the oppressed become the oppressors by re-inscribing and drawing upon the same apparatuses of violence.

Although I have learned this history throughout my lifespan, whether at family gatherings, church events, or in classes throughout my education, it was/ is always presented as normative and benign—a manifest destiny from which I and others like me are naturally "supposed to" benefit. I recognize now the fallacy of the narrative of this "destiny," but it has taken years for me to unpack and see; years for me to admit to myself that I was born into an unjust system from which I benefit; and yet more years to move beyond the guilt that prevented me from doing anything to counter this injustice.[44]

However, while recognizing his privilege, Talbot also noted his opposite experiences as a minority in other respects: As a gay man, he reported having been the victim of harassment, violent threats, discrimination, and "constantly living with the feeling that you must work harder than everyone around you so that no one can ever use that as an excuse when they try to get rid of you for 'other' reasons."[45]

In essence, no one is fully guilty or fully innocent of any injustice: We are all products of our society, educational structures, and cultural background. That said, we all have an opportunity to do our individual parts to make things better in the future than they were in the past. Brent Talbot similarly recognized his place as "both colonizer and colonized,"[46] and concluded that we all might see the world from our own unique vantage points, speak out against injustice, and work together to make our educational community more equitable for everyone. He stated:

The types of hybridities I represent echo in many of us. . . . Each one of us speaks and views the world from multiple locations. . . . By speaking out, we render visible and challenge the power structures at play in our field.[47]

It is imperative, then, to speak up, change the discourse, and help bring the "hidden curriculum" to light. However, as our Facebook generation is starting to understand, being aggressive or defiant in standing up for the rights of others is not likely to convert anyone else to our point of view. Rather, it may be much more effective to gently and carefully note differences in worldviews and seek to understand one another through honest and genuine conversations, both in the classroom and beyond.[48] In the chapter that follows, I continue the conversation of inclusion to discuss how building a musical community in our classrooms and studios can help provide every student with a place to belong.

Reflection Questions

1. What stories of inclusion (or the lack thereof) in this chapter most resonate with you? Why?
2. What pedagogical practices have you simply taken for granted that might actually privilege some students over others?
3. What words or language have you taken for granted that might serve to reinforce hurtful stereotypes or injustices?
4. In what ways do you currently lack resources, ideas, or assistance to meet the needs of particular students you teach? How might you advocate for and/or acquire the support that you need?

NOTES

1. "Training the Mind, Verse 2," The Office of His Holiness the Dalai Lama, para. 2, accessed February 27, 2017, https://www.dalailama.com/teachings/training-the-mind/training-the-mind-verse-2.

2. This name has been changed.

3. Karin S. Hendricks, Tawnya D. Smith, and Jennifer Stanuch, "Creating Safe Spaces for Music Learning," *Music Educators Journal* 101, no. 1 (2014): 35–40.

4. Jens Manuel Krogstad and Richard Fry, "Dept. of Ed. Projects Public Schools Will Be 'Majority-Minority' This Fall," The Pew Research Center, last modified August 18, 2014, accessed August 3, 2017, http://www.pewresearch.org/fact-tank/2014/08/18/u-s-public-schools-expected-to-be-majority-minority-starting-this-fall.

5. Ibid.

6. Jacqueline Kelly-McHale, "The Influence of Music Teacher Beliefs and Practices on the Expression of Musical Identity in an Elementary General Music Classroom," *Journal of Research in Music Education* 61, no. 2 (2013): 195–216.

7. See, for example, Randall. E. Allsup and Catherine Benedict, "The Problems of Band: An Inquiry into the Future of Instrumental Music Education," *Philosophy of Music Education Review* 16, no. 2 (2008): 156–73; John Kratus, "Music Education at the Tipping Point," *Music Educators Journal* 94, no. 2 (2007): 42–48; Roger Mantie and Lynn Tucker, "Closing the Gap: Does Music-Making Have to Stop upon Graduation?," *International Journal of Community Music* 1, no. 2 (2008): 217–27; J. L. Shively, "In the Face of Tradition: Questioning the Roles of Conductors and Ensemble Members in School Bands, Choirs, and Orchestras," in *Questioning the Music Education Paradigm*, ed. Lee Bartel (Toronto: Canadian Music Educators Association, 2004), 179–90.

8. All CMT quotes are from interviews with the author, unless otherwise cited.

9. See Maurianne Adams, Larissa E. Hopkins, and Davey Shlasko, "Classism," in *Teaching for Diversity and Social Justice,* 3rd ed., ed. Maurianne Adams and Lee Anne Bell (New York: Routledge, 2016); Ruth Wright, "Music Education and Social

Reproduction: Breaking Cycles of Injustice," in *the Oxford Handbook of Social Justice in Music Education*, ed. Cathy Benedict, Patrick Schmidt, Gary Spruce, and Paul Woodford (New York: Oxford University Press, 2015), 340–71.

10. Don Ester and Kristin Turner, "The Impact of a School Loaner-Instrument Program on the Attitudes and Achievement of Low-Income Music Students," *Contributions to Music Education* 36, no. 1 (2009): 55.

11. Adams, Hopkins, and Shlasko, "Classism," 218.

12. Quote shared with permission.

13. Gloria Ladson-Billings, "You Gotta Fight the Power: The Place of Music in Social Justice Education," in *The Oxford Handbook of Social Justice in Music Education,* ed. Cathy Benedict, Patrick Schmidt, Gary Spruce, and Paul Woodford (New York: Oxford University Press, 2015), 406–19.

14. Kenneth Elpus, "Music Teacher Licensure Candidates in the United States: A Demographic Profile and Analysis of Licensure Examination Scores," *Journal of Research in Music Education* 63, no. 3 (2015): 314–35; Constance L. McKoy, "Effects of Selected Demographic Variables on Music Student Teachers' Self-Reported Cross-Cultural Competence," *Journal of Research in Music Education* 60, no. 4 (2013): 375–94.

15. Ibid., 317.

16. See, for example, Michael Cooper, "Music Education Group's Leader Departs after Remarks on Diversity," *New York Times,* May 12, 2016. Accessed August 3, 2017, http://www.nytimes.com/2016/05/13/arts/music/music-education-groups-leader-departs-after-remarks-on-diversity.html?_r=0.

17. Deejay Robinson and Karin S. Hendricks, "Black Keys on a White Piano: A Negro Narrative of Double-Consciousness in Music Education," in *Marginalized Voices in Music Education,* ed. Brent C. Talbot (New York: Routledge, in press), 28–30.

18. Karin S. Hendricks and Dorothy, "Negotiating Communities of Practice in Music Education: Dorothy's Narrative," in *Marginalized Voices in Music Education,* ed. Brent C. Talbot (New York: Routledge, 2017), 74.

19. Paul L. Morgan, George Farkas, Marianne M. Hillemeier, and Steve Maczuga, "Replicated Evidence of Racial and Ethnic Disparities in Disability Identification in U. S. Schools," *Educational Researcher* 46, no. 6 (2017): 305–22.

20. Judith A. Jellison, "Including Everyone," in *The Child as Musician,* ed. Gary E. McPherson (New York: Oxford University Press, 2006), 257.

21. Kimberly VanWeelden and Jennifer Whipple, "Music Educators' Perceived Effectiveness of Inclusion," *Journal of Research in Music Education* 62, no. 2 (2014): 148–60.

22. Ibid., 152.

23. Jellison, "Including Everyone," 257.

24. Karen Salvador, "Who Isn't a Special Learner? A Survey of How Music Teacher Education Programs Prepare Future Educators to Work with Exceptional Populations," *Journal of Music Teacher Education* 20, no. 1 (2010): 27–38.

25. Alice M. Hammel and Ryan M. Hourigan, *Teaching Music to Students with Special Needs: A Label-Free Approach* (New York: Oxford University Press, 2011).

26. Alice M. Hammel, Roberta Y. Hickox, and Ryan M. Hourigan, *Teaching Individual Differences in Music Classroom and Ensemble Settings* (New York: Oxford University Press, 2016).

27. Hammel, Hickox, and Hourigan, *Teaching Individual Differences,* 2–4; see also Kevin W. Gerrity, Ryan M. Hourigan, and Patrick W. Horton, "Conditions That Facilitate Music Learning among Students with Special Needs: A Mixed-Methods Inquiry," *Journal of Research in Music Education* 61, no. 2 (2013): 144–59.

28. Salvador, "Who Isn't a Special Learner?" 37.

29. Deborah Bradley, "Music Education, Multiculturalism and Anti-Racism: Can We Talk," *Action, Criticism, and Theory for Music Education* 5, no. 2 (2006): 2–30; Deborah Bradley, "The Sounds of Silence: Talking Race in Music Education," *Action, Criticism, and Theory for Music Education* 6, no. 4 (2007): 132–62.

30. Bradley, "Music Education, Multiculturalism and Anti-Racism," 3.

31. Bradley, "The Sounds of Silence," 133.

32. Juliet Hess, " 'How Does That Apply to Me?' The Gross Injustice of Having to Translate," *Bulletin of the Council for Research in Music Education* 207–208 (2016): 81–100.

33. Derald Wing Sue, *Microaggressions in Everyday Life: Race, Gender, and Sexual Orientation* (Hoboken, NJ: John Wiley & Sons, 2010), 24; as cited in Hess, " 'How Does That Apply to Me?' " 84.

34. Sue, *Microaggressions in Everyday Life*, 191; as cited in Hess, " 'How Does That Apply to Me?' " 84.

35. Hess cited a number of sources that address this compounding effect, including Lindsay Pérez Huber and Daniel G. Solorzano, "Racial Microaggressions as a Tool for Critical Race Research," *Race Ethnicity and Education* 18, no. 3 (2015): 297–320; Daniel Solorzano, Miguel Ceja, and Tara Yosso, "Critical Race Theory, Racial Microaggressions, and Campus Racial Climate: The Experiences of African American College Students," *Journal of Negro Education* 69, no. 1/2 (2000): 60–73; Derald Wing Sue, Christina M. Capodilupo, Gina C. Torino, Jennifer M. Bucceri, Aisha Holder, Kevin L. Nadal, and Marta Esquilin, "Racial Microaggressions in Everyday Life: Implications for Clinical Practice," *American Psychologist* 62, no. 4 (2007): 271–86; Tara Yosso, William Smith, Miguel Ceja, and Daniel Solórzano, "Critical Race Theory, Racial Microaggressions, and Campus Racial Climate for Latina/o Undergraduates," *Harvard Educational Review* 79, no. 4 (2009): 659–91.

36. Hess, " 'How Does That Apply to Me?' " 81.

37. Ibid.

38. See Patrick Slattery, *Curriculum Development in the Postmodern Era,* 3rd ed. (New York: Routledge, 2013).

39. Maxine Greene, "Introduction," in *The Hidden Curriculum and Moral Education,* ed. Henry Giroux and David Purpel (Berkeley, CA: McCutchan Publishing, 1983), 1–5.

40. Elizabeth Vallance, "Hiding the Hidden Curriculum: An Interpretation of the Language of Justification in Nineteenth-Century Educational Reform," in *The Hidden Curriculum and Moral Education,* ed. Henry Giroux and David Purpel (Berkeley, CA: McCutchan Publishing, 1983), 11.

41. Michael Apple and Nancy King, "What Do Schools Teach?" in *The Hidden Curriculum and Moral Education,* ed. Henry Giroux and David Purpel (Berkeley, CA: McCutchan Publishing, 1983), 82–99.

42. Greene, "Introduction," 4.

43. Paulo Freire, *Pedagogy of the Oppressed, 30th Anniversary Edition* (New York: Continuum, 2007).

44. Brent C. Talbot, "Introduction," in *Marginalized Voices in Music Education,* ed. Brent C. Talbot (New York: Routledge, in press), 6–7.

45. Ibid., 8.

46. Ibid.

47. Ibid.

48. Tawnya D. Smith, "Multiple Worldviews in the Classroom: Scaffolding for Differentiated Instruction and Social Justice Learning," unpublished manuscript.

Chapter 7

Community

The unity of many communities has been maintained by music.

—June Boyce-Tillman[1]

Music has lived side by side with humans throughout their existence and has served as a means of promoting and maintaining community identity across a variety of cultures.[2] As suggested in the preceding quote from music and spirituality author June Boyce-Tillman, music has had such a strong influence on the bonds shared between people that it has even served to bring and keep them together. Yet in recent history (particularly in the Western world), our extreme strivings toward individualism and independence have in many ways put us out of balance in our relationships with one another. Boyce-Tillman explained:

> The heroic journey model is essentially a lonely journey and is characterised by a search for absolute independence. . . . Its dangers lie in an abrogation of responsibility for anyone but oneself, a denial of any responsibility for the results of one's actions and a confusion between the private and the public. The results have been a fragmentation of communities as the [extreme] of the individual is stressed and fostered.[3]

Music offers people the possibility to balance their inherent need for individual accomplishment with an equally inherent need for community.[4] In the same moment, music allows each of us to express our own individual identity and to contribute an artistic product of our own efforts, while simultaneously mingling our sounds and resonance with that of others. Such musical blending of individual with community can be breathtaking, even to the point that countless communities and cultures have relied on music-making to evoke transcendent experiences.[5]

COMMUNITY AND CULTURE IN MUSIC TEACHING

It is not surprising that the words *community* and *culture* came up frequently in my interviews with each CMT. Brian Michaud celebrates the way in which his entire community comes together in support of children and their education. Community and culture combine for Renae Timbie; her aim is to bring people of different cultures together—in community—to understand one another. As she worked with people from Syria, Iran, and Afghanistan in the same camp, Timbie discovered a need "to give them voice, for them to share their music with one another."[6]

Marcus Santos spoke of fostering a culture at his school over his many years of teaching, so that students came to know what to expect when they took his class. For Santos, this built-in culture has "made life easier," in that he can focus on music-making and let the traditions do much of the talking. Similarly, Steve Massey used the word *culture* often to define the atmosphere of musical excellence he had fostered over three decades at Foxborough High School—a culture intrinsically focused on music, with students who genuinely encourage one another to perform at the highest possible levels. He remarked, "I really become to many of them a surrogate parent. And I don't mind that role. Probably even now a surrogate grandparent."

Dorothy DeLay was also a mother of sorts to her students: She was keenly interested in her students' lives beyond violin playing, and they interacted socially as well as musically. Through positive, frequent, and long-term interactions, she nurtured a sense of community in her studio. In fact, many of her students called DeLay their "mother away from home."[7] Her students remarked that DeLay's ability to empathetically listen, without judgment, made it so anyone felt safe to talk with her about anything.[8]

Yet, despite the twinkle in her eye and a soft, loving care for her students (complete with regular terms of endearment such as *sugarplum* or *sweetie*), DeLay has been described as "behaving more like a lioness, defending [her students] from outside predators"[9] when it came to ensuring that those in her musical community found successful jobs and were compensated well.[10] DeLay's nurturing approach resulted in dozens of high-level virtuosos, who—despite their attendance at one of the most intense music schools in the world—reportedly did not engage in competition with one another.[11] In each of the cases described earlier, the CMTs created a nurturing community for their students—a musical place to belong.

A Place to Belong

Space is physical, structural, and geographical. *Place* is alive with meaning.[12] We live in a space called a house; we thrive in a place called a home. Compassionate music teachers can transform any space into a place, whether it be a state-of-the-art rehearsal room with acoustical panels and practice rooms or a dilapidated trailer without air conditioning. The CMTs in this book have taught in these and other kinds of settings and have in each—through their focus on their students—created a place where students felt like they belonged.

Scholars have studied the phenomenon of *belonging* in a variety of "places" as diverse as families, business corporations, religions, and countries to demonstrate the universal appeal of belonging to someone and to something.[13] The need to belong is a "powerful, fundamental, and extremely pervasive motivation"[14] that allows us to understand why humans act and interact in the ways that they do. In psychologist Abraham Maslow's hierarchy of needs, love and belongingness are considered more basic human needs than receiving the esteem of others and of self, following only after basic needs such as food and physical safety.[15] According to belongingness scholars, the need to belong is satisfied through the combination of two experiences: frequent, positive interactions with an intimate group; and a stable relationship of mutual support and concern that endures over time.[16]

It is unlikely that anyone would be reading this book without having had some experience of belonging in a music-making setting. Music education programs have tremendous potential to provide a place of belonging for both students and teacher provided they are offered in a context of caring and mutual support. Programs in which students and teacher interact regularly, with mutual care and concern, and over the course of several years satisfy both criteria for belongingness described earlier, in that music-making takes place in frequent, positive settings and endures over a long period of time. Furthermore, music programs also utilize an art form of sound and vibration that can literally connect people together.

Feelings of belongingness have been found to occur in music-making settings in which there are opportunities for social interaction; an atmosphere of caring; and a sense of emotional safety. According to music teacher and researcher Nick Rzonsa, emotionally safe places that promote belongingness are those that lack demeaning judgment, intimidation, or competitiveness.[17] He further stated:

> Presumably, we want . . . happy and productive groups, but may tend to emphasize rehearsal strategies and classroom management, overlooking the creation

of a caring and stress-free environment. As a teacher, I often overlook what is important in favor of getting done what needs to be done. . . . This study suggests that an ideal learning environment should place importance on social events, which will allow for more bonds to be made. Sub-groups such as chamber music and community service groups offer additional outlets for members to get to know one another, build bonds, and interact more frequently.[18]

The "stress-free environment" recommended by Rzonsa certainly does not mean "challenge-free." Otherwise, there would be no true growth or "flow" experiences, and therefore no real enjoyment.[19] However, just as music performance anxiety can develop in demeaning or overly critical settings, performance confidence can be developed in settings where students feel emotionally safe enough to take ever-increasing musical risks.[20]

Figure 7.1 shows a picture that Savana Ricker, a music teacher in the St. Joseph, Missouri, School District, drew for use in her orchestra classroom.[21] Ricker shows her students this picture and asks, "Which blob are you?" to foster a sense of belongingness amid difference, similar to what Renae Timbie called "diversity in togetherness."

Figure 7.1.   Savana Ricker, orchestra blob drawing. Used with permission.

The idea for Ricker's illustration was based on the "blob tree" images of Pip Wilson and Ian Long,[22] which they intentionally drew without features of gender, age, or race:

> The Blobs are neither male nor female, young nor old, European nor African, ancient nor modern. They are outside of culture. Blobs are the best of us and the worst of us. They don't tell us what we ought to do, or what we mustn't do . . . they merely show us how a variety of people feel.[23]

By drawing this picture, Ricker sought to provide her students with an opportunity to tap into their feelings, actions, and dispositions by identifying with any combination of images. What I find most fascinating about Ricker's picture is how all "blobs," no matter their state of being, nevertheless have a place of belonging in the picture. Whether intentional or not, the diagram provides a "microaffirmation"[24] that everyone, no matter where they are situated within the image of the violin, is a part of the musical picture. Even the individual falling from the violin's G peg has a platform below to break the fall!

Community, Hospitality, and a Return to Vulnerability

A compassionate and inclusive community is not only welcoming of different people, approaches, and needs, but it is also hospitable. Although it embraces its members, their traditions, and their shared identity, it also provides a welcoming place to guests from beyond those community boundaries. Hospitality goes beyond mere kindness, as it requires us to be open to the viewpoints and ideas of any newcomer. According to educator Parker Palmer,

> Hospitality in the classroom requires not only that we treat our students with civility and compassion but also that we invite our students and their insights into the conversation. The good host is not merely polite to the guest—the good host assumes that the guest has stories to tell.[25]

As a result, any act of hospitality requires vulnerability and risk on the part of the host. To music educator Lee Higgins, "Community means an open-door policy, a greeting to strangers, extended in advance and without full knowledge of its consequences."[26] As we invite new and previously unknown individuals to be a part of our social circles, these people bring their own lives, backgrounds, and worldviews with them—thereby potentially challenging and even changing our group identity. Similarly, when we as music teachers invite student voices to be heard, we risk vulnerability in terms of our own teaching, curriculum, and perceived authority.

However, similar to Higgins's "safety without safety" idea addressed in chapter 3, only by taking risks can we really open up possibilities for creativity and insight. In a musical community with decades of tradition, the idea of opening up to new approaches and musics may seem impossible or simply unimportant. However, the act of welcoming new kinds of music, people, and approaches beyond our present circle can be empowering and inspiring beyond our imagination. As Palmer stated, "Good teaching is an act of hospitality toward the young, and hospitality is always an act that benefits the host even more than the guest.[27]

The Importance of Professional Boundaries

Finally, in this discussion of belonging and community, it is important to clarify the need for professional boundaries between teachers and students. Far too many teachers lose a sense of personal and professional boundaries and get into trouble—something that I wish were unnecessary to discuss, but something that lawsuits and prison sentences for inappropriate behavior warrant mentioning. When I asked Steve Massey how he had learned to balance his deep concern for his students with appropriate professional boundaries, he offered the following advice:

> You need to start out an extremely professional relationship: *High-task, low-sociability.* I have a very high task, low sociability relationship with freshmen. But as students who achieve over their four years in high school, that relationship gradually changes to more high-task, high-sociability. But that's an evolving relationship that's earned by achievement. And by sociable, I'm not hanging around and going anywhere with them. It's just that we sometimes talk more about college plans, family issues, those kinds of things. I would not set out to do that as a beginning teacher. I would set out to teach music at a high-task level with great enthusiasm, and then see where that goes.[28]

As discussed in chapter 4, those of us in serving professions need to ensure that we provide ourselves sufficient self-care and get professional and personal support apart from those whom we serve. That way, we reduce the need to rely on students to fulfill any of our personal, social, or emotional needs.

COLLABORATION AND COMPETITION

When considering the importance of community building, belongingness, and safety in risk-taking, we need to thoughtfully and carefully consider the use of competition among our students as a motivational strategy. As Steve Massey pointed out in his interview, much of what we do in United States music education is a result of our relationship with athletics. Competitions, trophies, and medals are one example, which the music industry further promotes.

The Power of Collaborative Learning and Achievement

On one hand, competitions provide a thrilling and powerful opportunity for students to work together in community, to strive for their highest potential, and stun audiences—even stun themselves—with the outcomes they are able to produce. The experience of working together collaboratively, over a long period of time, to produce something positive and expressive can lead to a sense of belonging Furthermore, the time and effort that can go into preparing for a musical event can be a powerful way to foster student learning, teamwork, and cooperation. Many of us would not be in the business today if it weren't for the life-changing experiences we had as we prepared for major performances such as these.

Secondly, as noted in discussions of self-efficacy throughout this book, the process of working toward an achievement can increase students' beliefs in their ability to perform. The ability to observe others and compare our respective strengths and weaknesses may, in some cases, help students fairly and honestly assess their abilities and learn how to improve. These kinds of "vicarious experiences" can be powerful reinforcements to help students more accurately understand their own capabilities.[29]

Hidden Messages of Competition

On the other hand, competitive performance structures in which students are ranked against each other often carry a "hidden curriculum" of their own. When we rank students or groups against each other, we often make the assumption that all other things are equal between them. In truth, however, each school and each student come with a unique background, level of family support, and amount (or lack) of financial resources that might play just as large a role in the success of a performance as does the amount of hard work. Returning to the "myth of meritocracy" discussed in the previous chapter, it is possible that rank-based competitions provide further rewards to those who already have more to begin with, thereby increasing the divide between them and others. I provide one example from a music teacher who offered a story specifically for this book.

COMPETITION AND UNFAIR ADVANTAGE: JORDAN'S STORY

Jordan[30] once taught music at Prospect High School, a rural, low-income school district in the Midwest. Jordan described experiencing a "serious wakeup call" when preparing these low-income students for

marching band competition. Having grown up in a thriving band program with tremendous parent support, and having won both individual
and group awards for marching band in college, Jordan was at the top of
the class as far as readiness to help students achieve. However, Jordan
was unprepared to face the impact of poverty on the students' ability to
compete against other schools who had far more in terms of resources
than Prospect High students could even imagine.

The financial disparity in Jordan's state is astounding. Although
Prospect High students had very little in terms of financial resources,
other affluent parts of the state are home to some of the nation's wealthiest families. Students in these prosperous public schools have private
music lessons and chamber music coaching during the school day (paid
for by the district); state-of-the-art musical instruments for use at school
and at home; and regularly scheduled European performance tours.
These affluent students also live near a major symphony, and many of
them take additional lessons from symphony players.

In Jordan's district, however, students lived in dire poverty, with single
parents working multiple part-time jobs, students unable to afford instruments, and marching uniforms that Jordan reported were "held together
with safety pins and duct tape." Private lessons were certainly not an
option for these students, as neither district nor families could afford
them (nor did any qualified teachers live in the area). As their school
band teacher, Jordan devoted every free hour after school and in the
summer to provide private lessons for students of every instrument, at no
cost—asking them only to help organize music and other tasks in return.

Believing that competition was what music students did (because that
is what Jordan had been taught), Jordan made a tremendous effort to
prepare the students to compete:

> Much of it I was starting from scratch, and I knew it wasn't sustainable
> from the director standpoint. I had no one to help me do it. But I wrote a
> simple field show, which the students could handle. The amount of learn-
> ing my students did was off the charts. We went from not marching at all
> to being able to pull off the field show. They worked really hard.
>
> But I don't think there was a single student who left the competition
> feeling good about what they had accomplished, because they compared
> themselves to students who had more resources. The students were horri-
> fied at just how basic our show was, and how basic our ability was to do
> a field show. And I think that was really deflating for them.
>
> It's like having your students play a solo before they are ready in pub-
> lic: I took a marching band that didn't have the supports they needed to be
> a marching band in a competitive situation. And it was really devastating

for my students. So we didn't go again. We did simple field forms, and we played on the marching band field during games, but we didn't attempt anything like that again, because I realized it was a waste of time and it only served to make my students feel even more disadvantaged than they already did feel.

When you put students in situations where there is not a reasonable chance that they can actually compete, it's just not really fair. And it certainly deflates the students' beliefs in themselves. Even if they are totally prepared musically, all they need to have a totally awful experience is to realize, "Wow, these people are light-years ahead of where we are." And it's hard to help students get over that.

I really regret having put them in that situation, but I was just doing what I thought I was supposed to do as a band teacher. Competition is what I learned band was supposed to be all about. I had been taught that competitions were what motivated students to learn. I didn't question that as a new teacher at all. But once that experience happened, I rethought everything.

As noted in chapter 5, students can be engaged in school music and feel a sense of belonging and connection no matter their financial or other resources. However, in cases such as Jordan's, a sense of musical engagement and belonging might best come through other avenues beyond competition against others who have already been set up with the resources to win. Rather than attempting to motivate students simply out of tradition, therefore, it is imperative for teachers to know the respective needs of their students and engage them in musical activities in which they can sense authentic achievement, collaboration, and community, no matter their circumstances.

Focusing on Music-Making

Despite the vast amount of emphasis on trophies, medals, and comparative rankings in our music programs, research has not provided sufficient evidence that competition itself is intrinsically motivational to students, nor that it influences achievement.[31] On the contrary, research suggests that an emphasis on competition can distract students from the musical task, interfere with musical expression, promote a fixed rather than growth mindset, and/or discourage students from persisting when things get difficult.[32]

Steve Massey similarly suggested that our music education profession's obsession with competitions can interfere with a focus on music-making, which he sees as the greatest and most authentic reward. Over the past three decades at Foxborough High School, Massey has gradually shifted the philosophy and focus of his community to one in which everyone's prime priority is the musical experience—including regular commissions with famous composers, artists in residence, and jazz-artist collaborations—to the point that his students and their parents have begun to view awards as ridiculous and irrelevant. He offered the following explanation and story:

> We certainly never celebrate any kind of awards or recognition publicly, like stand around and cheer that we got a gold medal or stuff like that. In fact, our kids don't really even think about medals. They do expect to get gold medals because they always do, but they don't care when they get the medal. They don't stand up and scream. They just go, "Thank you very much. Now on to the next musical experience." And at the end of the year, I throw a lot of them out. And no kids ever say, "Did you throw out the trophy from Philadelphia? Because I look at that every day." No, they don't; they don't care about them.
>
> I did have one group, about 25 years ago, on a Washington, D.C. tour when the trophies . . . they weren't boxed, they were huge and gaudy and awful looking, and they couldn't stand in the back of the bus without falling over. They wanted to know, "Do you mind if we throw these out? We can't fit them on the bus." This is before we even left Virginia.
>
> I had to really think about that one, and I finally said to the band officers, "What do you think?" They said, "I think we should throw them out; they're stupid looking." I said, "Do you think that represents the feelings of all the kids, or will some kids be hurt by that?" They had to think about that for a minute, but they said, "We'll talk it over." I said, "All right, I'll let you make the decision, but please be respectful of all the other kids." I said, "Personally, I don't care about them. I didn't come here for those."
>
> I was so excited at that moment. I thought, this culture has broken through to the next level where the kids are starting to understand what counts. When you have a young program, it's that first trophy that gets them running around, screaming about. I do understand the PR power of award-winning. So you've got to find a balance, and you've got to teach your kids what's important. I think it's actually that simple.

To Steve Massey, what is "important" is the music-making itself. Notably, upon his retirement in 2017, his parent booster club honored him, not with a plaque or some other framed piece of memorabilia, but with a musical commission from a noted composer. His parents understood that it was the music, not a memory of his own accomplishments, that he wanted to keep alive after he left the building for the last time. Massey further noted how he has tried to help other younger teachers catch the vision of putting music first:

> Sometimes you should teach your staff, if you have young immature staff members who actually validate themselves as teachers based on competitions. A lot of young teachers do. They think, "I'm a good teacher because we won a medal." And the truth is that there's not a correlation. It doesn't make you a great teacher. Great teachers do more than win medals; they change lives.

Emphasizing Group Cohesion and Peer Support

As stated previously, certain students and musical communities may thrive through participation in competitive events, while others may do better with alternative approaches to music-making. Of particular benefit in either case may be festivals where students receive feedback, something that many school administrators have recently begun to consider as a part of a teacher's evaluation portfolio. In these cases, teachers and students can determine what approaches fit with particular needs, values, and interests. However, when considering the benefits to the student and the fostering of community within a group, it is an entirely different issue to ask students in the same ensemble or studio to compete against one another for seating placements, solos, and the like, all in the name of "motivation." As suggested by the quote from Nicholas Rzonsa earlier, such internal competition within a group can negatively affect a student's sense of belonging in that musical community.

Furthermore, competition against our peers does not necessarily produce the motivation to practice that we might hope for, but it may also take away the enjoyment itself. "Flow" expert and psychologist Mihalyi Csikszentmihalyi put it this way:

> The challenges of competition can be stimulating and enjoyable. But when beating the opponent takes precedence in the mind over performing as well as possible, enjoyment tends to disappear. Competition is enjoyable only when it is a means to perfect one's skills; when it becomes an end in itself, it ceases to be fun.[33]

Seating Placements

Some music teachers might use chair-placement auditions and challenges simply out of tradition, without considering other options that might have a stronger music-learning impact. However, teachers of various kinds of ensembles have found tremendous *musical* benefits by seating students in rotations (both leaders and section members), pairing students according to complementary strengths and weaknesses, and encouraging peer mentoring.[34] Steve Massey described his philosophy behind seating in his band:

> I assign parts at the beginning of the year, but we never have challenges for chairs. If you're unhappy with the part you're playing, come talk to me, and I'll think about that. But I think you have to have criteria and you have to say, "Yes, this is your principal player. This is the best player right now, or two best players."
>
> But that old school band bureaucracy where you could have once-a-week seat challenges: It would be all about you! Not about the band. And not about the quality of the music. Instead it would be about, "I'm better than her, and she's better than me . . ." Again, I think that's also kind of an athletic paradigm. It doesn't seem that's a trust situation. It seems like it's fear and intimidation.

And it puts the director in a position of judge and jury, not in the position of advisor and guide.

We also rotate parts quite a bit: "You play first on this piece and second on that," depending on if they have the skill sets to do it. And again, if you have multiple groups like we do, then the kid might be playing third trumpet in the concert band, but in the symphonic winds (the younger one), they might be the principal trumpet player there. So, we are trying to find ways for kids to be successful at different levels depending on which ensemble they're actually in.

Massey further encourages his students to leave their own egos aside for the good of the ensemble:

I want people helping each other, not trying to beat each other. Sometimes I make them crazy when I say to the section leader, she'll say—always flute players—"Who should play the solo at letter B?" And I'll say, "Well, who do you think has the best *sound* for that solo?" "Well, I'm not sure." "Well, think about it, and then have them try it the next time, and then we'll talk about it."

So I want her, rather than saying, "Well, I do. I'm the principal player," to think instead, "Well, yeah, you're the principal player and you're going to get lots of solos. Who do you want to reach out to on this one? Who are you trying to help get better?" And once you just think in those terms, then I think everybody wins.

Rotating chairs and using leadership as an opportunity for peer mentoring may reap benefits in balancing out certain student strengths and weaknesses across the ensemble, thereby strengthening the group sound as a whole. However, as high school orchestra director John Findlay and I previously wrote, "when teachers implement a seating approach that is different than the norm, it is important to communicate this both to students and to parents (who sometimes are more concerned about seating status than are the students themselves)."[35]

Brian Michaud places his choir members not by ability, but by "comfortability," meaning that he invites the students to choose by whom they stand—provided they choose neighbors who will encourage them to be the best students and musicians they can be. He further explained how he teaches them to value every part in the ensemble:

I do a demonstration to show the students that every single one of them is important. I take my guitar out and I say, "How many strings are on this guitar? OK, there are six strings. All right." And I'll strum the guitar, and I'll ask, "Does it sound good?" They'll say, "Yeah." "OK, I'm going to knock one string out of tune. Now I've got five strings in tune and I've got one of tune," and I'll play it. They'll groan and exclaim, "Oh that was terrible!" So, I say, "Every one of you is important. Every one of you has a very important job in here, so don't feel like you're not important because you all work together toward the whole."

Opening Our Arms Wider:
Finding Multiple Ways to Engage Students in Music

Competitive environments influence students in different ways, whether because of their gender, cultural background, ability level, or prior musical experiences.[36] Using competition as a default form of motivation can, therefore, continue to privilege certain types of students over others—and may continue the pattern of attrition and disconnect with school music discussed in chapter 6. In research I conducted with Gary McPherson, we found that, in general, students in the United States ranked music classes as one of their least-valued subjects taught in school.[37] However, these same students valued autonomous musical activities outside of school the highest of any activity, equal only to their valuing of sports.

While many music students are currently satisfied with their school music experiences, it may be that there are likely far more students in our schools who might yet find a place in school music communities. We concluded:

A broader emphasis and opportunities for autonomous and student-directed musical activity may . . . be inviting to students who are not presently served

Figure 7.2. Brian Michaud on guitar. Figure courtesy of Brian Michaud.

within the American music education system. Providing more extensive, enriching, and more varied musical experiences at school may make music more
accessible to a larger and more diverse population of students, and help students
to experience first-hand the value that music can have in their lives.[38]

In addition to widening our musical communities by offering varied musical
experiences for a larger number of students, we can provide more differentiated means of engaging with students currently in our programs, in intrinsically musical ways.

Intrinsic Motivation

External rewards may have a short-term effect, similar to the short-term effect
of punishment described by Brian Michaud in chapter 5. However, there are
other, more internal, and lasting ways in which students can be motivated to
engage in music. Intrinsic motivation is present when students experience
three basic psychological needs: *relatedness,* or the development of social
bonds and a sense of belongingness (discussed at length earlier in this chapter); *competence,* or their effectiveness at particular skills; and *autonomy*, or
a sense of freedom and control over one's own learning and success.[39]
    Music education in the past few centuries has capitalized on the develop-
ment of competence in musical skills. Throughout this book, I have outlined
a number of ways that task-specific competence, or self-efficacy, can be fostered both individually and collectively. In brief review, teachers can foster a
strong sense of competence by:

1. Providing students with multiple opportunities to experience success first-
   hand, with increasing levels of mastery over time;
2. Creating a supportive musical community in which students observe and
   share in the successes of their peers;
3. Providing encouraging, honest, and specific feedback; and
4. Encouraging students to maintain physical and emotional well-being so
   that they perform and feel at their best.[40]

Autonomy may be another area where music educators can look for additional ways to engage a broader range of students. Music psychologist Paul
Evans suggested,

> Music has traditionally been an area in which teaching practices tend not to
> support autonomy. The student tends to have little input into the subject of the
> lessons, with the teacher charting the direction of the student's music learning,
> often including the choice of repertoire.[41]

The CMTs in this book, however, have shown how their student-centered approaches place more of the onus of control and responsibility on the students, and simultaneously help to build a sense of community among them. Marcus Santos described the amount of student ownership, engagement, and sense of community that is possible when he lets students lead themselves:

> Students will have a lot more fun if they see all their peers playing leadership roles, or being the conductors, or putting themselves in front of the group, instead of the teachers. They will pay a lot more attention, you know? And the students also, depending on the age, they're going to do funnier things than the teachers. Say, for example, that we're drumming in the middle school, and we're doing dynamics: When the conductor has their hands up we play loud. When the conductor has their hands down, we play soft. Some kids go on the floor and then they start doing the worm, and everybody's playing soft and cracking up laughing. It makes it a much more enjoyable way to reach our goal.

Emphasizing Expressive Goals

Preparing for performance competitions and festivals may, for some students, be a powerful way to bring a sense of musical community. Furthermore, as much of our Western society runs on competitive structures, the act of winning and losing can also be critical for students to learn important life lessons beyond those of music. However, using social comparison as a primary means of motivating students to practice may also cause a breach of trust among some students and potentially steer them away from much more meaningful musical goals. Focusing on winning awards as a means to get students engaged in music programs may actually invite and keep in our programs the kinds of students who are, in fact, more interested in competition in the first place, thereby isolating other would-be music-makers.

Band director and researcher Al Legutki noted that competitive festivals play a fundamental and important role in many school music programs.[42] However, just as with any extrinsic kind of feedback (e.g., stickers, charts, grading), he posited that competition can be used either in *informing* or in *controlling* ways. Rather than doing away with all forms of competition—something not likely to happen any time soon in our current society—Legutki suggested that teachers might, instead, engage students musically by focusing on the ways in which competition can be informing rather than controlling, thereby fostering a sense of autonomy, competence, and intrinsic motivation.[43]

A sense of community is supported when teachers emphasize informing aspects of competition, such as specific tracking of individual or collective progress, rather than ranking or comparison with others. Legutki recommended that teachers also emphasize the *music*-specific aspects of any competition, including "listening to their peers, performing for new audiences, and having an opportunity to get feedback that will help them improve their musical skills."[44] Rather than simply relying on certain external structures to do the motivational talking—which may continue to serve certain students, while isolating others—we may do well to shift the focus to one of community building and shared musical expression. String teacher and researcher Rebecca Roesler offered the following in this regard:

> Teachers' aspirations for their students' positive musical experiences may be realized when learners seek to connect with their audiences and evoke responses in listeners. Instead of anxiety-promoting concerns over judgment, students can be concerned with communicating. Instead of learning isolated techniques [such as intonation and rhythm] with no apparent meaning, learners can acquire skills and knowledge that serve to realize expressive ends. Authentic, interpersonal goals can enhance expression and connect knowledge in meaningful ways.[45]

Finally, teachers may find greater success in engaging students musically by observing individual differences in student motivational patterns, and differentiate approaches according to individual student needs. Meanwhile, a more diverse array of students in our public schools might be welcomed into our school music community if we provide a broader, richer menu of musical offerings and/or use other, more *music*-specific means of motivation. As I have written elsewhere, "Variations in individual student needs and motivational influences may be limitless, since students are each unique and are also continually growing and developing."[46] No matter the case, as Steve Massey's quotes suggest, nothing can replace the aesthetic experience of music-making in a community where music itself is the reward.

CONCLUSION

Perhaps of any qualities of compassion, inclusion and community seem to relate most in a universal way to all other qualities. We foster compassion in our own educational landscape by building *trust* within a community of learners, which has been found to enhance equity in schools.[47] The CMTs expressed how *empathy* is the key to caring about the concerns of those who are different than they are, with Marcus Santos adding that "being inclusive is very important for human development." We exercise *patience* with those of varying ability levels. Finally, we offer hospitality to others who may still be learning to recognize the inherent dignity in all people, as becoming more compassionate is a lifelong journey for all of us. In the following chapter,

Figure 7.3.   Steve Massey conducting at a holiday concert. Figure credit: Brian Doherty.

I continue the conversation of inclusion and community to suggest that music has a unique and remarkable potential to create authentic and ineffable connections between people.

Reflection Questions

1. In what ways does your classroom or studio feel like a "home away from home" for you and your students?
2. How might you practice hospitality with those beyond your classroom or studio whom you have previously not reached musically?
3. What are some ways that competition plays an extrinsically motivating or "controlling" role with your students? How might you modify these approaches to create intrinsically motivating or "informing" experiences?
4. How might you transform practices of seating placements, studio performance, and/or student leadership to create a sense of community and musical ownership in your classroom or studio?

NOTES

1. June Boyce-Tillman, *Constructing Musical Healing: The Wounds That Sing* (London: Jessica Kingsley Publishers, 2000), Kindle edition, Kindle location 342.

2. See, for instance, Patricia Shehan Campbell and Trevor Wiggins, eds., *The Oxford Handbook of Children's Musical Cultures* (New York: Oxford University Press, 2012).

3. Boyce-Tillman, *Constructing Musical Healing,* Kindle locations 323–25.

4. Ibid., location 399.

5. Ibid.; June Boyce-Tillman, *Experiencing Music-Restoring the Spiritual* (New York: Peter Lang, 2016).

6. All CMT quotes are from interviews with the author, unless otherwise cited.

7. Dijana Ihas, unpublished research; used with permission.

8. Ibid.

9. Barbara Lourie Sand, *Teaching Genius: Dorothy DeLay and the Making of a Musician* (Portland, OR: Amadeus Press, 2000), 16.

10. Dijana Ihas, unpublished research; used with permission.

11. Ibid.

12. Yi-Fu Tuan, *Space and Place: The Perspective of Experience* (Minneapolis: University of Minnesota Press, 1977).

13. Roy F. Baumeister and Mark R. Leary, "The Need to Belong: Desire for Interpersonal Attachments as a Fundamental Human Motivation," *Psychological Bulletin* 117, no. 3 (1995): 497–529.

14. Ibid.

15. Abraham H. Maslow, "A Theory of Human Motivation," *Psychological Review* 50, no. 4 (1943): 370–96.

16. Baumeister and Leary, "The Need to Belong," 497.

17. Nicholas M. Rzonsa, "Perceptions and Meanings of Belongingness within an Orchestra: A Narrative Study" (PhD diss., Boston University, 2016).

18. Ibid., 144.

19. Mihaly Csikszentmihalyi, *Flow: The Psychology of Optimal Performance* (New York: Harper & Row, 1990).

20. Casey McGrath, Karin S. Hendricks, and Tawnya D. Smith, *Performance Anxiety Strategies: A Musician's Guide to Managing Stage Fright* (Lanham, MD: Rowman & Littlefield, 2016).

21. Used with permission.

22. Pip Wilson and Ian Long, *The Big Book of Blob Trees* (New York: Routledge, 2017); see also Blobshop, "What Are the Blobs? A Feelosophy," last modified 2017, accessed August 5, 2017, https://www.blobtree.com/pages/frontpage.

23. Blobshop, "What Are the Blobs? A Feelosophy," para. 2–3.

24. See chapter 6.

25. Parker J. Palmer, *The Courage to Teach: Exploring the Inner Landscape of a Teacher's Life* (San Francisco, CA: John Wiley & Sons, 2007), 82. Kindle edition.

26. Lee Higgins, "The Impossible Future," *Action, Criticism, and Theory for Music Education* 6, no. 3 (2007), http://act.maydaygroup.org/articles/Higgins6_3.pdf, 83.

27. Parker J. Palmer, *The Courage to Teach: Exploring the Inner Landscape of a Teacher's Life* (San Francisco, CA: John Wiley & Sons, 2007), 51. Kindle edition.

28. Steve Massey has drawn many of his ideas from a "situational leadership" approach. See Paul Hersey, Kenneth H. Blanchard, and Walter E. Natemeyer, "Situational Leadership, Perception, and the Impact of Power," *Group & Organization Studies* 4, no. 4 (1979): 418–28.

29. Albert Bandura, *Self-Efficacy: The Exercise of Control* (New York: Macmillan, 1997); Karin S. Hendricks, "The Sources of Self-Efficacy: Educational Research and Implications for Music," *Update: Applications of Research in Music Education* 35, no. 1 (2016): 32–38.

30. Pseudonym used for both teacher's name and school; story and quote used with permission.

31. James R. Austin, "Competitive and Non-Competitive Goal Structures: An Analysis of Motivation and Achievement among Elementary Band Students," *Psychology of Music* 19, no. 2 (1991): 142–58; Charles P. Schmidt, "Relations among Motivation, Performance Achievement, and Music Experience Variables in Secondary Instrumental Music Students," *Journal of Research in Music Education* 53, no. 2 (2005): 134–47; Walter P. Vispoel and James R. Austin, "Constructive Response to Failure in Music: The Role of Attribution Feedback and Classroom Goal Structure," *British Journal of Educational Psychology* 63, no. 1 (1993): 110–29; see also Karin S. Hendricks, Tawnya D. Smith, and Jennifer Stanuch, "Creating Safe Spaces for Music Learning," *Music Educators Journal* 101, no. 1 (2014): 35–40; Rebecca A. Roesler, "Musically Meaningful: The Interpersonal Goals of Performance," *Music Educators Journal* 100, no. 3 (2014): 39–43.

32. See Carole Ames, "Classrooms: Goals, Structures, and Student Motivation," *Journal of Educational Psychology* 84, no. 3 (1992): 261–71; Carole Ames and Russell Ames, "Goal Structures and Motivation," *The Elementary School Journal* 85, no. 1 (1984): 39–52; James R. Austin, "The Effect of Music Contest Format on Self-Concept, Motivation, Achievement, and Attitude of Elementary Band Students," *Journal of Research in Music Education* 36, no. 2 (1988): 95–107; James R. Austin, "Competition: Is Music Education the Loser?" *Music Educators Journal* 76, no. 6 (1990): 21–25; James R. Austin, "Competitive and Non-competitive Goal Structures: An Analysis of Motivation and Achievement among Elementary Band Students," *Psychology of Music* 19, no. 2 (1991): 142–58; Vernon Burnsed, James Sochinski, and Dennis Hinkle, "The Attitude of College Band Students toward High School Marching Band Competition," *Journal of Band Research* 19, no. 1 (1983): 11–17; Karin S. Hendricks, "Relationships between the Sources of Self-Efficacy and Changes in Competence Perceptions of Music Students during an All-State Orchestra Event" (PhD diss., University of Illinois at Urbana-Champaign, 2009); G. L. Rogers, "Attitudes of High School Band Directors, Band Members, Parents, and Principals toward Marching Contests," *Update: Applications of Research in Music Education* 2, no. 4 (1984): 11–15.

33. Csikszentmihalyi, *Flow,* 50.

34. Louis S. Bergonzi, "'Whadya Get?': Evaluation, Recognition, Motivation, Competition, and School Orchestra Programs," in *Teaching Music through Performance in Orchestra* volume 2, ed. David Littrell, (Chicago, IL: GIA, 2003), 15–39; John Findlay and Karin S. Hendricks, "Seating Assignments: Are They Necessary?" *Utah Music Educators Journal* 57, no. 1 (2011): 30–32; Andrew Goodrich, "Peer Mentoring in a High School Jazz Ensemble," *Journal of Research in Music Education* 55, no. 2 (2007): 94–114; Karin S. Hendricks, Rebecca A. Roesler, Clark C. Chaffee, and Jonathan Glawe, "Orchestra Student Leadership: Developing Motivation, Trust, and Musicianship," *American String Teacher* 62, no. 3 (2012), 36–40.

35. Findlay and Hendricks, "Seating Assignments," 32.

36. Hendricks, "The Sources of Self-Efficacy"; Karin S. Hendricks, "Changes in Self-Efficacy Beliefs over Time: Contextual Influences of Gender, Rank-Based Placement, and Social Support in a Competitive Orchestra Environment," *Psychology*

of Music 42, no. 3 (2014), 347–65; Karin S. Hendricks, Tawnya D. Smith, and Allen R. Legutki, "Competitive Comparison in Music: Influences upon Self-Efficacy Belief by Gender," *Gender and Education* 28, no. 7 (2016), 918–34.

37. Gary E. McPherson and Karin S. Hendricks, "Students' Motivation to Study Music: The United States of America," *Research Studies in Music Education* 32, no. 2 (2010): 201–13.

38. McPherson and Hendricks, "Students' Motivation," 210.

39. Edward L. Deci and Richard M. Ryan, *Intrinsic Motivation and Self-Determination in Human Behavior* (New York: Plenum Press, 1985); Paul Evans, "Self-Determination Theory: An Approach to Motivation in Music Education," *Musicae Scientiae* 19, no. 1 (2015): 65–83; Allen R. Legutki, "Self-Determined Music Participation: The Role of Psychological Needs Satisfaction, Intrinsic Motivation, and Self-Regulation in the High School Band Experience" (PhD diss., University of Illinois at Urbana-Champaign, 2010); Richard M. Ryan and Edward L. Deci, "Intrinsic and Extrinsic Motivations: Classic Definitions and New Directions," *Contemporary Educational Psychology* 25, no. 1 (2000): 54–67.

40. Bandura, *Self-Efficacy: The Exercise of Control*; Hendricks, "The Sources of Self-Efficacy: Educational Research and Implications for Music."

41. Evans, "Self-Determination Theory," 70.

42. Legutki, "Self-Determined Music Participation," 6.

43. Ibid., 186.

44. Ibid.

45. Rebecca A. Roesler, "Musically Meaningful: The Interpersonal Goals of Performance." *Music Educators Journal* 100, no. 3 (2014): 39.

46. Hendricks, "Changes in Self-Efficacy Beliefs Over Time," 362.

47. Dimitri van Maele, Mieke Van Houtte, and Patrick B. Forsyth, "Introduction: Trust as a Matter of Equity and Excellence in Education," in *Trust and School Life,* ed. Dimitri van Maele, Mieke Van Houtte, and Patrick B. Forsyth (Dordrecht: Springer, 2014), 1–36.

Chapter 8

Authentic Connection

Perhaps the healing of the world rests on [a] shift in our way of seeing, a coming to know that in our suffering and our joy we are connected to one another with unbreakable and compelling human bonds. In that knowing, all of us become less vulnerable and alone. The heart, which can see these connections, may be far more powerful a source of healing than the mind.

—Rachel Naomi Remen[1]

Rachel Naomi Remen is a physician, professor, and best-selling author who has studied the ways in which cancer patients—in the darkest and most pivotal times of their lives—have come to know themselves and deepen their relationships with others.[2] Ironically, many of Remen's patients expressed how their cancer diagnosis helped them to understand a sense of "aloneness" within themselves that they had taken for granted all their lives, *until* their diagnosis. Then, when things appeared most grim, "the profoundly isolating experiences of illness [began] to heal this sense of aloneness" and spark a profound connection to self and to others.

While many of Remen's patients developed a "genuine sense of connection, belonging, and altruism" over time and with deep reflection, others discovered it instantly and by surprise.[3] Still others came to experience what Remen called "the great simplicity of living with an open heart" through great suffering, "by crawling a long way on [their] knees in the dark."[4] In this latter case, being open to their feelings and being truly authentic with themselves "burned away the habits of thought and belief that had separated [them] from

other people, and left [them] with an unshakable sense of belonging and connection."[5] Remen wrote:

> The opening of the heart seems to go far beyond love to an experience of
> belonging which heals our most profound wounds. When people look at others
> in this way, the connection they experience makes it a simpler thing to forgive,
> to have compassion, to serve, and to love. As my patient told me, "When I was
> able to connect honestly to myself, I found that I was connected to everyone
> else, too."[6]

Remen's work with many who had learned to authentically connect with others led her to conclude that "compassion emerges from a sense of belonging.
. . . When we know ourselves to be connected to all others, acting compas-
sionately is simply the natural thing to do."[7]

Throughout this book, I have touched on the ways in which music has a
unique capacity for bringing people together in empathy and community, providing us with meaningful, restorative, and even life-giving ways to express
ourselves. In this chapter, I consider more specifically the ways in which we
can use music as a means of connecting deeply with ourselves and with
others. I begin by outlining research about our capacity for human connection, and then turn to a discussion of music as a means of creating authentic
relationships. The chapter concludes with a more personal reflection regarding the ways in which we might similarly help students use music to forge
authentic connections with self and others.

HUMAN CONNECTION AND COHERENCE

Groundbreaking research has uncovered remarkable, previously immea-
surable connections that exist between humans. Neuroscientists have demonstrated evidence of mirror neurons—brain cells that fire the same way
whether we engage in an activity ourselves or merely observe someone
else engaging in that activity.[8] Furthermore, researchers have suggested
that we might use this system of brain cells to understand the intentions
of others.[9]

Other researchers have found similar coherence between human hearts.
Scientists at the HeartMath Institute[10] in Boulder Creek, California, speak
of "heart intelligence," suggesting that the heart is much more than "just a
ten-ounce muscle that pumps blood and maintains circulation."[11] In fact, this
amazing organ contains at least 40,000 neurons and has been found to communicate with the brain in ways that the brain understands and obeys. Subsequently, messages from heart waves have been found to influence cognitive

processing, and, as a result, human behavior. Various emotions also affect heart activity, creating a continual cycle of influence between our heart, brain, and action.[12]

Here's where this gets interesting: Scientists have observed energy exchanges not only between one person's heart and head but also from *person to person*. Using electrocardiogram (ECG) and electroencephalogram (EEG) technology, researchers have discovered that heart waves in one person can influence brain and heart activity in another person who is nearby.[13] One report states, "While this signal is strongest when people are in contact [i.e., physically touching], it is still detectable when subjects are in proximity without contact."[14]

Quantum physics takes this even further through the concept of "quantum entanglement," providing evidence that two particles that were once connected continue to mirror one another even when they are no longer in proximity.[15] In their discussion of the nonlocal connection between particles, quantum physicists David Bohm and Basil Hiley envision how this connectedness might extend to human experience:

> It takes only a little reflection to see that [this connection] . . . will apply even more directly and obviously to consciousness, with its constant flow of evanescent thoughts, feelings, desires, urges, and impulses. All of these flow into and out of each other.[16]

When we put this all together and reflect on the interplay of heart, brain, and emotion within each one of us—and then consider how our own expressions might find (and even create) resonance with other people—we recognize the capacity for our behaviors, actions, and even feelings to influence others. HeartMath researchers Doc Childre and Howard Martin said it this way:

> Of course, we communicate emotional states in other ways as well; we learn to read each other through a complicated set of cues. . . . But even without body language and additional cues, we transmit a subtle signal. We can't keep it in. All of us affect each other.[17]

We may be able to relate to the experience of shared energy among a group of people. A common expression such as "tension filled the room" is a negative example, but those of us who have been involved in group music-making can attest to a kind of shared synergy we have experienced that is much more than an interplay of pitch and rhythms. Notably, the HeartMath Institute refers to the collective energy of a group of people with the words *vibration* and *pitch*.[18] This might lead us to wonder just how much a "buzz" of excitement might be stimulated or enhanced by shared music-making.

Musical Tone and Human Connection:
Suzuki and the Living Soul

Violin pedagogue Shinichi Suzuki taught the importance of human-to-human connection, which he believed to be both musical and spiritual. Similar to the opinions of scientists mentioned earlier, Suzuki believed in a literal vibration that connected individuals to one another. The following Suzuki quotes illustrate how he perceived the musical ear and the compassionate heart to be inseparably connected:

"The heart that feels music will feel people."[19]
"Music is a language of the heart without words."[20]
"The ear loses the power to listen when the heart forgets to listen to the sounds."[21]
"Beautiful tone, beautiful heart."[22]

For Suzuki, music wasn't merely a way of getting people to connect; he believed that music—as a tangible manifestation of life force—was connection to life itself.[23] Music educator Merlin Thompson explained to a Western audience that Suzuki's common phrase "Beautiful tone with living soul, please," or "*Utsukushiki oto ni inochi o*," represents beauty (*utsukushiki*), tone (*oto*), and life force (*inochi*), where *i* represents "breath" and *chi* represents "dynamic energy."[24] Translated differently, *inochi* refers to living soul.[25] Music teacher Yui Kitamura provided further interpretation:

> Other information is based on the kanji, or the character, of *inochi*, which looks like this, 命. Like most [Japanese] characters, the origin is based on a picture, in this case of a person kneeling down under a roof, and praying to God. One thing to note is that the character for mouth, 口, is embedded in the character of *inochi*. Linguists say that the origin of this character is based on the person taking in the God's word or blessing, which is life itself. Hence, *inochi* is not just life, but it is also a direct connection to God.[26]

"Tone has a living soul," Suzuki is quoted as saying.[27] As the preceding translations suggest, Suzuki viewed musical tone as a direct and divine means of communication from soul to soul, which he perceived as being a part of an integrated spiritual whole. In an unpublished interview between Suzuki and William Starr, Suzuki expressed how he believed he was connected spiritually to the children he taught:

> *Suzuki*:   I have respect for all children. Living soul to living soul, same person. . . . The children feel my feeling, then change [to become better people]. . . . Many people do not have respect for the living soul. [Children and I are at the] same level. I must [nurture nobleness in] children.

Starr: When you teach a small child you don't know, you immediately feel respect for the living soul of the child. You think the child catches that feeling from you.

Suzuki: Yes. The child's living soul feels everything, even if the child does not understand in his mind.[28]

Suzuki emphasized in his violin teaching that there was no greater technical skill than the production of resonance with the instrument. For him, the outward manifestation of musical tone reflected the internal and interpersonal sensitivity of the performer.[29] As a part of an earlier research project, I interviewed several music teachers who personally worked with Suzuki, asking them to describe his careful attention to tone production for the sake of connection with self and others. The teachers were in virtually perfect agreement about how fundamental this idea was to Suzuki. Patricia D'Ercole, a prominent Suzuki teacher trainer, offered this description:

> Tone comes alive through [a performer's] expression. Your individuality comes through. [Suzuki] said he could tell the character of a person by the beauty of their tone. If they had a beautiful tone, they were probably a beautiful person with high sensitivity.[30]

Cellist Tanya Carey described her own experience with music and personal connection, as inspired by Suzuki:

> [Music] has the capacity to break through the layers of insulation from our environment to reach the "soul" to evoke a transformation in our relationship to ourselves, others, and connection to the spiritual. I don't know how it works. I can't define it. It is an "is" in my experience and I use it as a tool of communication and spiritual renewal.[31]

From Suzuki's words above and in many of his other writings,[32] it is clear that Suzuki's primary desire was to connect with students through music, using this "life force" to foster compassion in a way that he believed all children were capable of developing. Marcus Santos similarly senses a connection between music, his students, and life energy when they drum in a circle together: "There are feelings and there are articulations, and, most importantly, because it's a drumming ensemble, we are all communicating without using words by the energy that the drum is putting out into the universe."[33]

AUTHENTICITY

Making genuine connections with others—whether our students, colleagues, or musical audiences—requires a certain level of personal authenticity. Said differently, it is hard to authentically connect with others when you do not truly know yourself. Authenticity here is not defined in terms of musical or historical performance authenticity (although that conversation could also relate to the ways in which we musically connect with others). Instead, the definition of authenticity that I use here is one of *connection with our true selves, as well as the integrity we display in our interactions with others.*

Authenticity has been defined as "synonymous with such terms as genuineness or realness," in that it "encompasses the matter of being true to oneself and connects notions of personal grounding, sense of self, and identity with the matter of self-alignment."[34] As Parker Palmer expressed, "Good teaching cannot be reduced to technique; good teaching comes from the identity and integrity of the teacher."[35] Authenticity on the part of the teacher is a prerequisite for modeling integrity and wholeness in our students.[36]

Personal and Professional Integrity

Dorothy DeLay's personal and professional integrity was evident in the way that she "lived the role of teacher 24 hours a day, 365 days a year."[37] DeLay was what researcher Dijana Ihas called a "holistic mentor" to her students, providing support in psychosocial concerns, intentional socialization into the field, and being an expert role model for them.[38] The amount of time she spent being fully attentive to student after student—often leaving Juilliard at 2:00 a.m.—might exhaust many of us; however, teaching was such a part of who she was that she was able to spend decade after decade doing so.

Inauthenticity brings exhaustion; being true to oneself brings energy and life. Brian Michaud described how being true to himself—and allowing the natural "little boy" in his persona to come forth—has allowed him to authentically connect with his students:

> As somebody once said, children smile X amount of times a day and adults only smile a fraction of that. Maybe we're so caught up in what we're doing that we forget to enjoy ourselves. So one of the simple things that I do to be more "kid-like" is to smile more. Earlier in my career I had a student ask, "Are you sad, Mr. Michaud?" And I said, "No, I'm not sad." But maybe I was looking serious. And I thought, "Oh, you know, I should make a mental note of that."
>
> So I think about those things that kids do more naturally than adults, and I try and have that connection. When I see kids smiling at me, I smile back. And guess what? It feels good to smile. There's an electricity or magic in the air when a teacher truly connects with a group of students. You see them in front of their students, and they are smiling, and their students are smiling, and they're laughing, and there's something special about that connection because it's almost like they're one.

Marcus Santos amazed my university practicum students by his tireless ability to fill a room of sleepy teenagers with excitement, every morning at 8:00 a.m. When I asked him what his secret was, he responded:

> When you love what you do and you're not afraid to show it, it has a strong effect on your teaching and on others around you. If you're having fun, it doesn't matter how tired you are. Even though your body or mind is tired, you feed off of the energy because you love what you do, and because it's fun.

Integrity and Vulnerability

Integrity, authenticity, and vulnerability go hand in hand. Dorothy DeLay demonstrated integrity and opened herself up to vulnerability when she decided to establish her own studio, after serving as an assistant to Ivan Galamian for over a decade.[39] DeLay began as Galamian's student and then moved into an assistant role with him, even packing up her family each summer to teach with him in Upstate New York at Meadowmount, the institute Galamian founded.

It is difficult to imagine the strength of spirit and sense of self that DeLay had as a woman, to pick up the phone and tell an authoritarian man—who is remembered for "having a problem with women being successful"[40]—that she would not join him at Meadowmount, but would be teaching on her own at the Aspen Music Festival and School instead. As Dijana Ihas exclaimed, "How strong of a person one would have to be to say 'no' to Ivan Galamian?"[41]

DeLay was willing in this instance to risk the anger and retribution of the world's most legendary violin pedagogue—a fear that came to light, as he tried unsuccessfully to get her fired from Juilliard and otherwise attempted to make her life difficult for years to come. Yet, being true to herself, she followed her passion and launched her own studio, teaching in her own remarkable way. DeLay's students observed that the severing of that relationship led to a blossoming of her own creativity, as she was forced to build her career on her own.[42] Had she not followed her authentic voice, we may never have known who Dorothy DeLay was.

The Power in Saying "I Don't Know"

Dorothy DeLay demonstrated integrity to the point of vulnerability in that she unabashedly welcomed her students to bring the most challenging and innovative violin repertoire to their lessons, regardless of whether she was capable of playing those pieces herself. She was not afraid to let her students see her own technical weaknesses; she instead modeled technical concepts from virtuosic passages in extremely challenging repertoire via simpler means—on open strings, with scales, or with a very slow tempo—so that students could transfer the concepts into their own playing.[43] Much of DeLay's personal and professional identity involved a sense of curiosity and a desire to continually learn. Therefore, she placed the acquisition of new knowledge above her need to appear as the sole expert of everything she taught, thereby rendering limitless her students' capacity to learn and develop as musicians.

Renae Timbie also noted the importance of letting go of her own ego to allow students the space to learn without limits:

> Compassion is saying, "I want to do whatever it takes to show that I'm here for you. I'm going to come to whatever level it is that you are comfortable with." When I go into a refugee camp, even just walking around Greece in our concerts, I want to do whatever it takes to connect with these people. And shame on me if I expect them to come to me, to be my understanding of what they should be. I'm here to be with them, so I'm going to ask questions, and I'm going to risk being the one that does something stupid and just say, "Whoops, sorry; I didn't know," because I want them to know that they are worth being with. That's hard to do at times, and I don't think we're taught to do that because it's considered weakness, you know, as opposed to going in and saying, "Look! This is it, you are on my turf." So the power in saying, "I don't know," it makes their voice and their learning important.

Authenticity and Integrity in Music

Music and life were the same to Shinichi Suzuki, and Suzuki's relationship with music helped him to understand his relationship with life and with himself. As Merlin Thompson wrote:

> Beautiful tone, musical appreciation, and musical expression were intimate meaning-making experiences that prompted Suzuki's understanding of himself. The essence of art, the meaning of music in tone and sound was something that existed within his ordinary daily self, captured not only in musical performance, but in the way a person greets people or expresses one's self. His relationship with beauty in music led to an unanticipated yet empowered understanding of who he was as a person. It is as if beauty—surprise, curiosity, and wonder— pulled him into a heightened awareness of his own sense of self.[44]

Marcus Santos described his connection with music in a similar way to that of Suzuki: "It's that feeling of the energy of the music; there is a moral value of music, don't you think? And we're trying to project that energy through the music that we're playing."

Integrity is a word that jazz legend Wynton Marsalis used to describe Steve Massey, a term he defined as "belief in meaning and the value of meaning."[45] For Massey, integrity also comes through music-making, by ensuring that every class period is a sanctuary of sorts to an authentic musical experience:

> I try to get my students to understand we could play this piece of music right now and the experience—the aesthetic experience—could be as powerful and

as life-changing as playing that piece in Carnegie Hall. This flawed idea that we have to go away, and we have to pay lots of money, and we have to wear tuxes, and we have to have a big audience to make music powerful is a flawed premise that teachers are promoting. But I say, "Yes, it's great to play at Symphony Hall, it's so much fun . . . but what we're going to do right now in this room in here could be magical."

As a teacher, you've got to try to make at least one magical moment in every rehearsal. Every rehearsal has to have "a-ha" moments. And it's a moment that is emotionally thrilling. Then they come to every rehearsal with a little more intensity because this could be awesome. Those experiences can just as often be in the rehearsal as they are in a performance.

I don't have those post-concert talks. I never really even say anything about the concert or have post-concert celebrations. Like we need brownies to celebrate Grainger? Grainger is celebratory enough. A lot of programs get swept up in that kind of stuff, and the parents get involved in that kind of stuff too, and a lot of that is in cultures that are, in my opinion, a little immature musically. The culture is not thinking artistically yet. Here our parents are thinking about the piece we commissioned for the string orchestra this year, and about the composer in residence. If you build the program around celebrating music, that's going to be enough.

TEACHING CONNECTION

How can students connect authentically with others through music? In this technology-driven age, youth are in one sense more connected than ever with others through various messaging applications and social media. At the same time, the heads-down, thumbs-whizzing stance of adolescents is an embodiment of their disconnection from the people in their immediate proximity—those same people with whom, as discussed earlier, they might actually be sharing a biophysical connection. I believe, therefore, that seizing opportunities to encourage young people to reach out to others through music is not just about meeting a community-service quota but also about maintaining and preserving critical human connections.

My own life and musicianship were deeply influenced by my former orchestra teacher Ted Ashton, one of the most loving and compassionate men I have ever known. He had an amazing ability to facilitate connection among his family of students, which we experienced in a number of dimensions: connection to peers, connection to our communities, connection to ourselves, and shared connections with others. It seemed natural for him to foster this in us because he lived it. I am grateful for his example in helping me understand how to create this same kind of connection with my own students. In this section, I share aspects of what I learned from Ted, along with quotes from various music students and teachers,[46] about how experiences of connection influenced them.

Connecting with Peers

I explained in chapters 4 and 7 how competition can be healthy when it does not elicit a situation in which students are set up against each other, but instead allows for continual personal growth and challenge. Compassionate teachers can help students feel confident enough in their own abilities and potential so that they are willing and interested in helping their peers succeed as well. Students can connect to peers through positive interactions in which they are encouraged to work together, encourage each other's growth, and celebrate each other's successes. Such connections can happen in studio situations, ensembles, tutoring younger students, and student leadership opportunities. Encouraging peer interactions in music brings together complementary strengths and weaknesses, allowing for a special synergy when everyone can contribute what they do best to make the whole even better.[47]

As an orchestra director, I enjoy involving peers in the rehearsal process, asking them to listen and provide specific feedback to others. For example, I might ask the horn players which of a variety of articulation choices they like best when the viola section performs each for them. This approach takes more time than just telling the violas to "play short" but promotes independent thought, collective goal sharing, and a general development of musicianship skills in the long term. As discussed in chapter 5, taking a few minutes now to teach students to listen can save hours of future practice and rehearsal.

An approach to collective music learning and peer interaction gave Doug, a viola student, a place where he felt at home. He stated, "In school there's all these social classes and cliques. But in orchestra, everyone is equally important. We're all trying to be better, all playing together."[48]

Outreach and In-Reach

Visits to unfamiliar places such as hospitals and retirement communities can be scary for teenagers (OK, let's admit it—sometimes for the teachers too), but what better way can students learn compassion than by stepping outside of their comfort zones? In my experience, the discomfort is short-lived once students have an opportunity to interact and share music with listeners whose gratitude is apparent, even if not explicitly expressed. Here's what Gerry, age fifteen said, after a class holiday party in which student officers chose to take party attendees to sing at a local-assisted care facility:

> At first when we decided to go sing for the elderly a lot of people weren't very excited. As we started singing and getting to know some of the men and women there, I noticed that everyone's attitudes had changed for the best. Seeing all of the elderly clapping, singing, and even playing their harmonicas with us really

helped everyone to feel the holiday spirit. Although we went there to give service, I think we were the ones who were made better by the experience.

Teachers can also encourage other community connections through extracurricular music participation in amateur, intergenerational, community ensembles, garage bands, multicultural groups . . . and the list is endless. Whether for course credit or just for the love of it, students can enrich their musicianship as well as their sense of community by exercising their abilities in a variety of ways and with a variety of people.

Music in Prison

One of the most compelling examples of community outreach of which I am aware is the work of André de Quadros, who facilitates music classes at two prisons outside Boston. Prisoners are arguably the most neglected and oppressed population in the United States; de Quadros has suggested that people in the United States are "largely unaware of the full extent of its incarceration system in numbers, ethnicity, and economic and class parameters."[49] Consider these shocking figures: The United States makes up roughly 5 percent of the world's population, but an astounding 25 percent of the world's prisoners.[50] Research suggests that the rate of U.S. incarceration is on the rise—yet with no correlated improvements in our country's safety or health.[51] Racial inequities abound in prisons; for example, data suggest that black Americans go to prison for drug use at ten times the rate of white Americans, although white people report using illegal drugs at five times the rate of black people.[52]

Prison life is the antithesis of connection. Things most of us take for granted, such as touch and eye contact—let alone a meaningful conversation with someone about one's purpose in life—are not only rare in prison but are even purposefully avoided as a means of self-security.[53] I recently spoke with R. M., a man who had spent more than thirty years in prison on a life sentence he received as a teenager. R. M. told me about the loss of human dignity, identity, and purpose he had experienced in prison, with a sense of isolation and emotional numbness that I can't even begin to fathom.

R. M. was one of the participants in de Quadros's music class—a class in which de Quadros challenges prison norms by creating a space without hierarchies or authority, a place where prisoners sing, create, and express music together. The focus and fundamental priority is expressive freedom, and in these workshops, the prisoners (along with course facilitators and other visitors) interact with one another in various musical and artistic activities that include free improvisation and communal singing. One activity involves all of the participants holding hands in a circle and looking into each other's eyes while singing, "The road that I follow leads me on my way. I've got my eyes on tomorrow and my feet on today." The kind of musical connection in these classes is a vastly different experience than prisoners are accustomed to, but its intent is purposeful: De Quadros reports that such "activities serve to empower the participants and to allow them to experience a democratic classroom within a brutal penal system—a zone of safety, security, and integrity."[54]

What some might consider "community service" is more like "community connection" to de Quadros. He advocates that each of us revisits the notion of "outreach" to include a critical component of "in-reach," where we turn inward to better know and understand ourselves and allow ourselves to be touched by the lives and experiences of others.[55] This idea is reminiscent of the definition of compassion addressed in chapter 1, in which a person resists the notion of serving another person out of a sense of obligation, superiority, or pity, and instead focuses on equality, mutual respect, and appreciation for what each person brings to a relationship.

As de Quadros, the other facilitators, and other prison visitors first reach inward and allow themselves to model vulnerability, they invite the inmates to let down their emotional walls and risk feeling again—an experience that invites feelings of pain, of course, but also welcomes long-forgotten feelings of love and connection. One prisoner, G. C., reflected on how he was captivated by the visitors' first entrance to their classroom and their free expression of music—so much so that "the hairs on [his] arm stood up." Over time, the music classroom became for G. C. "our secret place, where a magic happens every week."

Music teacher Yui Kitamura, who accompanied de Quadros to the prison music and art classes, articulated the kind of connection that she felt with these complete strangers as they engaged in creative activities together. With her permission, I share a reflection she wrote after one visit:

The Gaze

The gaze of a stranger
Staring through my eyes,
Seeing my attributes & sins . . . so much that I feel naked.
Clothes don't mean anything . . . They don't mean anything if I can gaze in your eyes, telling me who you are on the inside.
Let me look into you, stranger. Your eyes, guiding me through the world you live In . . . just waiting to be seen.
What I do see when I stare in your eyes? you ask. Well, stranger, I see everything. Your smiles, your tears, your anguish, your fears. Your struggles, your pain, your hardships in life, and everything you wanna hide.
But don't . . .
Don't hide, because I'm just listening to you.
I ain't here to judge or condemn, because only God knows.

Only He knows you fully.
Can you hear me?
Because I wanna hear you.
Can you see me?
Because I wanna see you.
Let me look into you, stranger. . .
Let our gaze just go Beyond
going above & beyond both of our worlds.
Until we reach the heavens, where we can gaze, gaze into the same world . . .
because the world is really just one . . . with you & me.

Music in a Refugee Camp

The experience of connection that Kitamura experienced with prisoners is akin to that of Renae Timbie in Greece: In both situations, one person was allowed freedom to move beyond human-imposed boundaries that confined the other. Yet in both cases, both the boundary-crosser and the confined were deeply moved in life-changing ways. Timbie described her experience:

> When we were performing the very last concert of the week, the refugee kids came and joined us. We had brought "Dona Nobis Pacem," or "Grant Us Peace," and it was Latin, but they did it. We thought we would get a part of it, but they did the whole thing. I was able to turn and tell the audience, in Arabic, "This is what they're singing: 'Give us peace.' " You know? And how cool to say that to a room full of refugees who experienced so much. And so they did it again. The children sang it and the parents wanted the children to come back at the end too. The parents were taking pictures, and there was relief. And it was really incredible.
>
> While one of the directors was conducting, one of the kids was kind of hanging on her arms, as she connected with her all week. And the kid looked at her, and said, "You came for us?" It just kind of dawned on her. After this whole week of being with her, she asked, "You came all this way for *us*? Here? You did this for us?" Music is the easy avenue that we have to connect with others. It's just such an easy tool to bring dignity, to bring value to another person. Music can play a role in transforming lives.

Self-Expression

> It's not that hard to be able to play music, but putting your heart into it is another matter.
>
> —Tori, age fifteen

Music gives us an opportunity to connect with ourselves. Compassionate music teachers understand that music is, first and foremost, a vehicle for self-expression. Because it is personal, students require a safe emotional environment where they can feel free to be vulnerable, take risks, and let their authentic selves come through.[56] Certain musics and approaches lend themselves well to the facilitation of self-expression. For example, engaging with students in popular music, music of various world cultures, and student-selected music that reflects their own identities can expand students' musical and stylistic repertoires and give them an opportunity to explore new and innovative ways to say what is in their heart.

Jazz, folk music, and community and world music approaches that high-light improvisation evoke a large amount of self-expression. Whether this improvisation is semi-structured or completely free, it allows students to amplify their own voices and to experiment and explore musical forms and styles, as well as come to better understand themselves. For example, music educator Tawnya Smith has used free improvisation—including making "music" out of bats, balls, and various objects in the room—to help students explore inner emotions and overcome musical inhibitions and performance anxiety.[57]

In prior research, I found that students in a highly structured, competitive seating audition most closely associated their overall beliefs in their abilities with their capacity to impress an adjudicator, and least with their ability to perform expressively.[58] When an ensemble conductor gives all the "right" answers and players are expected to follow, there may be a strong sense of unity and precision, but self-expression is less likely—although not impossible. Similarly, playing classical music where every dynamic is dictated (Mahler and Tchaikovsky come to mind), the music can be wildly expressive, but not necessarily *self*-expressive.

"Authentic Self" Expression

Although musical styles and genres with freer forms may lend themselves more readily to self-expression, I believe "authentic you" performances are possible in any style or genre. We don't need to throw the classical music baby out with the bath water here; perhaps just be more flexible and explor-atory. For example, traditional ensemble directors might offer students an opportunity to have a greater voice and choice in music-making decisions, including repertoire selection, articulations, dynamics, phrasing, move-ment, and so on. Carmen, age eighteen, described how performing in such a democratic ensemble format fostered her own self-discovery: "It helped me find strengths and weaknesses within myself. . . . I have learned to react and engage in something I really love."

Similarly, students learning solo Bach works might be afforded the oppor-tunity to create their own dynamics and musical phrases, or teachers might encourage concerto soloists to improvise their own cadenzas. There are plenty of places where classical composers intended musicians to be spontaneous, but countless performers since the Romantic era have reverted to playing someone else's composed "improvisations" instead. I propose that it is time for a renaissance of self-expression, no matter the genre.

Twenty-first-century music technologies will likely to continue to amaze us with expressive possibilities as well. However, as splicing and pitch bending capabilities continue to encourage the "perfectifying" of music recordings, it might be worth a trip into the past with our students to share some imperfect—but truly authentic—moments of self-expression, as caught on unedited analog. Would Joe Cocker's "You Are So Beautiful" be nearly as memorable, for instance, without the crack in the final ". . . to me"? Would Chicago's "Colour My World" be nearly as colorful if the flute's extreme registers had been spliced to perfection? Would the rawness and authenticity in Louis Armstrong's trumpet and voice still move us to the same extent if "cleaned up" somehow?

As we aspire to create a compelling work of art, are we more consumed by producing a performance that is perfect, or one that is alive? How can we balance these priorities? I hope we can continue to celebrate the raw, heartfelt realness and connectedness of "musicking"[59] that has been a part of our human experience for millennia. With the 21st-century expansion in styles and awareness of differences that we have already observed, I am optimistic that we can.

Finally, compassionate music teachers might encourage self-expression just by allowing it to happen naturally, by modeling personal expression, by speaking openly to students about its importance, and by welcoming students to be their own unique versions of humanness. As we make more room for diversity and allow students a safe place to be whoever they feel they really are, I am hopeful that their expressions of self will naturally emerge.

SHARED EXPRESSION

I remember the first time that I finally realized that my musical talent wasn't just for scoring well in competition or for impressing people with my technique. Someone who listened to my performance told me afterward that they felt like they had become better acquainted with me through the way that I had played. Now when I perform, instead of focusing on trying to get a perfect score, I focus on giving a part of myself to my audience.

—Hilary, age eighteen

At various times in my career, I have had the unfortunate experience of witnessing the untimely deaths of several students at the schools in which I taught.

In one case, one student drove her car full of student passengers through a stop light right outside the school parking lot during lunch, apparently attempting to outrun a double-trailered sugar beet truck. The accident was in full view for everyone at school to see. In other cases, students died unexpectedly, with many of their friends not finding out until they arrived at school the next day, right before the concertmaster was to give the signal to start tuning.

There is nothing more difficult than standing in front of students on their first day back after a tragedy has occurred. What do you do? What do you say? Can you really say anything? In these moments and in others like them (such as the morning of September 11, 2001), I told my students that I thought the best thing we could do was make music. I invited students who needed to talk to go to the counseling center, but for those who wanted to stay, we would use our instruments to express our feelings together. Rather than rehearse our standard repertoire, however, I let them select pieces from the library, and we just *played*.

One freshman group, after unexpectedly losing their classmate Jocie, requested to play "Rhosymedre" by Ralph Vaughan Williams. As we reached the climax at the middle of the piece we were all in tears (conductor included), feeling a sense of peace in honoring Jocie's life with such beautiful music. As days progressed and these students continued to work through their grief, we kept the song in our folders.

Later in the year, the students asked if they could perform "Rhosymedre" at the state orchestra festival, in honor of Jocie. As we took our two and a half-hour bus drive to the competition, several of the students told me how they cared less about the adjudicator's opinions and more about having an opportunity to honor their friend. Even though months had passed, their memory of Jocie had not faded, and they found in music a way to release their grief while also expressing to others just how much her friendship meant to them.

Connection with others via musical expression is my first priority in teaching. For me, all roads of practice and technical exactness lead here. For this reason, when on the podium I often look students in the eye and tap my heart before beginning a piece, to remind them where my focus would be and invite them to join me there. This is the reason that many of us—along with each of our CMTs, no matter the student age, background, or genre—regularly have students form one large circle around the room, and encourage them to attune to one another in our own kind of musical community. For this reason, many of us have ensembles perform without a conductor so that they learn to express what is *theirs* to express, without anyone else in the way. I hope that it has made a difference. According to Emily, age seventeen, it has:

> Music is an amazing thing. I don't think the composer can ever know what their music can do for people. I always try to have some purpose for playing and it

always works best when it is for someone else. Today it was for my aunt whose husband just left her and her seven-month-old baby.

Then I thought about it and not three feet away was [a member of the ensemble] who needed something to lift her up, too. I, just like the composer, can't know if my thoughts and reasons for the music ever reached her, but look what it's done for me. It allowed me to play for someone else to try and lift them up, and that is what I have been taught by wonderful and understanding teachers who know exactly what music is supposed to be all about.

We may each have our own opinions about "what music is supposed to be all about," but Emily joins many others quoted throughout this chapter to suggest that music is about connection to others—to the composer, a family member, a friend, her teachers, and even connection to herself. As her teacher, I couldn't have asked for more than this.

Reflection Questions

1. In what ways have you felt a connection to other people while making music?
2. Consider a music teacher you know who displays professional integrity. What are some ways that this integrity has an impact on that teacher's students?
3. What kinds of "community connection" activities have you done with your students? How have those activities been received, both by the students and by the community with which they engaged?
4. What is a way that you might reach beyond your present musical and/or pedagogical comfort level, to connect more authentically with others when you perform and/or teach?

NOTES

1. Rachel Naomi Remen, *Kitchen Table Wisdom* (New York: Riverhead, 2006), 140.
2. Rachel Naomi Remen, "Educating for Mission, Meaning, and Compassion," in *The Heart of Learning: Spirituality in Education,* ed. Steven Glazer (New York: Jeremy P. Tarcher/Putnam, 1999), 33–49.
3. Rachel Naomi Remen, *Kitchen Table Wisdom*, 140.
4. Ibid.
5. Ibid.
6. Ibid.
7. Remen, "Educating for Mission, Meaning, and Compassion," 34.
8. Giacomo Rizzolatti and Laila Craighero, "The Mirror-Neuron System," *Annual Review of Neuroscience* 27 (March 2004): 169–92.
9. Marco Iacoboni, Istvan Molnar-Szakacs, Vittorio Gallese, Giovanni Buccino, John C. Mazziotta, and Giacomo Rizzolatti, "Grasping the Intentions of Others with

One's Own Mirror Neuron System," *PLoS Biology* 3, no. 3 (2005): e79, https://doi.org/10.1371/journal.pbio.0030079.

10. The HeartMath Institute website is http://www.heartmath.org; see also Doc Childre and Howard Martin, *The HeartMath Solution* (New York: HarperCollins, 1999).

11. Childre and Martin, *The HeartMath Solution*, 9.

12. Robert C. Frysinger and Ronald M. Harper, "Cardiac and Respiratory Correlations with Unit Discharge in Human Amygdala and Hippocampus," *Electroencephalography and Clinical Neurophysiology* 72, no. 6 (1989): 463–70; Robert C. Frysinger and Ronald M. Harper, "Cardiac and Respiratory Correlations with Unit Discharge in Epileptic Human Temporal Lobe," *Epilepsia* 31, no. 2 (1990): 162–71; John I. Lacey and Beatrice C. Lacey, "Some Autonomic-Central Nervous System Interrelationships," in *Physiological Correlates of Emotion,* ed. Perry Black (New York, Academic Press, 1970), 205–27; R. McCraty, W. A. Tiller, and M. Atkinson, "Head-Heart Entrainment: A Preliminary Survey" (paper presentation, Key West Brain-Mind, Applied Neurophysiology, EEG Biofeedback 4th Annual Advanced Colloquium, 1996); R. Schandry, B. Sparrer, and R. Weitkunat. "From the Heart to the Brain: A Study of Heartbeat Contingent Scalp Potentials," *International Journal of Neuroscience* 30, no. 4 (1986): 261–75.

13. Rollin McCraty, "The Energetic Heart: Bioelectromagnetic Communication within and between People," in *Bioelectromagnetic Medicine*, ed. Paul J. Rosch and Marko S. Markov (New York: Marcel Dekker, 2004), 541–62; Rollin McCraty, Mike Atkinson, Dana Tomasino, and William A. Tiller, "The Electricity of Touch: Detection and Measurement of Cardiac Energy Exchange between People," in *Brain and Values: Is a Biological Science of Values Possible,* ed. Karl H. Pribram (Mahwah, NJ: Lawrence Erlbaum Associates, 1998), 359–79; Linda G. Russek and Gary E. Schwartz. "Interpersonal Heart-Brain Registration and the Perception of Parental Love: A 42 Year Follow-Up of the Harvard Mastery of Stress Study," *Subtle Energies & Energy Medicine Journal Archives* 5, no. 3 (1994): 195–208.

14. McCraty et al., "The Electricity of Touch," 359.

15. Scott Hill and William K. Wootters, "Entanglement of a Pair of Quantum Bits," *Physical Review Letters* 78, no. 26 (1997): 5022, http://dx.doi.org/10.1103/PhysRevLett.78.5022; Rysszard Ryszard, Paweł Horodecki, Michał Horodecki, and Karol Horodecki, "Quantum Entanglement," *Reviews of Modern Physics* 81, no. 2 (2009): 865, http://dx.doi.org/10.1103/RevModPhys.81.865; William K. Wootters, "Entanglement of Formation of an Arbitrary State of Two Qubits," *Physical Review Letters* 80, no. 10 (1998): 2245, http://dx.doi.org/10.1103/PhysRevLett.80.2245.

16. David Bohm and Basil J. Hiley, *The Undivided Universe* (London: Routledge, 1993), 382, as cited in Childre and Martin, *The HeartMath Solution,* 257.

17. Childre and Martin, *The HeartMath Solution,* 161.

18. Institute of HeartMath, "Each Individual Impacts the Field Environment," last modified September 10, 2012, accessed August 4, 2016, http://www.heartmath.org/free-services/articles-of-the-heart/each-individual-impacts-field-environment.html.

19. Shinichi Suzuki, *Ability Development from Age Zero,* trans. Mary Louise Nagata (Miami, FL: Summy-Birchard, 1981), 40.

20. Suzuki Association of the Americas, *Every Child Can: An Introduction to Suzuki Education* (Boulder, CO: Suzuki Association of the Americas, 2003), 2.

21. Shinichi Suzuki, *Where Love Is Deep: The Writings of Shinichi Suzuki*, trans. Kyoko Selden (New Albany, IN: World-Wide Press, 1982).

22. Martha Shackford, "Beautiful Tone, Beautiful Heart," *American Suzuki Journal* 24, no. 4 (1996): 25.

23. Karin S. Hendricks, "The Philosophy of Shinichi Suzuki: Music Education as Love Education," *Philosophy of Music Education Review* 19, no. 2 (2011): 136–54; Merlin Thompson, "Authenticity, Shinichi Suzuki, and 'Beautiful Tone with Living Soul, Please,'" *Philosophy of Music Education Review* 24, no. 2 (2016).

24. Thompson, "Authenticity, Shinichi Suzuki, and 'Beautiful Tone with Living Soul, Please,'" 182.

25. Yui Kitamura, personal communication with the author, March 26, 2017.

26. Ibid.

27. Takeo Mizushima and Tanya Lesinsky Carey, "Another Look at Ability Development," *American Suzuki Journal* 27, no. 2 (1999), 32; Thompson, "Authenticity, Shinichi Suzuki, and 'Beautiful Tone with Living Soul, Please,'" 181–83.

28. William Starr, unpublished transcript, used with permission.

29. Hendricks, "The Philosophy of Shinichi Suzuki."

30. Patricia D'Ercole, e-mail message to author, October 25, 2006, previously published in Hendricks, "The Philosophy of Shinichi Suzuki," 143.

31. Tanya Carey, e-mail message to author, October 29, 2006, previously published in Hendricks, "The Philosophy of Shinichi Suzuki," 143.

32. See previous endnotes 13–20, as well as Shinichi Suzuki, *Nurtured by Love: A New Approach to Talent Education,* trans. Waltraud Suzuki (Miami, FL: Summy-Birchard, [1969] 1983).

33. All CMT quotes are from interviews with the author, unless otherwise cited.

34. Thompson, "Authenticity, Shinichi Suzuki, and 'Beautiful Tone with Living Soul, Please,'" 172.

35. Parker J. Palmer, *The Courage to Teach* (San Francisco, CA: John Wiley and Sons, 2007), 10.

36. See Estelle R. Jorgensen, *The Art of Teaching Music* (Bloomington, IN: Indiana University Press, 2008), 2–4; "Authenticity, Shinichi Suzuki, and 'Beautiful Tone with Living Soul, Please,'" 173.

37. Dijana Ihas, personal interview, June 29, 2017.

38. Dijana Ihas, "Full Service Violin Teacher: Mentoring Practices of Miss Dorothy DeLay," Unpublished manuscript.

39. Dijana Ihas, personal interview, June 29, 2017; Barbara Lourie Sand, *Teaching Genius: Dorothy DeLay and the Making of a Musician* (Portland, OR: Amadeus Press, 2000).

40. Ibid.

41. Ibid.

42. Dijana Ihas, unpublished research, used with permission.

43. Dijana Ihas, unpublished research, used with permission.

44. Thompson, "Authenticity, Shinichi Suzuki, and 'Beautiful Tone with Living Soul, Please,'" 178.

45. Wynton Marsalis, tribute to Steve Massey at the Foxborough High School Pops Concert, May 7, 2017, transcript from video "Wynton Marsalis Surprise Visit to Honor Steve Massey," last modified May 9, 2017, accessed July 28, 2017, at https://www.youtube.com/watch?v=jf_lPe3U23w.

46. These quotes were volunteered by students for public use; all names have been changed.

47. Karin S. Hendricks, Rebecca A. Roesler, Clark C. Chaffee, and Jonathan Glawe, "Orchestra Student Leadership: Developing Motivation, Trust, and Musicianship," *American String Teacher* 62, no. 3 (2012), 36–40.

48. Brooke Nelson, "Music in Academics: How One Teacher Works Miracles through Orchestra," *Hard News Cafe*, May 18, 2005, http://hardnews.ansci.usu.edu/archive/may2005/051805_misshen.html; Doug is the student's actual name.

49. André de Quadros, "Rescuing Choral Music from the Realms of the Elite: Models for Twenty-First Century Music Making—Two Case Illustrations," in *The Oxford Handbook of Social Justice in Music Education*, ed. Cathy Benedict, Patrick Schmidt, Gary Spruce, and Paul Woodford (New York: Oxford University Press, 2016), 503.

50. de Quadros, "Rescuing Choral Music," 503; see also Glenn C. Loury, *Race, Incarceration, and American Values* (Cambridge, MA: MIT Press, 2008); World Prison Brief, "United States of America," modified August 23, 2017, accessed August 27, 2017, http://www.prisonstudies.org/country/united-states-america.

51. Ibid.

52. National Association for the Advancement of Colored People (NAACP), "Criminal Justice Fact Sheet," accessed August 27, 2017, http://www.naacp.org/criminal-justice-fact-sheet, as cited in de Quadros, "Rescuing Choral Music," 503–4.

53. de Quadros, "Rescuing Choral Music."

54. Ibid., 505.

55. André de Quadros, personal communication with the author, June 2016.

56. Karin S. Hendricks, Tawnya D. Smith, and Jennifer Stanuch, "Creating Safe Spaces for Music Learning," *Music Educators Journal* 101, no. 1 (2014): 35–40; Lee Higgins, "The Creative Music Workshop: Event, Facilitation, Gift," *International Journal of Music Education* 26, no. 4 (2008): 326–38; Lee Higgins and Patricia Shehan Campbell, *Free to Be Musical: Group Improvisation in Music* (Lanham, MD: Rowman & Littlefield, 2010).

57. Tawnya D. Smith, "Using the Expressive Arts to Facilitate Group Music Improvisation and Individual Reflection: Expanding Consciousness in Music Learning for Self-Development" (PhD diss., University of Illinois at Urbana-Champaign, 2014); see also Casey McGrath, Karin S. Hendricks, and Tawnya D. Smith, *Performance Anxiety Strategies: A Musician's Guide to Managing Stage Fright* (Lanham, MD: Rowman & Littlefield, 2017).

58. Karin S. Hendricks, "Relationships between the Sources of Self-Efficacy and Changes in Competence Perceptions of Music Students during an All-State Orchestra Event" (PhD diss., University of Illinois at Urbana-Champaign, 2009); Tawnya D. Smith and Karin S. Hendricks, "Playful Spaces for Musical Expression and

Creativity: An Ethnodrama," in *Online Proceedings of the Leading Music Education International Conference,* ed. Ruth Wright (London, ON: University of Western Ontario, 2011), http://ir.lib.uwo.ca/lme/May31/Program/9.

59. Christopher Small, *Musicking: The Meanings of Performing and Listening* (Hanover, NH: Wesleyan University Press, 1998).

Afterword

Psychologists have used the term *Michelangelo phenomenon* to define close interpersonal relationships in which partners are able to envision one another's ideal or best self, and then strive to bring that ideal self out in the other person.[1] The term was derived from a description of master artist Michelangelo, who is said to have sculpted in such a way that he saw an image of a person or angel in the stone, and chipped away until the image was set free.[2] The Michelangelo phenomenon was first coined in reference to close, healthy relationships in which partners could sense the "ideal self" of another and affirm those behaviors that would bring them closer to that ideal.

In her writings on Dorothy DeLay, Dijana Ihas described how DeLay similarly exemplified this phenomenon in her teaching relationships with students: She envisioned the unique artistic potential of her students and patiently "carved away" until a violin virtuoso emerged.[3] This process could only take place through her keen ability to know exactly when and how to "carve," coupled with her careful and thoughtful attention to each student's unique strengths.

All of the compassionate music teachers described in this book share a capacity for the Michelangelo phenomenon. They exude a sense of trust in the musical potential of their students—regardless of whether that potential is yet evident to anyone else. They empathically consider each student's needs, to determine the best approaches for bringing out that potential. Then they patiently keep the end goal in mind during the process of musical development, chipping away as each individualized step requires. Because they are more interested in facilitating an aesthetic experience over any personal reward, they make a musical "place" for everyone and delight in the opportunity to learn themselves and to share in the process of creation itself. Finally, the integrity of the artist is reflected in the integrity of the artwork, as their students each emerge as independent musicians and create authentic and expressive performances of their own.

In this book, I have resisted using the term *heroic* to describe compassionate music teachers, suggesting that such a term immediately places a teacher in a position of superiority over students. Such an imbalance of power (and subsequent imbalance of responsibility) benefits neither student nor teacher. However, I am intrigued by the notion of calling compassionate teachers "artists" who, like Michelangelo, are so inspired by the beauty of what *could be* that they are compelled to bring that beauty out for the sake of beauty itself.

In the vision of Michelangelo, the hero was actually the one dwelling in the marble—"the slumbering figure that lay hidden in the stone was something heroic, vibrant, and divine."[4] I recognize this same potential for vibrancy and divinity in all of us. Consequently, I envision a future where compassionate music teachers, who continue to learn and grow along with their students, emerge from the "marble" all around us and help to create a more compassionate world.

NOTES

1. Stephen M. Drigotas, Caryl E. Rusbult, Jennifer Wieselquist, and Sarah W. Whitton, "Close Partner as Sculptor of the Ideal Self: Behavioral Affirmation and the Michelangelo Phenomenon," *Journal of Personality and Social Psychology* 77, no. 2 (1999): 293–323.

2. Caryl E. Rusbult, Eli J. Finkel, and Madoka Kumashiro, "The Michelangelo Phenomenon," *Current Directions in Psychological Science* 18, no. 6 (2009): 305–9.

3. Dijana Ihas, "Sculpting Musical Artists: A Tribute to Miss Dorothy DeLay" *American String Teacher* 67, no. 4 (2017), 14–17.

4. Drigotas, Rusbult, Wieselquist, and Whitton, "Close Partner as Sculptor of the Ideal Self," 294.

Bibliography

Adams, Maurianne, Larissa E. Hopkins, and Davey Shlasko. "Classism." In *Teaching for Diversity and Social Justice,* 3rd ed., edited by Maurianne Adams and Lee Anne Bell, 213–53. New York: Routledge, 2016.

Allsup, Randall Everett. "Democracy and One Hundred Years of Music Education." *Music Educators Journal* 93, no. 5 (2007): 52–56.

Allsup, Randall Everett. "Mutual Learning and Democratic Action in Instrumental Music Education." *Journal of Research in Music Education* 51, no. 1 (2003): 24–37.

Allsup, Randall Everett, and Catherine Benedict. "The Problems of Band: An Inquiry into the Future of Instrumental Music Education." *Philosophy of Music Education Review* 16, no. 2 (2008): 156–73.

Ames, Carole. "Classrooms: Goals, Structures, and Student Motivation." *Journal of Educational Psychology* 84, no. 3 (1992): 261–71.

Ames, Carole, and Russell Ames. "Goal Structures and Motivation." *The Elementary School Journal* 85, no. 1 (1984): 39–52.

Apple, Michael, and Nancy King. "What Do Schools Teach?" In *The Hidden Curriculum and Moral Education,* edited by Henry Giroux and David Purpel, 82–99. Berkeley, CA: McCutchan Publishing, 1983.

Austin, James R. "Competition: Is Music Education the Loser?" *Music Educators Journal* 76, no. 6 (1990): 21–25.

Austin, James R. "Competitive and Non-Competitive Goal Structures: An Analysis of Motivation and Achievement among Elementary Band Students." *Psychology of Music* 19, no. 2 (1991): 142–58.

Austin, James R. "The Effect of Music Contest Format on Self-Concept, Motivation, Achievement, and Attitude of Elementary Band Students." *Journal of Research in Music Education* 36, no. 2 (1988): 95–107.

Baier, Annette. "Trust and Antitrust." *Ethics* 96, no. 2 (1986): 231–60.

Bandura, Albert. *Self-Efficacy: The Exercise of Control.* London: Macmillan, 1997.

Barnett, Mark A. "Empathy and Related Responses in Children." In *Empathy and Its Development,* edited by Nancy Eisenberg and Janet Strayer, 146–62. New York: Cambridge University Press, 1987.

Barnett, Mark A., Karen A. Matthews, and Jeffrey A. Howard. "Relationship between Competitiveness and Empathy in 6- and 7-Year-Olds." *Developmental Psychology* 15, no. 2 (1979): 221–22.

Baron-Cohen, Simon. *The Essential Difference.* London: Penguin UK, 2004.

Baron-Cohen, Simon. *Zero Degrees of Empathy: A New Theory of Human Cruelty.* London: Penguin UK, 2011.

Barrett, Janet R. "Forecasting the Future of Professional Associations in Music Education." *New Directions in Music Education* 1, no. 1. Accessed August 19, 2017. https://www.newdirectionsmsu.org/issue-1/barrett-forecasting-the-future-of-professional-associations-in-music-education.

Baumeister, Roy F., and Mark R. Leary. "The Need to Belong: Desire for Interpersonal Attachments as a Fundamental Human Motivation." *Psychological Bulletin* 117, no. 3 (1995): 497–529.

Berg, Margaret H., and Peter Miksza. "An Investigation of Preservice Music Teacher Development and Concerns." *Journal of Music Teacher Education* 20, no. 1 (2010): 39–55.

Bergonzi, Louis S. "To See in Living Color and to Hear the Sound of Silence: Preparing String Teachers for Culturally Diverse Classrooms." In *String Teaching in America: Strategies for a Diverse Society,* edited by Jane Linn Aten, 77–100. Alexandria, VA: American String Teachers Association, 2006.

Bergonzi, Louis S. "'Whadya Get?': Evaluation, Recognition, Motivation, Competition, and School Orchestra Programs." In *Teaching Music through Performance in Orchestra*, volume 2, edited by David Littrell, 15–39. Chicago, IL: GIA, 2003.

Bierman, Karen L., and Stephen A. Erath. "Promoting Social Competence in Early Childhood: Classroom Curricula and Social Skills Coaching Programs." In *Blackwell Handbook of Early Childhood Development,* edited by Kathleen McCartney and Deborah Phillips, 595–615. Malden, MA: Blackwell, 2006.

Blair, Deborah V. "Stepping Aside: Teaching in a Student-Centered Music Classroom." *Music Educators Journal* 95, no. 3 (2009): 42–45.

Blake, M., and A. J. MacNeil. "Trust: The Quality Required for Successful Management." *Creating High Functioning Schools: Practice and Research,* edited by Yvonne Cano, Fred H. Wood, and Jan C. Simmons, 29–37. Springfield, IL: Charles C. Thomas, 1998.

Blobshop. "What Are the Blobs? A Feelosophy." Last modified 2017. Accessed August 5, 2017. https://www.blobtree.com/pages/frontpage.

Bohm, David, and Basil J. Hiley. *The Undivided Universe.* London: Routledge, 1993.

Boeije, Hennie. "A Purposeful Approach to the Constant Comparative Method in the Analysis of Qualitative Interviews." *Quality & Quantity* 36 (2002): 391–409.

Bowman, Wayne. *Philosophical Perspectives on Music.* New York: Oxford University Press, 1998.

Boyce-Tillman, June. *Constructing Musical Healing: The Wounds That Sing.* London: Jessica Kingsley Publishers, 2000. Kindle edition.

Bradley, Deborah. "Music Education, Multiculturalism and Anti-Racism: Can We Talk." *Action, Criticism, and Theory for Music Education* 5, no. 2 (2006): 2–30.

Bradley, Deborah. "The Sounds of Silence: Talking Race in Music Education." *Action, Criticism, and Theory for Music Education* 6, no. 4 (2007): 132–62.

Brewster, Cori, and Jennifer Railsback. *Building Trusting Relationships for School Improvement: Implications for Principals and Teachers*. Northwest Regional Educational Laboratory, 2003. Accessed March 7, 2017. educationnorthwest.org/sites/default/files/trust.pdf.

Brower, Holly H., Scott W. Lester, M. Audrey Korsgaard, Brian R. Dineen. "A Closer Look at Trust between Managers and Subordinates: Understanding the Effect of Both Trusting and Being Trusted on Subordinate Outcomes." *Journal of Management* 35, no. 2 (2009): 327–47.

Brown, Brené. "Shame Resilience Theory: A Grounded Theory Study on Women and Shame." *Families in Society* 87, no. 1 (2006): 43–52.

Bryk, Anthony S., and Barbara Schneider. *Trust in Schools: A Core Resource for Improvement*. New York: Russell Sage Foundation, 2002.

Bryk, Anthony S., and Barbara Schneider. "Trust in Schools: A Core Resource for School Reform." *Educational Leadership* 60, no. 6 (2003): 40–45.

Burnsed, Vernon, James Sochinski, and Dennis Hinkle. "The Attitude of College Band Students toward High School Marching Band Competition." *Journal of Band Research* 19, no. 1 (1983): 11–17.

Campbell, Patricia Shehan, and Trevor Wiggins, eds. *The Oxford Handbook of Children's Musical Cultures*. New York: Oxford University Press, 2012.

Carey, Tanya. "President's Message." *American Suzuki Journal* 18, no. 7 (Winter 1990): 3.

Casper, David Carl. "The Relationship between Collective Student Trust and Student Achievement." EdD diss., University of Oklahoma, Norman, OK, 2012.

Cassell, Eric J. "Compassion." In *The Oxford Handbook of Positive Psychology*, edited by C. R. Snyder and Shane J. Lopez, 393–403. New York: Oxford University Press, 2009.

Charter for Compassion International. "About the Charter for Compassion." *Charter for Compassion*. Accessed July 25, 2014. http://charterforcompassion.org/about-charter.

Charter for Compassion International. "The Charter for Compassion." *Charter for Compassion*. Accessed July 25, 2014. http://www.charterforcompassion.org.

Charter for Compassion International. "The Charter for Compassion." *Charter for Compassion*. Accessed August 4, 2016. http://www.charterforcompassion.org/index.php/charter.

Childre, Doc, and Howard Martin. *The HeartMath Solution*. New York: HarperCollins, 1999.

Chödrön, Pema. *The Places That Scare You: A Guide to Fearlessness in Difficult Times*. Boston, MA: Shambhala Publications, 2007.

Chou, Li-Fang, An-Chih Wang, Ting-Yu Wang, Min-Ping Huang, and Bor-Shiuan Cheng. "Shared Work Values and Team Member Effectiveness: The Mediation of Trustfulness and Trustworthiness." *Human Relations* 61, no. 12 (2008): 1713–42.

Cirelli, Laura K., Kathleen M. Einarson, and Laurel J. Trainor. "Interpersonal Synchrony Increases Prosocial Behavior in Infants." *Developmental Science* 17, no. 6 (2014): 1003–11.

Cohen, Jonathan D. "The Vulcanization of the Human Brain: A Neural Perspective on Interactions between Cognition and Emotion." *Journal of Economic Perspectives* 19, no. 4 (2005): 3–24.

Collaborative for Academic, Social, and Emotional Learning. "What Is Social and Emotional Learning?" *Collaborative for Academic, Social, and Emotional Learning.* Accessed August 4, 2016. http://www.casel.org/social-and-emotional-learning.

Cooper, Michael. "Music Education Group's Leader Departs after Remarks on Diversity." *New York Times,* May 12, 2016. Accessed August 3, 2017. http://www. nytimes.com/2016/05/13/arts/music/music-education-groups-leader-departs-after-remarks-on-diversity.html?_r=0.

Corrigall, Kathleen A., and E. Glenn Schellenberg. "Predicting Who Takes Music Lessons: Parent and Child Characteristics." *Frontiers in Psychology* 6 (2015). Accessed December 7, 2017. https://www.ncbi.nlm.nih.gov/pmc/articles/ PMC4371583/.

Corrigall, Kathleen A., E. Glenn Schellenberg, and Nicole M. Misura. "Music Training, Cognition, and Personality." *Frontiers in Psychology* 4 (2013). Accessed December 7, 2017. https://www.ncbi.nlm.nih.gov/pmc/articles/PMC3639373/.

Costa, Ana Cristina. "Work Team Trust and Effectiveness." *Personnel Review* 32, no. 5 (2003): 605–22.

Cowan, Philip A., Carolyn Pape Cowan, and Neera Mehta. "Feeling Like Partners." In *The Compassionate Instinct,* edited by Dacher Keltner, Jason Marsh, and Jeremy Adam Smith, 100–110. New York: W. W. Norton, 2010.

Csikszentmihalyi, Mihaly. *Flow: The Psychology of Optimal Performance.* New York: Harper & Row, 1990.

Cunningham, J. B., and J. MacGregor. "Trust and the Design of Work: Complementary Constructs in Satisfaction and Performance." *Human Relations* 53, no. 12 (2000): 1575–91.

Curwin, Richard L., and Allen N. Mendler. *Discipline with Dignity.* Alexandria, VA: ASCD, 1988.

Cutietta, Robert A. "During the Renaissance I Want to Be a Suzuki Teacher." Keynote address, International Research Symposium on Talent Education, Minneapolis, MN, May 22, 2014.

Dadds, Mark R., Kirsten Hunter, David J. Hawes, Aaron D. J. Frost, Shane Vassallo, Paul Bunn, Sabine Merz, and Yasmeen El Masry. "A Measure of Cognitive and Affective Empathy in Children Using Parent Ratings." *Child Psychiatry and Human Development* 39, no. 2 (2008): 111–22.

Debrot, Ruth. "Social Constructionism in the Middle School Chorus: A Collaborative Approach." DMA diss., Boston University, 2016.

Deci, Edward L., and Richard M. Ryan. *Intrinsic Motivation and Self-Determination in Human Behavior.* New York: Plenum Press, 1985.

de Quadros, André. "Rescuing Choral Music from the Realms of the Elite: Models for Twenty-First Century Music Making—Two Case Illustrations." In *The Oxford*

Handbook of Social Justice in Music Education, edited by Cathy Benedict, Patrick Schmidt, Gary Spruce, and Paul Woodford, 501–12. New York: Oxford University Press, 2016.

de Waal, Frans. "The Evolution of Empathy." In *The Compassionate Instinct,* edited by Dacher Keltner, Jason Marsh, and Jeremy Adam Smith, 16–25. New York: W. W. Norton, 2010.

Drigotas, Stephen M., Caryl E. Rusbult, Jennifer Wieselquist, and Sarah W. Whitton. "Close Partner as Sculptor of the Ideal Self: Behavioral Affirmation and the Michelangelo Phenomenon." *Journal of Personality and Social Psychology* 77, no. 2 (1999): 293–323.

Duke, Robert A., and Jacqueline C. Henninger. "Effects of Verbal Corrections on Student Attitude and Performance." *Journal of Research in Music Education* 46, no. 4 (1998): 482–95.

Duke, Robert A., and Jacqueline C. Henninger. "Teachers' Verbal Corrections and Observers' Perceptions of Teaching and Learning." *Journal of Research in Music Education* 50, no. 1 (2002): 75–87.

Dweck, Carol S. *Mindset: The New Psychology of Success.* New York: Random House, 2006.

Edgar, Scott N. *Music Education and Social Emotional Learning: The Heart of Teaching Music.* Chicago, IL: GIA Publications, 2017.

Einarson, Kathleen M., Karin S. Hendricks, Nancy Mitchell, Elizabeth Guerriero, and Patricia D'Ercole. "Empathy Level in Young Children Is Associated with Persistence in Group Music Training and with Parental Beliefs and Values." Unpublished manuscript.

Eisenberg, Nancy, and Paul Miller, "Empathy, Sympathy, and Altruism." In *Empathy and Its Development,* edited by Nancy Eisenberg and Janet Strayer, 292–316. New York: Cambridge University Press, 1987.

Eisenberg, Nancy, and Paul Henry Mussen. *The Roots of Prosocial Behavior in Children.* New York: Cambridge University Press, 1989.

Ekman, Paul. *Emotional Awareness: Overcoming the Obstacles to Psychological Balance and Compassion.* New York: Henry Holt, 2008.

Elpus, Kenneth. "Music Teacher Licensure Candidates in the United States: A Demographic Profile and Analysis of Licensure Examination Scores." *Journal of Research in Music Education* 63, no. 3 (2015): 314–35.

Ester, Don, and Kristin Turner. "The Impact of a School Loaner-Instrument Program on the Attitudes and Achievement of Low-Income Music Students." *Contributions to Music Education* 36, no. 1 (2009): 53–71.

Evans, Paul. "Self-Determination Theory: An Approach to Motivation in Music Education." *Musicae Scientiae* 19, no. 1 (2015): 65–83.

Fay, Jim, and Foster W. Cline. *Discipline with Love and Logic: Resource Guide.* Golden, CO: Love and Logic Press, 1997.

Fay, Jim, and Charles Fay. *Teaching with Love and Logic.* 2nd ed. Golden, CO: Love and Logic Press, 2016.

Feldman, Christina. *Compassion: Listening to the Cries of the World.* Berkeley, CA: Rodmell Press, 2005.

Feshbach, Norma Deitch. "Parental Empathy and Child (Mal)adjustment." In *Empathy and Its Development,* edited by Nancy Eisenberg and Janet Strayer, 271–91. New York: Cambridge University Press, 1987.

Findlay, John, and Karin S. Hendricks. "Seating Assignments: Are They Necessary?" *Utah Music Educators Journal* 57 no. 1 (2011), 30–32.

Forsyth, Patrick B., Curt M. Adams, and Wayne K. Hoy. *Collective Trust: Why Schools Can't Improve without It.* New York: Teachers College Press, 2011.

Forsyth, Patrick B., Laura L. B. Barnes, and Curt M. Adams. "Trust-Effectiveness Patterns in Schools." *Journal of Educational Administration* 44, no. 2 (2006): 122–41.

Freeman, Nicole P. M. "Credibility and the Professor: The Juxtaposition of Student Perceptions and Instructor Beliefs." PhD diss., University of Central Missouri, Warrensburg, MO, 2011.

Freire, Paulo. *Pedagogy of the Oppressed, 30th Anniversary Edition.* New York: Continuum, 2007.

Frysinger, Robert C., and Ronald M. Harper. "Cardiac and Respiratory Correlations with Unit Discharge in Epileptic Human Temporal Lobe." *Epilepsia* 31, no. 2 (1990): 162–71.

Frysinger, Robert C., and Ronald M. Harper. "Cardiac and Respiratory Correlations with Unit Discharge in Human Amygdala and Hippocampus." *Electroencephalography and Clinical Neurophysiology* 72, no. 6 (1989): 463–70.

Gabarro, John J. "The Development of Trust, Influence, and Expectations." In *Interpersonal Behavior: Communication and Understanding in Relationships,* 290–303. Englewood Cliffs, NJ: Prentice Hall, 1978.

Gagné, Françoys. "Transforming Gifts into Talents: The DMGT as a Developmental Theory." *High Ability Studies* 15, no. 2 (2004): 119–47.

Gagné, Françoys, and Gary E. McPherson. "Analyzing Musical Prodigiousness Using Gagné's Integrative Model of Talent Development." In *Music Prodigies: Interpretations from Psychology, Education, Musicology and Ethnomusicology,* edited by Gary E. McPherson, 3–114. New York: Oxford University Press, 2016.

Gerrity, Kevin W., Ryan M. Hourigan, and Patrick W. Horton. "Conditions That Facilitate Music Learning among Students with Special Needs: A Mixed-Methods Inquiry." *Journal of Research in Music Education* 61, no. 2 (2013): 144–59.

Gerry, David, Andrea Unrau, and Laurel J. Trainor. "Active Music Classes in Infancy Enhance Musical, Communicative and Social Development." *Developmental Science* 15, no. 3 (2012): 398–407.

Gholson, Sylvia A. "Proximal Positioning: A Strategy of Practice in Violin Pedagogy." *Journal of Research in Music Education* 46, no. 4, 535–45.

Glaser, Barney G. "The Constant Comparative Method of Qualitative Analysis." *Social Problems* 12, no. 4 (1965): 436–45.

Goddard, Roger D. "Relational Networks, Social Trust, and Norms: A Social Capital Perspective on Students' Chances of Academic Success." *Educational Evaluation and Policy Analysis* 25, no. 1 (2003): 59–74.

Goleman, Daniel. *Emotional Intelligence.* New York: Bantam, 2006.

Goleman, Daniel. "Hot to Help." In *The Compassionate Instinct,* edited by Dacher Keltner, Jason Marsh, and Jeremy Adam Smith, 171–74. New York: W. W. Norton, 2010.

Goodrich, Andrew. "Peer Mentoring in a High School Jazz Ensemble." *Journal of Research in Music Education* 55, no. 2 (2007): 94–114.

Goolsby, Thomas W. "Time Use in Instrumental Rehearsals: A Comparison of Experienced, Novice, and Student Teachers." *Journal of Research in Music Education* 44, no. 4 (1996): 286–303.

Gordon, Edwin E. *Learning Sequences in Music: Skill, Content, and Patterns.* Chicago, IL: GIA, 2003.

Govier, Trudy. "Distrust as a Practical Problem." *Journal of Social Philosophy* 23, no. 1 (1992): 52–63.

Green, Lucy. *How Popular Musicians Learn: A Way Ahead for Music Education.* Burlington, VT: Ashgate, 2002.

Green, Lucy. *Music, Informal Learning and the School: A New Classroom Pedagogy.* Burlington, VT: Ashgate, 2008.

Greene, Joshua D., R. Brian Sommerville, Leigh E. Nystrom, John M. Darley, and Jonathan D. Cohen. "An fMRI Investigation of Emotional Engagement in Moral Judgment." *Science* 293, no. 5537 (2001): 2105–08.

Greene, Maxine. "Introduction." In *The Hidden Curriculum and Moral Education,* edited by Henry Giroux and David Purpel, 1–5. Berkeley, CA: McCutchan Publishing, 1983.

Grieser, Diane. R., and Karin S. Hendricks. Pedagogical Content Knowledge and Preparation of String Teachers. Unpublished manuscript, under review.

Hammel, Alice M., Roberta Y. Hickox, and Ryan M. Hourigan. *Teaching Individual Differences in Music Classroom and Ensemble Settings.* New York: Oxford University Press, 2016.

Hammel, Alice M., and Ryan M. Hourigan. *Teaching Music to Students with Special Needs: A Label-Free Approach.* New York: Oxford University Press, 2011.

Hendricks, Karin S. "Changes in Self-Efficacy Beliefs over Time: Contextual Influences of Gender, Rank-Based Placement, and Social Support in a Competitive Orchestra Environment." *Psychology of Music* 42, no. 3 (2014): 347–65.

Hendricks, Karin S. "Investing Time: Teacher Research Observing the Influence of Music History and Theory Lessons upon Student Engagement and Expressive Performance of an Advanced High School String Quartet." *Bulletin of the Council for Research in Music Education* 184 (Spring 2010): 65–78.

Hendricks, Karin S. "Music Education, Character Development, and Advocacy: The Philosophy of Shinichi Suzuki." In *Pedagogies of Kindness and Respect: On the Lives and Education of Children,* edited by Paul L. Thomas, Julie A. Gorlewski, and Brad J. Porfilio, 171–84. New York: Peter Lang, 2015.

Hendricks, Karin S. "The Philosophy of Shinichi Suzuki: Music Education as Love Education." *Philosophy of Music Education Review* 19, no. 2 (2011): 136–54.

Hendricks, Karin S. "Relationships between the Sources of Self-Efficacy and Changes in Competence Perceptions of Music Students during an All-State Orchestra Event." PhD diss., University of Illinois at Urbana-Champaign, 2009.

Hendricks, Karin S. "Songs My Student Taught Me: Narrative of an Early Childhood Cello Teacher." *International Journal of Education & the Arts* 14, no. SI 1.4 (2013): 13. Accessed August 27, 2017. http://www.ijea.org/v14si1/.

Hendricks, Karin S. "The Sources of Self-Efficacy: Educational Research and Implications for Music." *Update: Applications of Research in Music Education* 35, no. 1 (2016): 32–38.

Hendricks, Karin S., and Dorothy. "Negotiating Communities of Practice in Music Education: Dorothy's Narrative." In *Marginalized Voices in Music Education*, edited by Brent C. Talbot, 65–79. New York: Routledge, 2017.

Hendricks, Karin S. and Ann M. Hicks. "Socio-Musical Connections and Teacher Identity Development in a University Methods Course and Community Youth Symphony Partnership." *String Research Journal* 7 (2017): 99–116.

Hendricks, Karin S., and Ann M. Hicks. "Uses of Technology in an 'Immersive Learning' Teacher Preparation Course." In *Music and Media Infused Lives: Music Education in a Digital Age*, edited by Susan A. O'Neill, 327–42. Waterloo, ON: Canadian Music Educators Association, 2014.

Hendricks, Karin S., and Gary E. McPherson. "Early Stages of Musical Development: Relationships between Sensory Integration Dysfunction, Parental Influence, and Musical Disposition of a Three-Year-Old 'Maestro.'" *International Journal of Music Education* 28, no. 1 (2010): 88–103.

Hendricks, Karin. S., Rebecca. A. Roesler, Clark. C. Chaffee, and Jonathan Glawe. "Orchestra Student Leadership: Developing Motivation, Trust, and Musicianship." *American String Teacher* 62, no. 3 (2012): 36–40.

Hendricks, Karin S., Tawnya D. Smith, and Allen R. Legutki. "Competitive Comparison in Music: Influences upon Self-Efficacy Belief by Gender." *Gender and Education* 28, no. 7 (2016): 918–34.

Hendricks, Karin S., Tawnya D. Smith, and Jennifer Stanuch. "Creating Safe Spaces for Music Learning." *Music Educators Journal* 101, no. 1 (2014): 35–40.

Hersey, Paul, Kenneth H. Blanchard, and Walter E. Natemeyer. "Situational Leadership, Perception, and the Impact of Power." *Group & Organization Studies* 4, no. 4 (1979): 418–28.

Hess, Juliet. "'How Does That Apply to Me?' The Gross Injustice of Having to Translate." *Bulletin of the Council for Research in Music Education* 207–208 (Winter/Spring 2016): 81–100.

Hietolahti-Ansten, Merja, and Mirja Kalliopuska. "Self-Esteem and Empathy among Children Actively Involved in Music." *Perceptual and Motor Skills* 71, no. 3 (1990): 1364–66.

Higgins, Lee. "The Creative Music Workshop: Event, Facilitation, Gift." *International Journal of Music Education* 26, no. 4 (2008): 326–38.

Higgins, Lee. "The Impossible Future." *Action, Criticism, and Theory for Music Education* 6, no. 3 (2007). http://act.maydaygroup.org/articles/Higgins6_3.pdf.

Higgins, Lee. "Safety without Safety: Participation, the Workshop, and the Welcome." *Musiké: The International Journal of Ethnomusicological Studies* 3 (2007): 65–84.

Higgins, Lee, and Patricia Shehan Campbell. *Free to Be Musical: Group Improvisation in Music.* Lanham, MD: Rowman & Littlefield, 2010.

Hill, Scott and William K. Wootters. "Entanglement of a Pair of Quantum Bits." *Physical Review Letters* 78, no. 26 (1997): 5022. http://dx.doi.org/10.1103/PhysRevLett.78.5022.

Hoffman, Martin L. *Empathy and Moral Development: Implications for Caring and Justice.* New York: Cambridge University Press, 2001.

Hoffman, Martin L. "Empathy: Justice and Moral Judgment." In *Empathy and Its Development,* edited by Nancy Eisenberg and Janet Strayer, 47–80. New York: Cambridge University Press, 1987.

Howe, David. *Empathy: What It Is and Why It Matters.* London: Palgrave Macmillan, 2013.

Howe, Michael J. A., Jane W. Davidson, and John A. Sloboda. "Innate Talents: Reality or Myth?" *Behavioral and Brain Sciences* 21, no. 03 (1998): 399–407.

Hoy, Wayne K., and Dennis J. Sabo. *Quality Middle Schools: Open and Healthy.* Thousand Oaks, CA: Corwin Press, Inc., 1998.

Hoy, Wayne K., and Megan Tschannen-Moran. "Five Faces of Trust: An Empirical Confirmation in Urban Elementary Schools." *Journal of School Leadership* 9, no. 3 (1999): 184–208.

Iacoboni, Marco, Istvan Molnar-Szakacs, Vittorio Gallese, Giovanni Buccino, John C. Mazziotta, and Giacomo Rizzolatti. "Grasping the Intentions of Others with One's Own Mirror Neuron System." *PLoS Biology* 3, no. 3 (2005): e79. https://doi.org/10.1371/journal.pbio.0030079.

Ihas, Dijana. "Full Service Violin Teacher: Mentoring Practices of Miss Dorothy DeLay." Unpublished manuscript.

Ihas, Dijana. "Sculpting Musical Artists: A Tribute to Miss Dorothy DeLay" *American String Teacher* 67, no. 4 (2017): 14–17.

Inglis, Anne. "Obituary: Dorothy DeLay: Unconventional Teacher behind the World's Greatest Violinists." *The Guardian,* last modified April 2, 2002. Accessed July 28, 2017. https://www.theguardian.com/news/2002/apr/02/guardianobituaries.schools.

Institute of HeartMath. "Each Individual Impacts the Field Environment." Last modified September 10, 2012. Accessed August 4, 2016. http://www.heartmath.org/free-services/articles-of-the-heart/each-individual-impacts-field-environment.html.

Jimenez, Sherlyn. "Compassion." *The Encyclopedia of Positive Psychology, Volume I,* edited by Shane J. Lopez, 209–15. Malden, MA: Blackwell, 2009.

Jellison, Judith A. "Including Everyone." In *The Child as Musician,* edited by Gary E. McPherson, 257–72. New York: Oxford University Press, 2006.

Jensen, Eric E. *Teaching with the Brain in Mind.* Alexandria, VA: Association for Supervision and Curriculum Development, 1998.

Jorgensen, Estelle R. *The Art of Teaching Music.* Bloomington: Indiana University Press, 2008.

Kalliopuska, Mirja, and Inkeri Ruokonen. "A Study with a Follow-Up of the Effects of Music Education on Holistic Development of Empathy." *Perceptual and Motor Skills* 76, no. 1 (1993): 131–37.

Keene, James A. *A History of Music Education in the United States.* Hanover: University Press of New England, 1982.

Kelly-McHale, Jacqueline. "The Influence of Music Teacher Beliefs and Practices on the Expression of Musical Identity in an Elementary General Music Classroom." *Journal of Research in Music Education* 61, no. 2 (2013): 195–216.

Keltner, Dacher. "The Compassionate Instinct." In *The Compassionate Instinct: The Science of Human Goodness,* edited by Dacher Keltner, Jason Marsh, and Jeremy Adam Smith, 8–15. New York: Norton, 2010.

Kirschner, Sebastian, and Michael Tomasello. "Joint Music Making Promotes Pro-social Behavior in 4-Year-Old Children." *Evolution and Human Behavior* 31, no. 5 (2010): 354–64.

Kohn, Alfie. "A Different View." In *The Compassionate Instinct,* edited by Dacher Keltner, Jason Marsh, and Jeremy Adam Smith, 157–160. New York: W. W. Norton, 2010.

Kohn, Alfie. *Punished by Rewards: The Trouble with Gold Stars, Incentive Plans, A's, Praise, and Other Bribes.* Boston, MA: Houghton Mifflin, 1999.

Koornhof, Piet. "The Secrets of Violinist Dorothy DeLay's Teaching Methods." *Strad Magazine,* July 13, 2015, para. 9. Accessed March 7, 2017. http://www.thestrad.com/the-secrets-of-violinist-dorothy-delays-teaching-methods.

Kratus, John. "Music Education at the Tipping Point." *Music Educators Journal* 94, no. 2 (2007): 42–48.

Krogstad, Jens Manuel, and Richard Fry. "Dept. of Ed. Projects Public Schools Will Be 'Majority-Minority' This Fall." The Pew Research Center, last modified August 18, 2014, accessed August 3, 2017. http://www.pewresearch.org/fact-tank/2014/08/18/us-public-schools-expected-to-be-majority-minority-starting-this-fall.

Lacey, John I., and Beatrice C. Lacey. "Some Autonomic-Central Nervous System Interrelationships." In *Physiological Correlates of Emotion,* edited by Perry Black, 205–27. New York: Academic Press, 1970.

Ladson-Billings, Gloria. "But That's Just Good Teaching! The Case for Culturally Relevant Pedagogy." *Theory into Practice* 34, no. 3 (1995): 159–65.

Ladson-Billings, Gloria. "Toward a Theory of Culturally Relevant Pedagogy." *American Educational Research Journal* 32, no. 3 (1995): 465–91.

Ladson-Billings, Gloria. "You Gotta Fight the Power: The Place of Music in Social Justice Education." In *The Oxford Handbook of Social Justice in Music Education,* edited by Cathy Benedict, Patrick Schmidt, Gary Spruce, and Paul Woodford, 406–19. New York: Oxford University Press, 2015.

Lampert, Khen. *Compassionate Education: A Prolegomena for Radical Schooling.* Lanham, MD: University Press of America, 2003.

Lazare, Aaron. "Making Peace through Apology." In *The Compassionate Instinct,* edited by Dacher Keltner, Jason Marsh, and Jeremy Adam Smith, 246–54. New York: W. W. Norton, 2010.

Legutki, Allen R. "Self-Determined Music Participation: The Role of Psychological Needs Satisfaction, Intrinsic Motivation, and Self-Regulation in the High School Band Experience." PhD diss., University of Illinois at Urbana-Champaign, 2010.

Lerner, Harriet. *The Dance of Anger: A Woman's Guide to Changing the Patterns of Intimate Relationships,* 4th ed. New York: HarperCollins, 2014.

Loury, Glenn C. *Race, Incarceration, and American Values.* Cambridge, MA: MIT Press, 2008.

Mantie, Roger, and Lynn Tucker. "Closing the Gap: Does Music-Making Have to Stop upon Graduation?" *International Journal of Community Music* 1, no. 2 (2008): 217–27.

Mark, Michael, and Charles L. Gary. *A History of American Music Education.* Lanham, MD: Rowman & Littlefield Education, 2007.

Marsalis, Wynton. Tribute to Steve Massey at the Foxborough High School Pops Concert, May 7, 2017. Transcript from video "Wynton Marsalis Surprise Visit to Honor Steve Massey." Last modified May 9, 2017. Accessed July 28, 2017. https://www.youtube.com/watch?v=jf_lPe3U23w.

Marsh, Jason. "Can I Trust You? A Conversation between Paul Ekman and His Daughter Eve." In *The Compassionate Instinct: The Science of Human Goodness,* edited by Dacher Keltner, Jason Marsh, and Jeremy Adam Smith, 161–70. New York: W. W. Norton & Company, 2010.

Maslow, Abraham H. "A Theory of Human Motivation." *Psychological Review* 50, no. 4 (1943): 370–96.

McCarthy, Marie. "Widening Horizons with a Global Lens: MENC Responds to the New World Order, 1982–2007." *Journal of Historical Research in Music Education* 28, no. 2 (2007): 140–54.

McCraty, R., W. A. Tiller, and M. Atkinson. "Head-Heart Entrainment: A Preliminary Survey." Paper presentation, Key West Brain-Mind, Applied Neurophysiology, EEG Biofeedback 4th Annual Advanced Colloquium, 1996.

McCraty, Rollin. "The Energetic Heart: Bioelectromagnetic Communication within and between People." In *Bioelectromagnetic Medicine,* edited by Paul J. Rosch and Marko S. Markov, 541–62. New York: Marcel Dekker, 2004.

McCraty, Rollin, Mike Atkinson, Dana Tomasino, and William A. Tiller. "The Electricity of Touch: Detection and Measurement of Cardiac Energy Exchange between People." In *Brain and Values: Is a Biological Science of Values Possible,* edited by Karl H. Pribram, 359–79. Mahwah, NJ: Lawrence Erlbaum Associates, 1998.

McCroskey, James C., and Thomas J. Young. "Ethos and Credibility: The Construct and Its Measurement after Three Decades." *Communication Studies* 32, no. 1 (1981): 24–34.

McGrath, Casey, Karin S. Hendricks, and Tawnya D. Smith. *Performance Anxiety Strategies: A Musician's Guide to Managing Stage Fright.* Lanham, MD: Rowman & Littlefield, 2017.

McPherson, Gary E., Jane W. Davidson, and Paul Evans. "Playing an Instrument." In *The Child as Musician: A Handbook of Musical Development,* 331–51. New York: Oxford University Press, 2006.

McPherson, Gary E., and Karin S. Hendricks. "Students' Motivation to Study Music: The United States of America." *Research Studies in Music Education* 32, no. 2 (2010): 201–13.

McPherson, Gary E., and Graham F. Welch, eds. *The Oxford Handbook of Music Education.* New York: Oxford University Press, 2012.

McPherson, Gary E., and Aaron Williamon. "Building Gifts into Musical Talents." In *The Child as Musician: A Handbook of Musical Development,* 2nd ed, edited by Gary E. McPherson, 340–60. Oxford: Oxford University Press, 2016.

McPherson, Gary E., and Barry J. Zimmerman. "Self-Regulation of Musical Learning: A Social Cognitive Perspective." In *The New Handbook of Research on Music Teaching and Learning,* edited by Richard Colwell and Carol Richardson, 327–47. New York: Oxford University Press, 2002.

Millican, J. Si. "Describing Instrumental Music Teachers' Thinking: Implications for Understanding Pedagogical Content Knowledge." *Update: Applications of Research in Music Education* 31, no. 2 (2013): 45–53.

Millican, J. Si. "Describing Preservice Instrumental Music Educators' Pedagogical Content Knowledge." *Update: Applications of Research in Music Education* 34, no. 2 (2016): 61–68.

Mizushima, Takeo, and Tanya Lesinsky Carey. "Another Look at Ability Development." *American Suzuki Journal* 27, no. 2 (1999): 32.

McKoy, Constance L. "Effects of Selected Demographic Variables on Music Student Teachers' Self-Reported Cross-Cultural Competence." *Journal of Research in Music Education* 60, no. 4 (2013): 375–94.

Morgan, Paul L., George Farkas, Marianne M. Hillemeier, and Steve Maczuga. "Replicated Evidence of Racial and Ethnic Disparities in Disability Identification in U. S. Schools." *Educational Researcher* 46, no. 6 (2017): 305–22.

National Association for the Advancement of Colored People (NAACP). "Criminal Justice Fact Sheet." Accessed August 27, 2017. http://www.naacp.org/criminal-justice-fact-sheet.

Nelson, Brooke. "Music in Academics: How One Teacher Works Miracles through Orchestra." *Hard News Cafe*, May 18, 2005. http://hardnews.ansci.usu.edu/archive/may2005/051805_misshen.html.

Nieto, Sonia. "Solidarity, Courage and Heart: What Teacher Educators Can Learn from a New Generation of Teachers." *Intercultural Education* 17, no. 5 (2006): 457–73.

Nitschke, Jack B., Eric E. Nelson, Brett D. Rusch, Andrew S. Fox, Terrence R. Oakes, and Richard J. Davidson. "Orbitofrontal Cortex Tracks Positive Mood in Mothers Viewing Pictures of Their Newborn Infants." *Neuroimage* 21, no. 2 (2004): 583–92.

Noddings, Nel. *A Richer, Brighter Vision for American High Schools.* New York: Cambridge University Press, 2015.

Obermiller, Carl, Bryan Ruppert, and April Atwood. "Instructor Credibility across Disciplines: Identifying Students' Differentiated Expectations of Instructor Behaviors." *Business Communication Quarterly* 75, no. 2 (2012): 153–65.

The Office of His Holiness the Dalai Lama. "Training the Mind, Verse 2." Accessed February 27, 2017. https://www.dalailama.com/teachings/training-the-mind/training-the-mind-verse-2.

O'Neill, Susan A. "Perspectives and Narratives on Personhood and Music Learning." In *Personhood and Music Learning: Connecting Perspectives and Narratives,* edited by Susan A. O'Neill, 1–14. Waterloo, ON: Canadian Music Educators Association, 2014.

O'Neill, Susan A. "Youth Music Engagement in Diverse Contexts." In *Organized Activities as Context for Development: Extracurricular Activities, After-School Programs, and Community Programs,* edited by Joseph L. Mahoney, Reed W. Larson, and Jacquelynne S. Eccles, 255–73. Mahwah, NJ: Lawrence Erlbaum Associates, 2005.

Pajares, Frank. "Self-Efficacy during Childhood and Adolescence: Implications for Teachers and Parents." In *Self-Efficacy Beliefs of Adolescents*, edited by Frank Pajares and Tim Urdan, 339–67. Greenwich, CT: Information Age Publishing, 2006.

Palmer, Parker J. *The Courage to Teach Exploring the Inner Landscape of a Teacher's Life.* San Francisco, CA: John Wiley & Sons, 2007.

Pérez Huber, Lindsay, and Daniel G. Solorzano. "Racial Microaggressions as a Tool for Critical Race Research." *Race Ethnicity and Education* 18, no. 3 (2015): 297–320.

Pitts, Stephanie E., Jane W. Davidson, and Gary E. McPherson. "Models of Success and Failure in Instrumental Learning: Case Studies of Young Players in the First 20 Months of Learning." *Bulletin of the Council for Research in Music Education* 146 (Fall 2000): 51–69.

Pornpitakpan, Chanthika. "The Persuasiveness of Source Credibility: A Critical Review of Five Decades' Evidence." *Journal of Applied Social Psychology* 34, no. 2 (2004): 243–81.

Rabinowitch, Tal-Chen, Ian Cross, and Pamela Burnard. "Long-Term Musical Group Interaction Has a Positive Influence on Empathy in Children." *Psychology of Music* 41, no. 4 (2013): 484–98.

Ray, James, and Karin S. Hendricks. "Collective Efficacy Belief, Within-Group Agreement, and Performance Quality among Instrumental Chamber Ensembles." Unpublished manuscript, under review.

Remen, Rachel Naomi. "Educating for Mission, Meaning, and Compassion." In *The Heart of Learning: Spirituality in Education,* edited by Steven Glazer, 33–49. New York: Jeremy P. Tarcher/Putnam, 1999.

Remen, Rachel Naomi. *Kitchen Table Wisdom.* New York: Riverhead, 2006.

Renwick, James M., and Gary E. McPherson. "Interest and Choice: Student-Selected Repertoire and Its Effect on Practising Behaviour." *British Journal of Music Education* 19, no. 2 (2002): 173–88.

Rieh, Soo Young, and David R. Danielson. "Credibility: A Multidisciplinary Framework." *Annual Review of Information Science and Technology* 41, no. 1 (2007): 307–64.

Rizzolatti, Giacomo and Laila Craighero. "The Mirror-Neuron System." *Annual Review of Neuroscience* 27 (March 2004): 169–92.

Robinson, Deejay, and Karin S. Hendricks. "Black Keys on a White Piano: A Negro Narrative of Double-Consciousness in Music Education." In *Marginalized Voices in Music Education,* edited by Brent C. Talbot, 28–45. New York: Routledge, 2017.

Roesler, Rebecca A. "Musically Meaningful: The Interpersonal Goals of Performance." *Music Educators Journal* 100, no. 3 (2014): 39–43.

Roessing, Lesley. "Creating Empathetic Connections to Literature." *Quarterly-National Writing Project* 27, no. 2 (2005). Retrieved December 14, 2017, https://www.nwp.org/cs/public/print/resource/2229.

Rogers, G. L. "Attitudes of High School Band Directors, Band Members, Parents, and Principals toward Marching Contests." *Update: Applications of Research in Music Education* 2, no. 4 (1984): 11–15.

Rogoff, Barbara. *The Cultural Nature of Human Development.* New York: Oxford University Press, 2003.

Rosenthal, Robert, Judith A. Hall, M. Robin DiMatteo, Peter L. Rogers, and Dane Archer. *Sensitivity to Nonverbal Communication: The PONS Test.* Baltimore, MD: The Johns Hopkins University Press, 1979.

Rusbult, Caryl E., Eli J. Finkel, and Madoka Kumashiro. "The Michelangelo Phenomenon." *Current Directions in Psychological Science* 18, no. 6 (2009): 305–9.

Russek, Linda G., and Gary E. Schwartz. "Interpersonal Heart-Brain Registration and the Perception of Parental Love: A 42 Year Follow-Up of the Harvard Mastery of Stress Study." *Subtle Energies & Energy Medicine Journal Archives* 5, no. 3 (1994): 195–208.

Ryan, Richard M., and Edward L. Deci. "Intrinsic and Extrinsic Motivations: Classic Definitions and New Directions." *Contemporary Educational Psychology* 25, no. 1 (2000): 54–67.

Ryszard, Rysszard, Paweł Horodecki, Michał Horodecki, and Karol Horodecki. "Quantum Entanglement." *Reviews of Modern Physics* 81, no. 2 (2009): 865. http://dx.doi.org/10.1103/RevModPhys.81.865.

Rzonsa, Nicholas M. "Perceptions and Meanings of Belongingness within an Orchestra: A Narrative Study." PhD diss., Boston University, 2016.

Salvador, Karen. "Who Isn't a Special Learner? A Survey of How Music Teacher Education Programs Prepare Future Educators to Work with Exceptional Populations." *Journal of Music Teacher Education* 20, no. 1 (2010): 27–38.

Sand, Barbara Lourie. *Teaching Genius: Dorothy DeLay and the Making of a Musician*. Portland, OR: Amadeus Press, 2000.

Schandry, R., B. Sparrer, and R. Weitkunat. "From the Heart to the Brain: A Study of Heartbeat Contingent Scalp Potentials." *International Journal of Neuroscience* 30, no. 4 (1986): 261–75.

Schmidt, Charles P. "Relations among Motivation, Performance Achievement, and Music Experience Variables in Secondary Instrumental Music Students." *Journal of Research in Music Education* 53, no. 2 (2005): 134–47.

Sergiovanni, Thomas J. "The Virtues of Leadership." *The Educational Forum* 69, no. 2 (2005): 112–23.

Shackford, Martha. "Beautiful Tone, Beautiful Heart." *American Suzuki Journal* 24, no. 4 (1996): 25.

Shively, J. L. "In the Face of Tradition: Questioning the Roles of Conductors and Ensemble Members in School Bands, Choirs, and Orchestras." In *Questioning the Music Education Paradigm*, edited by Lee Bartel, 179–90. Toronto, Canada: Canadian Music Educators Association, 2004.

Slattery, Patrick. *Curriculum Development in the Postmodern Era*. 3rd ed. New York: Routledge, 2013.

Small, Christopher. *Musicking: The Meanings of Performing and Listening*. Hanover, NH: Wesleyan University Press, 1998.

Smith, Adam. *Theory of Moral Sentiments*. Indianapolis, IN: Liberty Classics, [1759] 1976.

Smith, Jeremy Adam, and Pamela Paxton. "America's Trust Fall." In *The Compassionate Instinct,* edited by Dacher Keltner, Jason Marsh, and Jeremy Adam Smith, 203–12. New York: W. W. Norton, 2010.

Smith, Tawnya D. "Multiple Worldviews in the Classroom: Scaffolding for Differentiated Instruction and Social Justice Learning." Unpublished manuscript.

Smith, Tawnya D. "Using the Expressive Arts to Facilitate Group Music Improvisation and Individual Reflection: Expanding Consciousness in Music Learning for Self-Development." PhD diss., University of Illinois at Urbana-Champaign, 2014.

Solorzano, Daniel, Miguel Ceja, and Tara Yosso. "Critical Race Theory, Racial Microaggressions, and Campus Racial Climate: The Experiences of African American College Students." *Journal of Negro Education* 69, no. 1/2 (2000): 60–73.

Strayer, Janet. "Affective and Cognitive Perspectives on Empathy." In *Empathy and Its Development,* edited by Nancy Eisenberg and Janet Strayer, 218–44. New York: Cambridge University Press, 1990.

Strayer, Janet. "Current Research in Affective Development." *Journal of Children in Contemporary Society* 17, no. 4 (1986): 37–55.

Sue, Derald Wing. *Microaggressions in Everyday Life: Race, Gender, and Sexual Orientation.* Hoboken, NJ: John Wiley & Sons, 2010.

Sue, Derald Wing, Christina M. Capodilupo, Gina C. Torino, Jennifer M. Bucceri, Aisha Holder, Kevin L. Nadal, and Marta Esquilin. "Racial Microaggressions in Everyday Life: Implications for Clinical Practice." *American Psychologist* 62, no. 4 (2007): 271–86.

Suzuki Association of the Americas. *Every Child Can: An Introduction to Suzuki Education.* Boulder, CO: Suzuki Association of the Americas, 2003.

Suzuki, Shinichi. *Ability Development from Age Zero,* trans. Mary Louise Nagata. Miami, FL: Summy-Birchard, 1981.

Suzuki, Shinichi. *Nurtured by Love: A New Approach to Talent Education,* trans. Waltraud Suzuki. Miami, FL: Summy-Birchard, [1969] 1983.

Suzuki, Shinichi. *Where Love Is Deep: The Writings of Shinichi Suzuki*, trans. Kyoko Selden. New Albany, IN: World-Wide Press, 1982.

Swinth, Robert L. "The Establishment of the Trust Relationship." *Journal of Conflict Resolution* 11, no. 3 (1967): 335–44.

Talbot, Brent C. "Introduction." In *Marginalized Voices in Music Education,* edited by Brent C. Talbot, 1–12. New York: Routledge, 2017.

Teven, Jason J., and James C. McCroskey. "The Relationship of Perceived Teacher Caring with Student Learning and Teacher Evaluation." *Communication Education* 46, no. 1 (1997): 1–9.

Thompson, Merlin. "Authenticity, Shinichi Suzuki, and 'Beautiful Tone with Living Soul, Please.'" *Philosophy of Music Education Review* 24, no. 2 (2016): 170–90.

Thompson, Ross A. "Empathy and Emotional Understanding: The Early Development of Empathy." In *Empathy and Its Development,* edited by Nancy Eisenberg and Janet Strayer, 119–45. New York: Cambridge University Press, 1987.

Timbie, Renae. "An Ethnographic Case Study of Collaborative Learning in a Higher Education Choral Ensemble." Doctoral diss., Ball State University, Muncie, IN, 2016.

Tschannen-Moran, Megan, and Wayne K. Hoy. "A Multidisciplinary Analysis of the Nature, Meaning, and Measurement of Trust." *Review of Educational Research* 70, no. 4 (2000): 547–93.

Tuan, Yi-Fu. *Space and Place: The Perspective of Experience.* Minneapolis: University of Minnesota Press, 1977.

Vallance, Elizabeth. "Hiding the Hidden Curriculum: An Interpretation of the Language of Justification in Nineteenth-Century Educational Reform." In *The Hidden Curriculum and Moral Education,* edited by Henry Giroux and David Purpel, 82–99. Berkeley, CA: McCutchan Publishing, 1983.

van Maele, Dimitri, Mieke Van Houtte, and Patrick B. Forsyth. "Introduction: Trust as a Matter of Equity and Excellence in Education." In *Trust and School Life,* edited by Dimitri van Maele, Mieke Van Houtte, and Patrick B. Forsyth, 1–36. Dordrecht: Springer, 2014.

VanWeelden, Kimberly, and Jennifer Whipple. "Music Educators' Perceived Effectiveness of Inclusion." *Journal of Research in Music Education* 62, no. 2 (2014): 148–60.

Vispoel, Walter P., and James R. Austin. "Constructive Response to Failure in Music: The Role of Attribution Feedback and Classroom Goal Structure." *British Journal of Educational Psychology* 63, no. 1 (1993): 110–29.

Vygotsky, Lev. "Interaction between Learning and Development." *Readings on the Development of Children* 23, no. 3 (1978): 34–41.

Vygotsky, L. S. *Mind in Society: The Development of Higher Psychological Process,* edited by Michael Cole, Vera John-Steiner, Sylvia Scribner, and Ellen Souberman. Cambridge, MA: Harvard University Press, 1978.

Weick, Karl E., David P. Gilfillan, and Thomas A. Keith. "The Effect of Composer Credibility on Orchestra Performance." *Sociometry* 36, no. 4 (1973): 435–62.

Wilson, Pip, and Ian Long. *The Big Book of Blob Trees.* New York: Routledge, 2017.

Wilson, S. M., L. S. Shulman, and A. E. Richert. "'150 Different Ways' of Knowing: Representations of Knowledge in Teaching." In *Exploring Teachers' Thinking,* edited by J. Calderhead, 104–24. London: Cassell, 1987.

Wispé, Lauren. "History of the Concept of Empathy." In *Empathy and Its Development,* edited by Nancy Eisenberg and Janet Strayer, 17–37. New York: Cambridge University Press, 1987.

Witt, Anne C. "Use of Class Time and Student Attentiveness in Secondary Instrumental Music Rehearsals." *Journal of Research in Music Education* 34, no. 1 (1986): 34–42.

World Prison Brief. "United States of America." Modified August 23, 2017. Accessed August 27, 2017. http://www.prisonstudies.org/country/united-states-america.

Wootters, William K. "Entanglement of Formation of an Arbitrary State of Two Qubits." *Physical Review Letters* 80, no. 10 (1998): 2245. http://dx.doi.org/10.1103/PhysRevLett.80.2245.

Wright, Ruth. "Music Education and Social Reproduction: Breaking Cycles of Injustice." In *The Oxford Handbook of Social Justice in Music Education,* edited by Cathy Benedict, Patrick Schmidt, Gary Spruce, and Paul Woodford, 340–71. New York: Oxford University Press, 2015.

Yosso, Tara, William Smith, Miguel Ceja, and Daniel Solórzano. "Critical Race Theory, Racial Microaggressions, and Campus Racial Climate for Latina/o Undergraduates." *Harvard Educational Review* 79, no. 4 (2009): 659–91.

Zand, Dale E. "Trust and Managerial Problem Solving." *Administrative Science Quarterly* 17, no. 2 (1972): 229–39.

Index

About the Author

Karin S. Hendricks is co-director of undergraduate studies in music and assistant professor of music education at Boston University. A regular presenter of research papers and practitioner workshops, Dr. Hendricks has served as an orchestra clinician and adjudicator throughout the United States and abroad. Karin currently serves as national secretary of the American String Teachers Association. She conducts research in music psychology, student motivation and engagement, and social justice, and has published papers in professional and peer-reviewed journals and books. She is co-author of *Performance Anxiety Strategies*.